W9-DEV-485

DISCARDED

DISCARDED

RAC[E]ING
TO THE
RIGHT

RAC[E]ING
TO THE
RIGHT

SELECTED ESSAYS
OF GEORGE S. SCHUYLER

Edited by
Jeffrey B. Leak

THE UNIVERSITY OF TENNESSEE PRESS / KNOXVILLE

Copyright © 2001 by The University of Tennessee Press / Knoxville.
All Rights Reserved. Manufactured in the United States of America.
First Edition.

All photographs are from the Philippa Schuyler Photograph Collection, Schomburg Center for Research in Black Culture, New York Public Library, and are reprinted by permission.

"The Caucasian Problem" (1944) by George S. Schuyler from *What the Negro Wants* by Rayford W. Logan. Copyright © 1944 by the University of North Carolina Press, renewed 1974 by Rayford W. Logan. Used by permission of the publisher.

"The Negro Art-Hokum" by George S. Schuyler from the June 16, 1926, issue of the *Nation*.

"George S. Schuyler, Writer," by Ishmael Reed from *Shrovetide in New Orleans*, with permission from Lowenstein Associates.

"Rise of the Black Internationale" (1938) from *Black Empire* by George S. Schuyler, edited by Robert A. Hill and R. Kent Rasmussen. Copyright © 1991 by Northeastern University Press and the Regents of the University of California. Reprinted with permission of Northeastern University Press.

"The Reds and I" (1968) and "Malcolm X: Better to Memorialize Benedict Arnold" (1973) by George S. Schuyler from *American Opinion*. Reprinted with permission from Gary Benoit, editor of the *New American*.

"The Case Against the Civil Rights Bill" (1963), "Rising Tide of Black Racism" (1967), "Future of the American Negro" (1967), and "Non-Violence Always Ends Violently" (1968) by George S. Schuyler, published with permission from the Syracuse University Library.

The paper used in this book meets the minimum requirements of ANSI/NISO Z39.48-1992 (R 1997) (Permanence of Paper). The binding materials have been chosen for strength and durability.

Library of Congress Cataloging-in-Publication Data

Schuyler, George Samuel, 1895–
Rac(e)ing to the right : selected essays of George S. Schuyler / [edited by] Jeffrey B. Leak.— 1st ed.
  p. cm.
Includes bibliographical references and index.
ISBN 1-57233-118-6 (cl.: alk. paper)
1. Afro-Americans—Politics and government—20th century. 2. Conservatism—United States—History—20th century. 3. Right and left (Political science). 4. Afro-Americans—Civil rights—History—20th century. 5. Afro-Americans—Intellectual life—20th century. 6. Schuyler, George Samuel, 1895–   —Political and social views. 7. United States—Race relations.
I. Title: Raceing to the right. II. Title: Racing to the right. III. Leak, Jeffrey B., 1968–   IV. Title.
E185.6 .S396 2001
305.896'073—dc21   00-010821

THIS BOOK IS DEDICATED TO
BRITTANY MONIQUE FRANKLIN,
JOSEPH MICHAEL FRANKLIN,
AND D'NYDIA RACHEL FRANKLIN:
COME TO KNOW THE GOD IN YOU,
AND YOU WILL DEVELOP YOUR TALENTS
TO THE FULLEST.

CONTENTS

ILLUSTRATIONS

PREFACE

In 1973 Michael W. Peplow conducted one of the last interviews with the inimitable George Samuel Schuyler, conservative black journalist and early commentator on the New Negro movement of the 1920s. Peplow asked him about his longstanding commitment to conservatism and hence his marginal status as an African American intellectual. To what degree, in other words, did he consider himself a lonely iconoclast? Schuyler's response revealed an aged but feisty tongue: "Am I an iconoclast? Sure! Lonely? Hell no! I've got lots of friends."[1] Contrary to Schuyler's invincible reply, Peplow reveals a man who was indeed lonely and isolated: in 1967 his only child, Philippa Duke Schuyler, met her premature death on assignment as a journalist in Vietnam at the age of thirty-six; in 1969 his wife of forty years, Josephine Cogdell Schuyler, committed suicide;[2] and on August 31, 1977, Schuyler himself would die alone in New York's Manhattan Hospital, culminating a rich, controversial, and fascinating life begun in 1895.

Schuyler occupied a marginal position in both mainstream American and African American political circles. Because of his unshakable commitment at times to the most extreme forms of conservatism, he created a place for himself on the periphery of American intellectual life. At turns journalist, novelist, socialist, and satirist, Schuyler advocated controversial political positions that contributed to his isolation and ostracism. His status as a black conservative has detracted from his numerous critical essays on race, culture, and the complexities of American identity, a body of important work spanning almost fifty years.

Conservatism in its various forms has always informed African American communities; therefore, Schuyler's invocation of broadly defined conservative principles at specific periods in his life placed him in the mainstream of African American life. Indeed, prior to the 1950s, many prominent African Americans, such as novelist Zora Neale Hurston, legendary baseball player Jackie Robinson, and Dr. Martin Luther King Jr., identified with the Republican Party.[3] African Americans' ties to the Republican Party were rooted in tradition, pragmatism, and perceived opportunity. As historian Elwood Watson notes,

> The primary reason so many African Americans were Republicans was that, historically speaking, the Republican Party was seen as the party most hospitable to the interests of African Americans, especially because of its role in abolishing slavery. As the first Republican president, Abraham Lincoln

was responsible for signing the Emancipation Proclamation.
. . . For the few blacks who could vote in the early twentieth
century, the Republican Party was the only alternative for
African Americans, due to the fact that the Democratic Party
had established an all-White primary, which included poll
taxes, grandfather clauses, arduous historical documents, and
other forms of restrictions that prohibited most African Americans from voting.[4]

The Republican foothold would be challenged during the Great Depression of the
1930s, as President Franklin Delano Roosevelt, a Democrat, advanced New Deal
policies that sought to address the overwhelming economic and social needs of
America's poor. By 1970, the majority of African Americans had shifted to the
Democratic Party, in light of its support of civil rights legislation in the 1950s and
1960s. Whereas the Republican Party of the nineteenth and early twentieth centuries was associated with progressive policies regarding African American advancement, the Democratic Party now occupies that space in the political imagination of
most African Americans. Interestingly, as we trace Schuyler's intellectual and
political development—which includes brief membership in the Socialist Party—
he began his move to the political right in the 1930s at approximately the same
time many African Americans began to depart from the Republican ranks. In marked
contrast, Schuyler aligned himself with the Republican Party, returning to the conservative principles of his childhood.

Schuyler's emergence as a conservative, for numerous and complex reasons,
was eventually perceived in terms of racial disloyalty. For contemporary black conservatives, these connotations still hold true. Black conservatism should not sig-
nify racial disloyalty, but some contemporary black conservatives, most notably
Supreme Court Justice Clarence Thomas, critique the liberal project to the point
where they deny the benefits to which they have fallen heir as a result of liberal
protest.[5] In his analysis of contemporary black conservatives, Cornel West argues
that in their zeal to resist "blind loyalty to the race," they have replaced it with
"blind loyalty to the nation."[6] In his essays of the 1930s and 1940s, Schuyler demonstrates an informed loyalty to both "race" and "nation," with a burgeoning skepticism for the communist project in the twentieth century. Frustrated with his
marginal position as a conservative intellectual in the 1950s and 1960s, Schuyler's
"blind loyalty to nation" becomes disturbingly apparent as he focuses on extreme
forms of conservative idealism rather than racial justice.

Therefore, Schuyler's essays on race, culture, and citizenship from the 1930s
to the 1970s evolve within the shifting domains of local, state, and national
politics in both majority and minority communities. Perhaps more than any
other black writer during the first half of the twentieth century, Schuyler enjoyed
an extensive and diverse audience. As journalist, editor, and serial novelist for

the *Pittsburgh Courier,* one of the leading black weeklies, he reached scores of African Americans during his forty-year tenure. Schuyler's essays also appeared in a cross-section of racial, religious, and political publications.

The essays I have chosen for this collection, which span from "Negro-Art Hokum" in 1926 to "Malcolm X: Better to Memorialize Benedict Arnold" in 1973, demonstrate the breadth, depth, and, yes, strangeness of Schuyler's positions on race, citizenship, politics, interracial marriage, and American culture. Part I, "Leaning to the Left," comprises Schuyler's essays on race, Western imperialism, and the hybrid dimensions of American culture. If we were to read no further, the essays in this section, with the exception of "Negro-Art Hokum," would cast Schuyler primarily as a radical liberal, focused on the gross economic imbalances produced by capitalism. Part II, "Moving to the Right," highlights Schuyler's cultural and political conservatism, the latter of which serves as a refutation of communism. Motivated primarily by the tragedy of the Scottsboro case in 1931 and the Communist Party's manipulation of that event, along with Nazi aggression in Europe, Schuyler committed himself to dismantling what he perceived as the communist machine in America. These essays locate Schuyler within the larger tradition of black conservative thought. Undoubtedly, he is the linchpin connecting early-twentieth-century conservatives such as Booker T. Washington and P. B. Young with contemporary conservatives such as Shelby Steele, Glen C. Loury, and Condoleeza Rice.[7] Part III, "Race, Conservatism, and Civil Rights," represents Schuyler at the most volatile and controversial point in his development. Given the liberal backdrop of the civil rights movement, Schuyler's tireless invocation of conservative ideology endeared him only to those positioned on the political far right. In their totality, the essays in this third and final section chart Schuyler's struggle with the competing ideologies of liberalism and conservatism.

In addition to tracing Schuyler's movement from radical liberalism to radical conservatism, this collection introduces to us ideas that anticipate many of our contemporary debates on the future of our racially and culturally diverse Republic. We have witnessed already a resurgence of interest in Schuyler's fiction through the republication of *Black No More* (1931), the first black science fiction novel, and *Slaves Today: A Story of Liberia* (1931), the first novel about Africa by an African American. Moreover, "between 1935 and 1939, [Schuyler] produced fifty-four short-stories and twenty novels/novellas in serialized form under such pen names as Samuel I. Brooks and Rachel Call. . . . To date, four of his serialized novels have been reprinted in two volumes: *Black Empire* (1991) and *Ethiopian Stories* (1995)."[8] *Rac(e)ing to the Right* brings together for the first time Schuyler's complex and controversial political and cultural ideas, essays that complement and complicate the racial worlds that emerge in his fiction. Through his essays we explore the controversial and taboo subjects of African American identity. Prone to exaggeration and sarcasm, Schuyler, in his unique capacity as cultural critic, has left us a road map of cultural insights and political miscues.

What are the principle factors in Schuyler's development as a black conservative? In what ways did his decision in 1929 to marry Josephine Cogdell, a white Texas heiress, inform his understanding of racial identity? Did black organizations such as the National Association for the Advancement of Colored People (NAACP) ostracize him unfairly? By the 1960s, Schuyler was refusing to offer political support to the traditional civil rights movement and, in particular, to Dr. Martin Luther King Jr.—to what can we attribute this unpopular stance? As journalist, cultural critic, and political iconoclast, how does Schuyler measure against today's black conservatives? To these and other questions we shall now turn, as we explore the life of one of the most prolific and provocative observers of African American life from the 1920s to the 1970s.

NOTES

1. Michael W. Peplow, *George S. Schuyler* (Boston: Twayne, 1980), 17.
2. Kathryn Talalay, *Composition in Black and White: The Life of Philippa Schuyler* (New York: Oxford Univ. Press, 1995), 278. By all measures Josephine invested an unhealthy amount of time in her daughter's life, and Philippa's untimely death created an enormous void. Josephine's sense of loneliness was exacerbated by the fact that over the years George's work required him to be away from home, and their marriage suffered as a result. George's history of philandering was no doubt another source of frustration.
3. Elwood Watson, "Guess What Came to American Politics?—Contemporary Black Conservatism," *Journal of Black Studies* 29, no. 1 (Sept. 1998): 74. Watson has an excellent general bibliography on black conservatism.
4. Ibid., 74–75.
5. Clarence Thomas, "No Room at the Inn: The Loneliness of the Black Conservative," in *Black and Right: The Bold New Voice of Black Conservatives in America,* ed. Stan Faryna (Westport, Conn.: Praeger, 1997), 3–14.
6. Cornel West, *Race Matters* (Boston: Beacon Press, 1993), 51.
7. Henry Lewis Suggs, "The Washingtonian Legacy, a History of Black Political Conservatism in America 1915–1944." In *Black Conservatism: Essays in Intellectual and Political History,* ed. Peter Eisenstadt (New York: Garland, 1999), 81–108.
8. Adenike Marie Davidson, "George S. Schuyler," in *Oxford Companion to African American Literature,* ed. William Andrews, Frances Smith Foster, and Trudier Harris (New York: Oxford Univ. Press, 1997), 645.

ACKNOWLEDGMENTS

I would like to give honor and praise to the Spirit, and also I would like to thank my cadre of family and friends—know that your love continues to sustain me. To the English Department at the University of Vermont, thank you for supporting this project in its early stages. To my colleagues in the English Department at the University of North Carolina at Charlotte, especially Sandra Govan, Malin Pereira, James H. McGavran, and Mark I. West, I appreciate your guidance and support. To the Graduate School at the University of North Carolina at Charlotte, thank you for supporting this project in its final stages. To my mentors, Rudolph P. Byrd, Mark A. Sanders, and Robert A. Brown, you continue to inspire and lead the way. Special thanks to Ron Lewis, Graphics Coordinator at the University of North Carolina at Charlotte, whose artistic vision and intellectual curiosity compelled me to expand my political and cultural vision. To my wife, Renée Anthony Leak, I delight in knowing that we are writing the ultimate book together.

Schuyler in the 1930s. Photographer unknown.

INTRODUCTION

I

A BLACK PERSON LEARNS VERY EARLY THAT HIS COLOR IS A
DISADVANTAGE IN THE WORLD OF WHITE FOLK. THIS BEING
AN UNALTERABLE CIRCUMSTANCE, ONE ALSO LEARNS VERY
EARLY TO MAKE THE BEST OF IT.
—GEORGE S. SCHUYLER, *Black and Conservative*

Schuyler was born on February 25, 1895, in Providence, Rhode Island, but reared in Syracuse, New York. His father, George Francis Schuyler, a chef, died early in Schuyler's childhood. The Schuyler family hailed from the Albany-Troy area in upstate New York, with a great-grandfather having served under Gen. Philip Schuyler during the Revolutionary War. His mother, Eliza Fischer Schuyler, who could trace her roots to Madagascar, was from a racially diverse family with American origins in New York and New Jersey. A woman of modest education, she managed to introduce her son to the world of books. Given his mother's passion for learning and the work ethic of his stepfather, Joseph E. Brown, Schuyler became a black Yankee with a middle-class upbringing. By middle class, I mean that Schuyler enjoyed a fairly stable financial environment during his childhood. He learned the Protestant work ethic—the belief that economic salvation is earned solely through persistent labor—but we should remember that there were many African American families that were on the lower end of the economic divide who believed in and practiced this brand of conservatism.

The failures of Reconstruction also shaped Schuyler's boyhood and adolescence. By 1895, the federal government and various state governments had created laws to deny African Americans the opportunity to realize the freedoms they had been guaranteed in the Emancipation Proclamation, as well as in the Thirteenth, Fourteenth, and Fifteenth Amendments to the United States Constitution. Interestingly, the year of Schuyler's birth was also a significant moment in the development of national black leadership. Frederick Douglass, the leading race man of the nineteenth century, was laid to rest; W. E. B. Du Bois, one of the leading black academicians of the twentieth century, became the first African American to earn a doctorate from Harvard University; and Booker T. Washington, considered by many the founding father of modern black conservatism, assumed, in de facto terms, the position of national race leader through his Cotton States Exposition Address in Atlanta. In his speech, which would become known as the "Atlanta Compromise," he advanced the notion of black vocational and entrepreneurial training and the acceptance of segregation at the expense of black political and educational equity.[1] Three years earlier, in 1892, Anna Julia Cooper had published *A Voice from the South,* examining the pitfalls of black leadership as they would emerge in the lives of Du Bois and Washington. Further on the political front, Ida B. Wells Barnett invoked Douglass's progressive tradition of leadership in her national anti-lynching campaign.

Through the lives of these race leaders we discern that even with the inequities that slavery produced and the shattered promises of Reconstruction, African Americans were preparing for the challenges of modern life. This undaunted optimism is often associated with black conservatism. "If later historians saw the period 1877 to 1915 as the 'nadir' of black history in the United States," writes Peter Eisenstadt, "conservatives such as Washington always emphasized the tremendous progress former slaves made in the few short decades since emancipation."[2] The infant Schuyler inherited a world in which racial uplift and self-reliance were simply part of the individual and national consciousness of many African Americans. This kind of black conservatism was imperative, as George entered a world ruled by racial violence and segregation. This fact was underscored the year after his birth, when the U.S. Supreme Court affirmed racial segregation in the landmark case of *Plessy v. Ferguson,* a ruling that would not be challenged successfully until *Brown v. Board of Education* in 1954. The chief lawyer in the latter case was Thurgood Marshall, whose liberalism, similar to that of Dr. Martin Luther King Jr., must have agitated Schuyler. In 1968, during the period in which Schuyler would offer his most searing critiques of black liberalism, Marshall became the first African American appointed to the Supreme Court.

From his earliest recollections of childhood in his autobiography, *Black and Conservative,* Schuyler reveals to us a family history rooted in racial and conservative pride. For Schuyler, black conservatism represented the ability to adapt to the changing world and marshal one's resources. The capacity to conserve and maintain one's resources was a daily requirement for African American survival during some three hundred years of enslavement. When we consider the aftermath of slavery and Reconstruction, it was even more necessary to embrace this kind of conservatism. We must remember, however, that the Schuyler family had a more distant view of African American bondage. They "boasted" of having no direct slave descendants, viewing those with bondage in their bloodlines with northern condescension. Schuyler is forthright in revealing this aspect of his family history:

> I learned very early in life that I was colored but from the
> beginning this fact of life did not distress, restrain, or overburden
> me. One takes things as they are, lives with them, and tries to
> turn them to one's advantage or seeks another locale where the
> opportunities are more favorable. This was the conservative

viewpoint of my parents and family. It has been mine through life, not consistently but most of the time. . . . If any of the family were ever slaves, it must have been before the Revolutionary War. . . . My folks boasted of having been free as far back as any of them could or wanted to remember, and they haughtily looked down upon those who had been in servitude. They neither cherished nor sang slave songs. Such prejudices did not die among Northern Negroes until after World War I and the inrush of Southern migrants. Many regarded the latter as illiterate, ignorant, ill-bred, and amoral; as people with whom they neither had nor wanted anything to do.[3]

Schuyler acknowledges the impact of America's racial caste system and its negative manifestations in African American communities, but he is able to mitigate this turbulent history through his belief in personal responsibility, along with his family's history of freedom. Put another way, his conception of race is wedded to his history of place, the relatively free North. In a fundamental sense Schuyler learned early in life to assume responsibility for his development. One of the primary arguments between liberals and conservatives involves the relationship between the individual and the government. In general, liberals believe government should improve and enhance the lives of its citizens; conservatives, on the other hand, believe government should oversee only the country's defense and foreign policy, with minimal intrusion in the lives of its citizens. Clearly, there are lines of intersection within these two schools of thought. As Claudia Tate suggests in her research on the African American novel and psychoanalysis, "Different occasions and social contexts allow individuals to activate and to be perceived by one or more of the various constituents of their identities."[4] Far too often, however, in American politics polemics take precedence over complexity. As liberalism and conservatism competed in the young and developing life of Schuyler, he looked to himself and his family, rather than the government, for support.

For Schuyler, the ability to adapt to change was crucial in his development. As a teenager, he realized his opportunities for advancement, with or without a high school diploma, were few. The decision was quite simple: since he could not envision a fruitful life in Syracuse beyond labor, he joined the United States Army. "Perhaps I should have stayed in school," Schuyler intimates, "but it must be remembered that the time was 1912, and no spirit of hopefulness pervaded the colored community. Opportunities were very slim, not only in Syracuse, but just about everywhere. In the army I could see the world I wanted to see and have a chance to advance myself. At any rate, I would be away from my hometown."[5]

Joining the army in 1912 at age seventeen, he served most of his time in Washington state and Hawaii, the latter of which did not become a state until

1959. During his six-year tenure, he would develop the basic tools as a writer that would result in a forty-year career as a journalist. Curiously, Schuyler was not always as patriotic as the rhetoric of *Black and Conservative* suggests. Kathryn Talalay, the biographer of his daughter Philippa, makes a stunning revelation concerning Schuyler's military involvement. In 1918 Schuyler was commissioned as a first lieutenant. During that summer, he traveled along the eastern corridor while awaiting reassignment at Camp Dix, New Jersey. One day in Philadelphia, on his way back to Camp Dix, Lieutenant Schuyler was refused service by a Greek bootblack. The refusal followed the logic of racial discrimination in America: Schuyler was a "nigger" and thus undeserving of equal treatment. Furious that he would receive this kind of racist treatment while serving in the U.S. Army, Schuyler deserted the Stars and Stripes: "I'm a son-of-a-bitch if I'll serve this country any longer!"[6] Schuyler was declared AWOL (absent without official leave) as he traveled clandestinely across the United States for nearly three months to the West Coast. He finally surrendered to military authorities in San Diego, California. Tried by a military court back east, he was sentenced to five years but served only nine months because he was a model inmate in the Castle Williams Penitentiary on New York's Governor's Island.

Given the large body of critical and autobiographical materials that Schuyler bequeathed to future generations, Talalay finds information regarding his imprisonment conspicuously absent from his published and recorded materials: "George kept this period of his life a deep secret until he met Josephine and confided in her a month after they had started dating. . . . Neither Schuyler's autobiography nor his oral history, recorded by Columbia University in 1960, mentions his desertion or imprisonment."[7] This revelation, which Talalay discovered in Schuyler's diary, is especially intriguing as we consider Schuyler's later move toward conservatism. In his encounter with this European immigrant, Schuyler faced the brutal reality of his marginal place in his native land. Even as an officer in the U.S. Army, he could be dismissed by European immigrants who had discovered the American advantages of whiteness. In my view, Schuyler must have repressed this period of his life, because this kind of experience provided much of the evidence for the liberal protest of the modern civil rights movement. Clearly, it reminded Schuyler of the fact that despite black accomplishments since slavery, the political and social bastions of white supremacy remained intact. To some degree, Schuyler repressed a painful part of his history in order to secure acceptance as an American patriot. Interestingly, black writers and activists such as James Baldwin, Dr. King, and Angela Davis have invoked their patriotism through the process of political dissent. Unlike Schuyler, they imagined experiences of incarceration as ritual periods of transformation and questioned the moral fitness of a society that would imprison persons for demanding their constitutional rights. Having spent nine months at Governor's Island, Schuyler would acknowledge neither the mistreatment that led to his imprisonment nor the effect of his incarceration upon his future development.

Following his release from prison in 1918, he moved to New York City, where, unable to earn money as a clerk and journalist, he became a dishwasher on Broadway. During this period, Schuyler became familiar with the underside of human experience: gambling, prostitution, theft, and homelessness. He adapted to street life, recalling the conservative tradition of self-help acquired during his formative years in Syracuse. Because Schuyler hailed from a fairly stable conservative home, he derived comfort from the knowledge that he could return to the security of familiar surroundings. In 1920, he returned to Syracuse and supported himself by performing various odd jobs that, unlike his jobs in New York City, did not require physical labor. Schuyler's flexible work schedule provided him the leisure to read and continue his autodidactic education:

> Syracuse had an excellent library, and my work was not so arduous that I had no inclination to read, as had been the case in New York on those twelve-hour jobs. Now I quit around four or four-thirty and was through dinner after six. I read Plato's *Republic*, books on astronomy, and geology, socialist books by Marx, Engels. . . . I found the writings of the socialists on the whole very tedious, and most of Marx was guaranteed to cure insomnia. It was quite an ordeal to wade through three volumes of Karl Marx's *Capital,* but I did.[8]

This opportunity to rekindle his intellectual passions, following his experience in the Bowery of New York City, prompted Schuyler to join the Socialist Party of America in 1921, but his membership in the party revolved more around his need for intellectual stimulation in Syracuse than a steadfast belief in socialism. As he explains, "The most active group in town, intellectually, was the Socialists, and it was not long before I began meeting with them in their forum and discussing the momentous happenings of the day, of which I discovered they knew little if anymore than I did. But it was exhilarating, and just the type of stimulation I had been hungering for. So in November, 1921, I joined the Socialist Party of America and got my red membership card."[9]

Indeed, 1921 represents Schuyler's symbolic initiation into American political and intellectual life. While he would not remain a socialist, many of Schuyler's essays in the 1920s, 1930s, and 1940s would invoke a socialist or anti-capitalist critique. Until the era of anti-communist sentiment led by Senator Joseph McCarthy in the 1950s, Schuyler often maintained a balance between his conservative background and liberal leanings. He continued a thoroughgoing critique of white economic and political exploitation; at the same time, he exercised a critical vigilance regarding the mission of many black organizations, such as the NAACP. As he developed his conservative philosophy, it was clear that his intellectual voice would transform forever the substance and form of American political commentary. Often referred to as the black H. L. Mencken—the libertarian editor of the *American Mercury* from 1923 to 1933 and mentor to the budding conservative—Schuyler would perfect his journalistic voice through political and cultural commentary that revered no one.

Two years after joining the Socialist Party, Schuyler decided to remain connected to the world of politics and culture, returning to New York City in 1923. That same year he joined the staff of the *Messenger,* a black socialist publication headed by A. Philip Randolph and Chandler Owen. Randolph's commitment to collective action would lead to the formation of the Brotherhood of Sleeping Car Porters and Maids in 1925. According to Schuyler, Owen was a sarcastic though insightful writer from North Carolina who demonstrated far less faith in the possibilities of socialist transformation. Poorly funded and understaffed, the *Messenger* was nonetheless, in Schuyler's words, "a good place for a tireless, versatile young fellow to get plenty of activity and exercise."[10]

His tenure at the magazine enabled Schuyler to study more closely the prospects of socialism and communism and their potential for realization in the United States. Most important, Schuyler's position at the *Messenger* placed him in a context of more rigorous intellectual debate. Randolph and Owen also founded an organization called the Friends of Negro Freedom, a collective of radical intellectuals, but like most of their organizations, this one faltered quickly. Although the organization failed, during its short life it became, according to historian Jervis Anderson,

> a sort of private intellectual forum for Randolph and friends of *The Messenger.* . . . On Sunday mornings, Randolph invited members of the Friends of Negro Freedom over to his apartment—then on West 142nd Street—between Lenox and Seventh—for breakfast and political discussion. The regulars were the disputatious Owen; Frank Crosswaith, a Socialist graduate of the Rand School; the priestly Robert Bragnall and the scholarly William Pickens, of the NAACP; George Schuyler, an acidulous young Socialist who, recently arrived from Syracuse, was finding his way among *The Messenger* intellectuals.[11]

Prior to his entrance into this circle of black socialist radicals, Schuyler already had begun to question the core tenets of socialism and liberal ideology. Before leaving Syracuse, he began to question whether "every occurrence could be explained on the basis of class struggle; that the poor were getting worse off all the time; that capitalism would destroy civilization; that a swarm of bureaucrats in Washington could run the country better than the decentralized free enterprise power structure."[12] To that end, Randolph himself would comment that Schuyler was more interested in intellectual debate than socialist ideology: "Schuyler was a Socialist when I met him. But he never took it seriously. He made fun of everything—including socialism. But he had an attractive writing style."[13]

From academicians such as Du Bois and Kelly Miller of Howard University, to cultural figures such as Countee Cullen and A'Lelia Walker, the ever loquacious Schuyler found himself in direct contact with many prominent African American political and cultural figures. Because he interacted with the black elite in New York City, the ambitious journalist was privy to invaluable knowledge regarding the strengths and weaknesses of black political and cultural leadership. Conversely, Schuyler maintained a keen understanding of black working-class communities. According to Arthur P. Davis, one of the pioneers in African American literary studies, "With the possible exception of Langston Hughes, [Schuyler] knew more about the Negro lower and working classes than any other major writer of the twenties and thirties."[14] I would amend Davis's observation by also including his colleague at Howard University, the poet Sterling A. Brown, whose modernist poetry, according to Brown scholar Mark A. Sanders, concentrated on the complex perspectives and extraliterary modes of lower- and working-class African Americans in both the North and South.[15]

In political terms Schuyler was especially cognizant of the economic struggles of working-class African Americans and searched for ideas that would empower the masses. As he considered the origins of American labor unions, however, he concluded that the idea of collective economic interests led to the denial of racism:

> Of course at that time no craft unions accepted Negro locals. To be sure, Negroes could join the clothing unions, which swore by Marx and Engels, but only as lower-paid cart-pushers and pressers. They were Jewish and Italian unions rather than labor unions. . . . These people paid lip service to the brotherhood of man and the universality of the labor interest, but they were not really talking about the Negro. Randolph's pious pronouncements of Socialist cant and clichés in the face of stark realities was, to say the least, disquieting, although he often had a twinkle in his eye. To be sure, the slogan "Black and White, Unite and Fight" was a good one, except that practically it meant nothing.[16]

Clearly, Schuyler's early socialist ideals informed his keen sense of racial inequity in the formation of the early-twentieth-century American labor movement and socialist movements in general. In the name of the general good, racial and individual interests were considered antithetical to the concept of collective agitation. Thus Schuyler's eventual rejection of socialism in America evolves from the stark reality that slogans such as "Black and White, Unite and Fight" had far more rhetorical power than social effect. Ironically, Schuyler rejected liberalism because he believed liberals were naïve to assume that every social ill could be addressed through government interventions; on the other hand, many liberals believed that Schuyler was naïve to assume that a free-market economy would inherently create solutions to vexing social problems.

Schuyler could not reconcile the rhetorical objectives of socialism and the racist realities of its program. In very impassioned terms, he questions the methods of the socialist program. He does not reject socialism's ultimate goal concerning the equitable distribution of wealth, but the means by which economic equity can be realized. In these observations, Schuyler anticipates contemporary black conservatives such as Shelby Steele, who argue against affirmative action, for example, but not against the larger goal of full African American inclusion in American society.[17] Schuyler would not forsake the ideals of socialism, but he began to explore their realization within a capitalist paradigm. In fact, he established the Young Negroes' Cooperative League in 1930, but it faltered quickly. The energetic journalist would continue to contemplate the most effective ways for African Americans to develop more economic and political capital, as well as offering provocative ideas regarding black cultural expression. Regarding the latter, one essay in particular would serve as a kind of literary albatross for the remainder of his life.

When "Negro-Art Hokum" appeared in the *Nation* (1926), a journal that continues to set the standard for thoughtful exploration of liberal ideas, it revealed the complex task Schuyler had set for himself: to demonstrate the hybrid dimensions of American cultural expression, to argue, that is, for the blackness and whiteness of American culture. To some degree, this kind of cultural synthesis was the aim of figures such as James Weldon Johnson, Du Bois, and the poet Anne Spencer, but Schuyler's condescension toward the very notion of authentic black expression would earn him the censure of these and other black intellectuals. "Art there has been, is, and will be among the numerous black nations of Africa," Schuyler proclaims, "but to suggest the possibility of any such development among the ten million colored people in this republic is self-evident foolishness."

Sarcastic and irreverent, Schuyler offers his assessment of black culture in rather biting terms. These observations emerged within the context of the Harlem Renaissance or New Negro movement. During this period of heightened black cultural production, generally designated as the 1920s, many African American artists began to explore in more concentrated fashion black America's relationship to Africa. Given the harsh realities of modern urban life, African Americans, most of whom were in the lower economic groups, embraced idealized and unrealistic notions about African history and culture. This desire to reclaim a glorious history was instrumental in the nominal success of Marcus Garvey's Universal Negro Improvement Association (UNIA), founded in Harlem in 1916 to facilitate the return of blacks to Africa. His organization shared the goals of the American Colonization Society of the nineteenth century in that both were created for the repatriation of African Americans to Africa. While an immensely popular figure among blacks both in the United States and Caribbean, in practical terms Garvey achieved mediocre success with his Back to Africa movement.

In Schuyler's view, such preoccupation with Africa denied the history of black people in America, the fact that African Americans had become, over a period of some three hundred years, an undeniable part of America's economic and cultural fabric. While his tone is acerbic, Schuyler's reading of America's cultural history resonates with some points of accuracy. Of the many comments for which Schuyler was lampooned, his comment that the "Aframerican [was] merely a lampblacked Anglo-Saxon" to this day causes even those sympathetic to his views on culture to question his judgment: "The dean of the Aframerican literati is W. E. B. DuBois, a product of Harvard and German universities; the foremost Aframerican sculptor is Meta Warwick Fuller, a graduate of leading American art schools and former student of Rodin. . . . This, of course, is easily understood, if one stops to realize that the Aframerican is merely a lampblacked Anglo-Saxon."

Schuyler would receive the most ridicule for this assertion. This idea of black assimilation to white culture is where intellectuals such as Locke and Du Bois had to distinguish themselves from Schuyler. All three believed in a common American culture that both blacks and whites created, but in this essay Schuyler refused to acknowledge the blackness of American culture. Along with Native American culture, African American cultural expression—in the form of slave narratives, work songs, folklore, spirituals, jazz, and the blues—constitutes one of the few cultural traditions indigenous to America. As such, it continues to unveil the possibilities of American democracy. In this sense Schuyler was bound by regional and class prejudices: "My folks boasted of having been free as far back as any of them could or wanted to remember, and they haughtily looked down upon those who had been in servitude. They neither cherished nor sang slave songs."[18] When Schuyler refutes the idea of black culture, more specifically the history of "slave songs," he is denying his historical connection to slavery, to the peculiar institution from which emerged many of the art forms of American culture. He claims no direct relationship to the most important moment in the formation of the Republic. He adopts this view despite the fact that many of the art forms indigenous to American culture emerge largely from the African American experience of bondage and freedom. To be fair, Schuyler demonstrates a knowledge and appreciation of black culture in "The Negro and Nordic Civilization" (1925) and "The Caucasian Problem" (1944), but these essays are less well known. In the essay that shaped Schuyler's reputation the most, he clearly ranks white culture higher than its darker counterpart.

Schuyler's general assertion of the reciprocal relationship between black and white culture cannot in the main be refuted. African Americans have been influenced by certain Euro-American institutions and traditions. To this day, most African Americans do not yearn to visit the African homeland. Moreover, Schuyler's critics failed to acknowledge the assertion that follows his idea that

black and white culture form a kind of incestuous union. He poses an inter-
rogative that unnerves today's Afrocentric cultural critics:

> If the European immigrant after two or three generations' expo-
> sure to our schools, politics, advertising, moral crusades, and
> restaurants becomes indistinguishable from the mass of Ameri-
> cans of the older stock (despite the influence of the foreign-
> language press), how much true it must be of the sons of
> Ham who have been subjected to what the uplifters call Ameri-
> canism for the last three hundred years. . . . The mere men-
> tion of the word "Negro" conjures up in the average white
> American's mind a composite stereotype of Bert Williams, Aunt
> Jemima, Uncle Tom, Jack Johnson, Florian Slappey, and the
> various monstrosities scrawled by the cartoonists. Your aver-
> age Aframerican no more resembles this stereotype than the
> average American resembles a composite of Andy Gump, Jim
> Jeffries, and a cartoon by Rube Goldberg.

Schuyler's fundamental point is quite credible. In many ways the idea of an American Republic predicates itself upon the presence of blacks in the United States.
Notions of white superiority, in other words, are bound to the African presence in
America. African Americans are the ultimate signposts of what, in theory at least,
whites are not: hypersexual, violent, incompetent, and ignorant. Ironically, these
stereotypes have been contradicted by whites themselves, given the history of
interracial encounters during slavery. As slave narratives and contemporary schol-
arship on slavery reveal, from sexual exploitation to consensual interracial relationships in various forms, blacks and whites often have shared intimate spaces.[19]
Schuyler believes that to deny the influence of African Americans on American
culture is a dishonest gesture. He insists on revealing the hybridity of American
culture, the ways in which Americans of European and African descent, despite
the context of racial bondage, have created a cultural space unlike any other.

The leadership of the Nation was so concerned about Schuyler's essay that
it enlisted Langston Hughes to issue, if not a direct response to Schuyler, at
least an alternative perspective on the nature of black cultural expression. In
"Negro Artist and the Racial Mountain" (1926) Hughes penned what would
become the artistic manifesto of the New Negro movement. His words reso-
nate with a youthfulness and independence that would reemerge during the
Black Arts movement of the 1960s:

> So I am ashamed for the black poet who says, "I want to be a
> poet, not a Negro poet," as though his own racial world were
> not as interesting as any other world. I am ashamed, too, for
> the colored artist who runs from the painting of Negro faces to
> the painting of sunsets after the manner of the academicians

because he fears the strange un-whiteness of his own features.
An artist must be free to choose what he does, certainly, but he
must also never be afraid to do what he might choose.[20]

Actually, Schuyler and Hughes offer complementary perspectives on black culture, but the political debate surrounding black cultural expression in the 1920s caused their views to be reduced to ideological mantras. In sum, both offered valuable insights of the artist vis-à-vis his or her community and the politics of black cultural production.

In "Negro-Art Hokum" Schuyler would introduce himself to the world of liberal white intellectuals. From this point forward he also would publish numerous essays in the *American Mercury* and other conservative publications, but his primary publishing podium would be the *Pittsburgh Courier,* one of the leading African American newspapers of the twentieth century. He would serve in numerous positions from 1924 to 1966 in the New York City bureau. Clearly, the 1920s was the touchstone decade in Schuyler's professional and intellectual development, and it would culminate with a personal decision that would complicate his later position as a conservative.

In 1928 Schuyler met Josephine Cogdell, a white Texas heiress and frequent contributor to Randolph's *Messenger.* On a visit to New York from San Francisco, she wanted to meet the editor with whom she had enjoyed a history of correspondence and whose ideas she found riveting. During this meeting, there was an immediate mutual attraction, and the couple wasted no time in solidifying their relationship through marriage in 1929. In light of the nuanced relationship between personal choices and public assertions, we must resist the inclination to collapse Schuyler's personal and political decisions. We must, in my view, accord the necessary space between one's private choices and political views. Nineteenth-century African Americans found themselves in a similar situation when Frederick Douglass in 1884, two years after the death of his first wife, Anna Murray Douglass, married his white secretary, Helen Pitts. As far as we know, George and Josephine experienced genuine love and its attendant complexities, but given the fact that marriages between blacks and whites were against the status quo in most states, this union posed a radical challenge to anti-miscegenation laws. In his monograph "Racial Intermarriage in the United States" (1929), Schuyler reminds us that Texas, the birthplace of his wife, forbade marriages "between persons of European blood and their descendants with persons of African blood and their descendants . . . establishing a *maximum* penalty of five years' imprisonment."[21] Despite the legal challenges and social rebukes this couple faced, Schuyler concentrated his energies on this woman whose mind and body he treasured:

She was blonde and shapely. . . . She was liberal on the race
question without being mawkish and mushy. She saw Negroes

as I saw whites, as individuals. She had been a Mack Sennet
girl in Hollywood, and a model and ballet dancer in San Francisco. She had a surpassing grasp of international politics,
and she had seen through both socialism and communism,
and their inevitable connection. This was rare in the intellectual milieu of the time when almost everyone was agog over
the Soviet "experiment."[22]

According to Schuyler, they fell in love with each other's minds, and of course
the exoticism embodied in their racial difference created even more romantic
intrigue. Through his marriage, Schuyler complicated the definitions of liberal
and conservative, demonstrating that human beings should not be reduced to
static categories. More to the point, a person's choice of spouse, while clearly
important and symbolic, does not necessarily coincide with a particular political
agenda. Schuyler created a domestic life based on a liberal or radical notion of
racial identity and of course love, but this personal decision did not prevent him
from eventually moving to the political far right. *Interracial* relationships, then,
do not necessarily denote progressive politics, and neither, for that matter, do
intraracial relationships. To complicate matters further, Schuyler's racial liberalism extended into his marriage with regard to his personal indulgences and his
sense of fidelity. As Talalay makes clear, "George was a dedicated epicure and an
unreconstructed womanizer. . . . Nothing in George's life since the Bible-reading
days on his mother's living room carpet had prepared him for fidelity or moderation."[23] This information underscores the fact that Schuyler's conservatism was
primarily political and cultural rather than social and domestic.

Unlike her husband, Josephine was more consistent in her politics. She
was, from all standard measures, an unwavering liberal. During her childhood
she witnessed racial miscegenation and the perils associated with it. She was
aware especially of the racial and sexual contradictions of the American South
through her own family's history: "A chronicle of one generation alone reads
more like a gothic tale than a saga of southern gentility. Josephine's father had
a black mistress for over forty years. Josephine's oldest brother, while still in
his teens, sired a daughter by a black woman. He was shot in the groin by the
woman's husband (whom he then proceeded to shoot at point-blank range)
and was never able to produce any children after that."[24] Despite his history of
infidelity and miscegenation, Josephine's father rendered her invisible after she
married George. Except for clandestine visits to her birthplace, she was banned
from her family. The couple would have their only child in 1931. In Philippa
Duke Schuyler, George and Josephine created an interracial prodigy. They lived
in the Sugar Hill section of Harlem, and "Philippa's birth was mentioned in all
the black newspapers. It was widely held that she was the product of the first
interracial celebrity marriage of the twentieth century."[25]

George and Josephine Schuyler's daughter, Philippa Duke Schuyler, in the 1950s. Photographer unknown.

Philippa's cognitive capacity and motor skills developed so rapidly that she was the subject of medical research, as she was able to read and write at age two, play the piano at age four, and compose at age five. For her iconoclastic parents, especially Josephine, she was the ultimate embodiment of the possibility represented by interracial unions:

> Josephine steadfastly attributed Philippa's amazing progress to two causes: "hybrid vigor" and a diet of raw food. The Cogdells were farmers and cattle ranchers. It is not surprising, then, that Josephine would have heard talk around the dinner table about hybridization, the crossing of independent strains of plants and animals. . . . Josephine was convinced that hybridization might well apply to human beings. . . . Perhaps the most avant-garde of her theories were her dietary ones. As early as fourteen-years-old, she had experimented with nutrition and now, as a young adult, firmly believed that all foods must be eaten raw, for cooking destroyed their valuable vitamin content. Even meats, especially liver and brains, were never cooked but simply run under hot water for several minutes to kill any lurking germs. No alcohol, tobacco, sugar, or anything artificial was allowed in the house. Philippa was being raised, and happily so, on the rather bizarre combination of mother's milk, cod liver oil, wheat germ, unpasteurized milk, and many fruits.[26]

Clearly, Josephine was the primary advocate of this radical diet, but both she and George believed in the possibilities represented by eugenics. For "the burgeoning field of eugenics in the first quarter of this century is a testament to both these beliefs: that the white U.S. population was simultaneously the strongest, most adept for modern life and the one threatened by unsupervised reproduction. Groups like the American Eugenics Society, the Population Association of America and the American Sociological Society worked hard to pass mandatory sterilization laws, first in Indiana in 1907 and then by 1915 in twelve other states as well."[27] Obviously, George and Josephine did not advocate racial purity in the form of the AES; to the contrary, they believed that the amalgamation of black and white would create the ultimate example of human beauty and intellectual ability.

One of the most visible proponents of such a concept during the 1920s and 1930s was writer-turned-philosopher Jean Toomer. Through *Cane* (1923), a collection of poems, short stories, and dramatic texts that focuses on the modern dilemmas of African American identity, Toomer achieved critical acclaim. While *Cane* is certainly a black text, Toomer did not define himself as an African American. According to Toomer scholar Rudolph P. Byrd, "For personal and political reasons, Toomer rejected all traditional classifications of race. Toomer's radical stance on an issue that inspired only the most conservative declarations in others was based on a precise knowledge of his varied ancestry. Toomer was physically white but racially mixed; therefore, he defined himself as 'neither black nor white' but as American."[28] Toomer reveals this belief in one of his autobiographical essays:

> There is a new race in America. I am a member of this new race. It is neither white nor black nor in-between. It is the American race, differing as much from white and black as white and black differ from each other. It is possible that there are Negro and Indian bloods in my descent along with English, Spanish, Welsh, Scotch, French, Dutch, and German. This is common in America. . . . But the old divisions into white, black, brown, red, are outworn in this country. They have had their day. Now is the time of a new order, a new vision, a new ideal of man. I proclaim this new order. My marriage to Margery Latimer is the marriage of two Americans.[29]

Like the Schuylers, Toomer envisions a more promising future through interracial unions, an idea upon which he would elaborate in his published poem "Blue Meridian." Like Toomer, the Schuylers believed that their commitment to the concept of hybridization or eugenics would produce a "new order." This visionary concept, however, would be appropriated in terms that solidified notions of Aryan superiority. During World War II, the Nazis would justify the eradication of Jews by invoking Aryan supremacy, an extreme form of eugenics.

While Philippa embodied the fruitful possibilities of interracial unions, her life was characterized by extreme isolation. Only she, her parents, and select others viewed the world and race in such experimental terms. The price she paid for literally embodying black and white was exorbitant. In terms of social isolation, Philippa was the tragic mulatto, the racially mixed, physically white character that emerges throughout African American fiction with varying degrees of acceptance in the black and white worlds. From William Wells Brown's *Clotel, or The President's Daughter* (1852) to Charles Johnson's *Oxherding Tale* (1982), the tragic mulatto constitutes an integral part of the black literary imagination, and these conflicts of identity emerge in the life of Philippa Schuyler. In fact, Philippa would come face-to-face with her own sense of racial conflict in 1965 when she found herself pregnant. As a cosmopolitan woman, she had experienced relationships with men of diverse racial backgrounds, but the father of her unborn child was black, and her "search for a mate was greatly influenced by her eugenic agenda. At heart, she considered her parents marriage, because of her own insurmountable difficulties, a mistake, even though it had produced a genius child. She wanted to correct this by marrying the Aryan type—a Maurice Raymond or an André Gascht—so that her children might not suffer as she had. Abortion seemed the only solution now."[30] With much pain and torment, Philippa would have this complex procedure performed in Tijuana, Mexico, as abortions were still illegal in the United States.

As the Schuylers continued to observe and marvel at the talents of their interracial child, and organizations such as the AES reached their peak of social and political influence, George would challenge certain notions of racial purity in *Black No More*, published in 1931.[31] This novel assures Schuyler a place in American literary history, as it inaugurated the tradition of African American science fiction reflected in the work of Octavia Butler, Samuel Delany, and Tananarieve Due. It also advanced the rich tradition of satire reflected in the work of Wallace Thurman, Charles Johnson, and Ishmael Reed. In fact, Reed's interview with Schuyler in 1973, which is republished in this collection, reveals his admiration for the elder satirist. According to Arthur P. Davis, *Black No More* "is a harsh, iconoclastic, 'galloping,' attack that slashes, primarily, at all American color shibboleths, black and white. It also slashes at other national weaknesses, among them greed. Highly audacious and irreverent, the work pokes fun at both the NAACP and the KKK."[32]

The story revolves around the dubious experiment of Dr. Junious Crookman, a black biologist who has discovered a means of turning "Negroes into Caucasians." Schuyler weaves this farce in the most incredulous fashion. The chief character is Max Disher, a black hustler from Atlanta. Upon his conversion to whiteness, he becomes Matthew Fisher. This newly acquired access to whiteness—which comes of course with a monetary and cultural price—ignites a series of racial dilemmas in America. As Dr. Crookman and his cronies establish sanitariums throughout the country to change black pigmentations to white, Caucasian communities are deluged suddenly with scores of Negroes who now possess a pale hue. Max (now Matthew) has not only passed into the white world but also infiltrated the Knights of Nordica (the Ku Klux Klan) and become one of its major leaders. He then marries the daughter of the Imperial Grand Wizard, an act that will produce considerable anxiety when she gives birth to what she believes will be a white baby. By the end of the farce, however, the racial caste system is restored. Those blacks who embody an artificial whiteness are a shade lighter. Racial segregation by skin color, therefore, is restored, but Max survives in his new white skin because he and his wife flee the country. *Black No More*, then, also can be placed into the category of "passing novels," texts in which a character who is socially defined as black bears the physical appearance of Euro-Americans and chooses to enter the white world. James Weldon Johnson's *Autobiography of an Ex-Colored Man* (1915) and Nella Larsen's *Passing* (1929) anticipate *Black No More*, as they explore this phenomenon in provocative terms.

By revealing the topsy-turvy nature of an America obsessed with race, Schuyler scoffs at the notion of white purity. In the end, whites must have a group or entity against which they can measure themselves. They fear a world of homogeneity because in such a world democracy would be realized more completely and individual achievement—as opposed to racial exploitation—would be the baseline for human interaction. Schuyler is at his satirical best in his exposé of racial pathology. As a result of "Black No More Incorporated," whites from the trailer park to the board room rush to find a solution to the latest challenge to white supremacy. In the novel we witness the depth of Euro-Americans' anxiety over losing their racial privilege in the fictitious *Oklahoma City Hatchet:* "There are times when the welfare of our race must take precedence over law. Opposed as we always have been to mob violence as the worst enemy of democratic government, we cannot help but feel that the intelligent white men and women of New York City who are interested in the purity and preservation of their race should not permit the challenge of Crookmanism to go unanswered, even though the black scoundrels may be within the law."[33]

Just as white racists are concerned with the implications of an all-white country in *Black No More,* so, too, are the race leaders in the black community. In this sense Schuyler seeks to reveal the questionable motives of many black and white race leaders. As Davis has aptly noted, no one escapes Schuyler's ridicule:

> Ever since the first sanitarium of Black–No More Incorporated started turning Negroes into Caucasians, the National Social Equality League's income had been decreasing. No dues had been collected in months and subscriptions to the national mouthpiece, the *Dilemma,* had dwindled to almost nothing. Officials, long since ensconced in palatial apartments, began to grow panic-stricken as pay days got farther apart. They began to envision the time when they would no longer be able for the sake of the Negro race to suffer the hardships of lunching on canvasback duck at the Urban Club surrounded by the white dilettante, endure the perils of first-class Transatlantic passage to stage Save-Dear-Africa Conferences or undergo the excruciating torture of rolling back and forth across the United States in drawing rooms to hear each other lecture on the Negro problem. . . . In a very private inner office of the N.S.E.L. suite, Dr. Shakespeare Agamemnon Beard, founder of the League and graduate of Harvard, Yale and Copenhagen (whose haughty bearing never failed to impress both Caucasians and Negroes) sat before a glass-topped desk. . . . In limpid prose he told of the sufferings and privations of the downtrodden black workers with whose lives he was totally and thankfully unfamiliar.[34]

Schuyler's primary critique of Du Bois and other race leaders centers on class prejudice. What could Du Bois and other black leaders with middle-class pretensions ultimately offer the black masses, those "downtrodden black workers with whose lives they were totally and thankfully unfamiliar"?

In the world of *Black No More*, stratified by race and class, the black middle class owes its sense of entitlement to the masses. Without them, these privileged few could not "endure the perils of first-class Transatlantic passage to stage Save-Dear-Africa conferences." This satirical treatment of Du Bois, cofounder of the NAACP and architect of modern pan-Africanism, asserts the idea that both blacks and whites can be governed by greed and self-preservation. If given the opportunity, any group will advance an economic and political program that assures it both dominance and privilege. In fact, Toni Morrison advances this thesis in her most recent novel, *Paradise* (1998), which explores black frontier life in the American West. By offering this kind of critique across racial lines, Schuyler's novel was praised by many. He so thoroughly impressed Du Bois with his satirical observations that the Victorian scholar offered an unequivocal endorsement of *Black No More* and the larger critical project to which Schuyler was committed; this, despite the unflattering portrait of Du Bois himself:

> The book is extremely significant in Negro American literature, and it will be—indeed it already has been—abundantly misunderstood. . . . But Mr. Schuyler's satire is frank, straight forward and universal. It carries not only scathing criticism of Negro leaders, but of the mass of Negroes, and then it passes over and slaps the white people just as hard and unflinchingly straight in the face. . . . At any rate, read the book. You are bound to enjoy it and to follow with joyous laughter the adventures of Max Disher and Bunny, Dr. Crookman and—we say it with all reservations— Dr. Agamemnon Shakespeare Beard.[35]

In "Criteria for Negro Art," Du Bois argues that art must possess a political dimension.[36] Younger artists such as Langston Hughes and Zora Neale Hurston argued for more expansive notions of black cultural expression that would be defined by the individual artist. Schuyler and Du Bois certainly did not share the same views on race and politics, but in this instance Du Bois embraces the political satire embodied in *Black No More;* for Dr. Agamemnon Shakespeare Beard, it was the ultimate form of political art.

Interestingly, Schuyler compels Du Bois and other African American leaders to consider the future implications of their race philosophy. In *Black No More* he reveals the limitations of race organizations that are defined narrowly, delineating the problem of constructing identity in exclusively racial terms. This critique is one of the key components of Schuyler's conservatism. His primary grievance with race organizations is that they are consumed with the rhetoric of oppression and victimization. As the 1920s ended and the Great Depression began, there were five major events in Schuyler's personal, literary, and political development: his marriage, the birth of Philippa, the failure of the Young Negroes' Cooperative League, the publication of *Black No More,* and the tragic events surrounding the lives of nine young black men in Scottsboro, Alabama.

II

In Sum, Homo Aframericanus is fundamentally
"Conservative" because, as Bert Williams used to
sing, "I May Be Crazy, But I Ain't No Fool"—
knowing that he has more to conserve in America
than elsewhere on the globe. . . . Thus I can claim
no uniqueness in being black and conservative, I
would be unique if I were not.
—George S. Schuyler, "The Reds and I"

In the epigraph above Schuyler demonstrates a wit and realism that recall the public rhetoric of Booker T. Washington. Ever the realist, Washington, in the early twentieth century, conceded the white majority's desire to limit black political power. In other words, as the century unfolded, African Americans found their political power greatly diminished, given the failed initiatives of Reconstruction. Moreover, racist organizations such as the Ku Klux Klan found themselves reinvigorated in light of the political assault on black advancement. From Washington's point of view, concession was a political imperative. In 1895, when Washington delivered his Cotton States Exposition Address in Atlanta, he preached that African Americans should work toward political equality in tragically incremental steps; meanwhile, whites would provide a limited number of economic opportunities in the South. Perhaps with the exception of Dr. King's "I Have a Dream" speech in 1963, no other African American political figure is as well known for a single public address. "In all things that are purely social we can be as separate as the fingers," Washington proclaimed to the segregated audience, "yet one as the hand in all things essential to mutual progress."[37] Washington preached that blacks would accept segregation if whites would provide them with economic opportunity. He offered blacks and whites a negotiated peace which was never realized, but this political surrender made him a national leader. Washington's Atlanta Compromise continues to characterize his very complex life. We now know that even Washington's public rhetoric did not always coincide with his private acts. As Louis Harlan reveals,

> He had frequent reminders that the violent race relations of
> the era could touch him as well as others, and several times
> when racial tensions were high he employed private detectives
> as bodyguards. Washington in these circumstances decided
> to launch a secret but direct attack on racially restrictive laws.
> He secretly paid for and directed a succession of court suits
> against discrimination in voting, exclusion of blacks from jury

panels, Jim Crow railroad facilities, and various kinds of
exploitation of the black poor.[38]

For obvious reasons, Washington kept these initiatives secret, but even with
such clandestine efforts his political concessions reverberated throughout the
South. In sum, Washington clearly sacrificed too much in terms of his public
positions on black equality. He arrived at his conservative position as a result
of powerful historical realities and his conscious decision to tailor his appeal
to the dominant society.

As Washington assumed the mantle of black leadership at the close of the
nineteenth century, the black political achievements of Reconstruction had been
supplanted by the more rabid racist ideology advanced by southern Demo-
crats. As Sandra Gunning has observed, "During this period lynching and white
mob violence aimed at African American individuals and communities alike
achieved their highest levels."[39] Thus the conservatism that Washington and
Schuyler would embrace emerged within the context of relentless political
oppression. Peter Eisenstadt provides a general definition of this brand of black
conservatism with two caveats:

> (1) It will not be true of all black conservatives, (2) it will be
> true of many individuals who are not conservatives. . . . .
> Perhaps the most basic tenet of black conservatism is a deep-
> seated respect for the culture and institutions of American
> society and Western civilization, and the related conviction
> and insistence that blacks, through their own resources, can
> make it within American society. This does not mean that
> black conservatives have either been indifferent to racism, or,
> opposed to government intervention in the social order to
> make black advancement possible. It is rather that black con-
> servatives place their focus on individual achievement rather
> than on government action and redress."[40]

In the face of unflinching racism, Washington clung to this definition, as he
considered the tragic consequences of the Reconstruction era. Schuyler would
also exercise a similar kind of response in relation to a very important and
tragic event.

In 1931 nine black youths were unjustly convicted of raping two white
women in Scottsboro, Alabama. Historian Dan T. Carter has chronicled the details of this American tragedy.[41] Eight of the young men were sentenced to life
in prison; four would be released in 1937, the other four between 1937 and
1976. The Scottsboro case was a cause célèbre for communists who had been
searching for inroads into poor and working-class black communities in the
South that would be decimated further by the Great Depression of the 1930s.
At the same time the more traditional black organizations such as the NAACP

were slow to respond to the legal plight of these young men. Clearly, the International Labor Defense (ILD), which served as the legal arm of the Communist Party, was concerned primarily with appropriating this unfortunate case to strengthen its case for what Carter calls "proletarian hegemony."[42] Carter argues further that "however much the Communists talked of a 'popular front,' leaders of such groups as the ACLU and the Socialist party—potentially the Communists' intellectual allies—rapidly learned that the slogans were a facade behind which the Party worked unscrupulously and unceasingly to 'win the masses away from their bourgeois and petty-bourgeois leaders.' In the Scottsboro campaign, the ILD demanded complete subservience to the leadership of the Communist party USA."[43]

Curiously, Langston Hughes would respond to this case by interrogating the class divide created by capitalism, while Schuyler would respond by advocating capitalism as a more realistic means of economic self-determination. Indeed, many artists and intellectuals were sympathetic to the communist cause, most notably Richard Wright and Ralph Ellison. Both writers, however, concluded that democracy in its purest form could not manifest itself in a totalitarian context. In a general sense, they grew more realistic, but unlike Schuyler, they did not journey to the extreme right. Despite the way in which the free-market economy failed her as a woman and as a writer, Hurston was the writer with whom Schuyler shared similar conservative views in the 1940s and 1950s.

Much like Hurston, from 1931 until his death in 1977, Schuyler would advance conservative arguments. Schuyler continued to reveal the absurdities of Jim Crow politics—which is certainly to his credit—but it is clear that he preferred the status quo of America, with all its imperfections and contradictions, to a totalitarian state. As he reflects on the communist program, he reveals that he was offended by the way in which communists manipulated the tragedy of Scottsboro to deluge working-class black communities with their propaganda:

> The most fantastic programs appeal to some elements of any population, and the inroads to Negro society by the Communists utilizing the Scottsboro case became very great in a short time. Volunteers to aid the International Labor Defense arose on every side. At least twice the number of Scottsboro mothers as there actually existed were sent about the country to appear in Negro churches. . . . Ordinary Negroes were won over because they did not see that the speakers sent to their churches were communists bent on destroying a way of life of which they approved, but saw them simply as advocates of justice for nine black boys caught in the toils of southern justice.[44]

In response to the Scottsboro case, Schuyler offered a legitimate critique of communism, but he would be unable to distinguish between communist ideologues and those devoted to the larger ideals of a socialist form of government.

According to Schuyler, the decade of the 1940s "was one of great importance. I wrote a variety of articles but aimed my shafts most often at the communist conspiracy, devoting at least fifty full-length columns to the subject in the *Pittsburgh Courier* alone."[45] Given the fact that Schuyler exercised his own form of radical protest through military desertion, it seems that he would have been able to empathize with the residents of poor black communities in the deep South as they tried to interpret the events surrounding the Scottsboro case.

By responding to Scottsboro with such virulent opposition, Schuyler alienated himself from most African American leaders. In an undated letter to Schuyler from E. Franklin Frazier, the renowned sociologist of Howard University, Frazier excoriates him as a race traitor. Infuriated by Schuyler's flippant response to the plight of the Scottsboro boys and his callous disregard for the trials of Angelo Herndon, a black communist whom the American government sought to demonize, Frazier's anger is palatable:

> We want to state unequivocally that your unprovoked attacks on the defense of the Scottsboro Boys and Angelo Herndon lend encouragement to the rulers in the South, who deny the Negro people all their elementary rights. This fact is driven home by the appearance in the *Jackson County Sentinel,* home paper of the lynchers in Scottsboro, Alabama, of your attack on the Scottsboro defense, which appeared in the *American Spectator.* The *Sentinel* reprints your article with a note of approval—and this is not an accident.[46]

For Frazier and other black political leaders, Schuyler's public ridicule of the disenfranchised southern black masses was unconscionable. Moreover, as Schuyler experienced an increasing discomfort with communism, he failed to understand the substantive elements of liberal critique that began to emerge as a result of the Great Depression and the aftermath of World War II. Having proved their patriotism in yet another war, African American soldiers encountered the same kind of racism at home that they risked their lives to eradicate abroad. From this point African Americans began to adopt more aggressive political strategies to address American racism.

To be sure, a rigorous analysis of liberal policies and black political naïveté was warranted, but Schuyler's uncompassionate response to the Scottsboro case and the larger issues involving black economic despair in the deep South forced potential allies to denounce him, positioning themselves on the far left by default. From a contemporary standpoint, Cornel West acknowledges that, like Schuyler, contemporary black conservatives have made some valid points regarding black liberal leadership: "Obviously, the idea that racial discrimination is the sole cause of the predicament of the black working poor and very poor is specious. And the idea that the courts and government can significantly enhance the plight of blacks by enforcing laws is even more spurious. White racism, though pernicious and potent, cannot fully explain the socioeconomic position of the majority of black Americans."[47] In this context, West speaks to the complexities of political orientation, revealing some of the flaws of liberalism in relation to race. West maintains, however, that the flaws of liberalism should not altogether discredit black liberal leadership. For it is also clear that most African Americans do not believe that diminished government regulation, free enterprise, and the revival of the Protestant work ethic are the ultimate panacea for black advancement into the economic and social mainstream. In other words, capitalism as an economic system will not ensure black progress, which is why traditional black leaders reacted so passionately to Schuyler's response to the Scottsboro case.

Nineteen years after Scottsboro, Schuyler would demonstrate the longevity of his anti-communist position in "The Negro Question Without Propaganda" (1950), an essay based on a speech delivered in 1950 to the Congress of Cultural Freedom in Berlin. In Schuyler's words, "This conference was to be the largest and most important of its kind in the long history of anti-communism, and would be held one hundred miles inside the Iron Curtain."[48] In this speech he sets forth a conservative response to the communist program as it relates to African Americans, arguing that they are far less oppressed than indicated in communist propaganda: "Actually, the progressive improvement of interracial relations in the United States is the most flattering of the many examples of the superiority of the free American civilization over the soul-shackling reactionism of totalitarian regimes. It is this capacity for change and adjustment inherent in the system of individual initiative and decentralized authority to which we must attribute the unprecedented economic, social, and educational progress of the Negroes of the United States."

Throughout the era spanning from the Depression to the modern civil rights movement, Schuyler would contend that African Americans, through the process of democratic politics, had risen in many standard indexes dating back to the abolition of slavery and the end of the Civil War. African Americans undoubtedly contributed to America's transformation from an agricultural to an industrial economy. With this convincing evidence, the irascible Schuyler found more reason to celebrate the accomplishments of black citizens than to lament the fact that in most states blacks were denied voting rights and equal access to public resources. Simply put, Schuyler was governed by black possibilities rather than black liabilities, a position more often associated with conservatism, but one those of diverse political persuasions could embrace. Like his conservative forbear Booker T. Washington, he created a hotbed of resentment in African American political circles with such categorical pronouncements because, to a degree, such public statements downplayed the injurious effects of slavery and southern apartheid on African American life. Unfortunately, Schuyler's often provocative and sometimes reckless comments made it difficult for moderate black conservatives in the middle of the twentieth century. As Eisenstadt makes clear, "Schuyler's message, not aided by his penchant for hyperbole and overstatement, fell largely on deaf ears in the 1950s and 1960s. The twenty-five years after the end of World War II probably mark the 'nadir' of black conservatism, either before or since."⁴⁹

The difference, however, between Washington and Schuyler involved influence and power. Washington was undoubtedly the most influential power broker of his generation. His relationships with northern industrialists, philanthropists, and presidents enabled him to exercise his brand of conservatism far more effectively. On the other hand, Schuyler lacked the material resources and political power that Washington possessed. Schuyler's strength lay in his voluminous essays and his commitment to political debate, although his perspective grew more polemical. As a result, Schuyler became "the most important black conservative in the middle decades of this [twentieth] century."⁵⁰

Like his conservative predecessors and successors, Schuyler believed that African American progress outweighed racial oppression. As we chart the evolution of Schuyler's conservatism, the critical sensibility that critiqued unbridled white power in essays such as "The Negro and Nordic Civilization" (1925) and "The Caucasian Problem" (1944) has been compromised significantly. More times than not, Schuyler chose to celebrate black achievement rather than focus on racial inequality. This emphasis on progress was not altogether wrongheaded, because part of the liberal protest formula rested too much on the idea of black oppression and pathology. In 1965, Senator Daniel Patrick Moynihan would issue *The Negro Family: The Case for National Action.*⁵¹ Commonly referred to as the "Moynihan Report," this government study defined the African American experience in pathological terms. Schuyler, as well as Dr. King, refused to embrace this narrow definition. For Schuyler, the historical record of African American progress refuted the claim of black pathology advanced by Moynihan, but this was as close as he would come in supporting Dr. King and the progressive efforts of other black liberals.

III

FROM DR. KING'S ORIGINAL EFFORT, THE MONTGOMERY IMPROVEMENT ASSOCIATION'S BOYCOTT, HE CONTRIBUTED VERY LITTLE TO THE SOLUTION OF THE TOUCHY PROBLEMS OF RACE RELATIONS IN THE UNITED STATES. IF THESE PROBLEMS ARE TO BE SOLVED, IT MUST BE IN MODERATION AND THROUGH INNUMERABLE COMPROMISES RATHER THAN BY USE OF ABRASIVE TACTICS THAT PRODUCE IRRITATION AND ILL-WILL RATHER THAN UNDERSTANDING AND COOPERATION.
—GEORGE S. SCHUYLER, "DR. KING: NON-VIOLENCE ALWAYS ENDS VIOLENTLY"

In his desire to combat what he believed to be the liberal view of black pathology, Schuyler would become more reactionary in his conservatism. As we sift through Schuyler's essays of the 1950s, 1960s, and 1970s, his ideological balance begins to waver. By the peak of the McCarthy era Schuyler's trenchant critiques of the white establishment are superseded often by insensitive and misguided appraisals of black leadership. In 1964 Dr. King would receive the Nobel Prize for Peace, and Schuyler would respond to this achievement by writing an article that in no way recalls the intellectual balance and cultural insight of previous essays. Black newspapers refused to publish his article, but the *Manchester Union Leader,* a bastion of ultraconservatism historically, embraced the opportunity. In "King: No Help to Peace," Schuyler argues that the person recognized throughout the world for demanding peace and justice for all citizens stands undeserving of such recognition by the world community:

> But neither directly nor indirectly has Dr. King made a contribution to the world (or even domestic) peace. Methinks the Lenin Prize would have been more appropriate for him, since it is no mean feat for one so young to acquire sixty Communist-front citations, according to the U.S. government. . . . Dr. King's principle contribution to world peace has been to roam the country like some sable typhoid-Mary, infecting the mentally disturbed with the perversion of Christian doctrine, and grabbing lecture fees from the shallow-pated. His incitement packed jails with Negroes and some whites, getting them beaten, bitten, and firehosed, thereby bankrupting communities, raising bail and fines, to the vast enrichment of southern law and order.

In this incendiary attack on Dr. King, Schuyler sounds more like J. Edgar Hoover and George Wallace, two of the most virulent opponents of racial equality in the segregated South and antagonists of Dr. King in the 1960s. We should remember, however, that Wallace repented for his transgressions, as Dan T. Carter details in *The Politics of Rage* (1996), a biography of Wallace. In his denunciation of Dr. King, we find that Schuyler has forfeited, to recall the observations of West, "blind loyalty to the race" for "blind loyalty to the nation." This, for me, is one of the most disconcerting documents in Schuyler's impressive and controversial body of writings. In this diatribe, Schuyler reveals the effects of an uncompassionate conservative ideology. He would contend further in "Non-Violence Leads to Violence" (1968) that Dr. King failed to understand the mental instability of the black masses. Mass protests, in his view, stoke the embers of resentment and frustration, causing ineffective civic unrest. Interestingly, Schuyler argues a legitimate point in terms of ideology and strategy, but the way in which he casts his argument undermines the progressive intentions of Dr. King. He fails to acknowledge the culpability of white America in the maintenance of racial inequality.

Moreover, he characterized Dr. King as a greedy race leader committed to self-indulgence. The irony of this verbal defamation lies in the fact that Dr. King was assassinated in Memphis, Tennessee, as he defended the rights of black sanitation workers. For Dr. King, the ultimate race involved fighting for what was right rather than racing to the right to occupy the category of political iconoclast. Dr. King was indeed the outsider, as he argued for America to demonstrate both a domestic and international morality, in light of the black freedom struggle and the burgeoning problems of American military involvement in Southeast Asia. At the very time he should have embraced Dr. King's progressive pursuit of non-violence in the beloved community, Schuyler chose political iconoclasm over social justice. He would pen other, more balanced speeches and essays, such as the "Future of the American Negro" (1967), in which he acknowledges that black advancement in many instances has been realized despite American racism, but by this point he had sacrificed his integrity and authority as an intellectual and commentator on black political affairs. Regardless of his growing isolation as a black conservative, Schuyler would seek to realize his ideas by running for political office. In 1964 he was nominated by the New York Conservative Party to run against embattled congressman Adam Clayton Powell, whose ethical problems left his reelection in question. In the end, Schuyler lost, as voters chose the man whose racial loyalties were beyond question.

In his contest with Powell, Schuyler exhibited many of the failings common to intellectuals who enter politics. He experienced tremendous difficulty transforming his political visions into realities, starting with the failed Young Negroes' Cooperative League in 1930 and concluding with his bid for political office in 1964. In my opinion, his inability to move from the abstract to the concrete, the fact that his political vision could not assume a material form, was a major source of angst. This ability to render concrete versions of political ideals was what caused the masses to commit themselves to luminaries such as Dr. King and El Haaj Malik El Shabazz, or Malcolm X. Because he did not receive comparable support, Schuyler began to specialize in sarcasm and irreverence. He became, that is, consumed with difference. Ironically, the man who had expounded upon the common concerns between black and white now found himself struggling to maintain a political niche based on difference.

Despite his reactionary response to Dr. King and others in 1964, Schuyler concludes his autobiography with a vision of human possibility:

> Relegating spurious racism to limbo, in our future America
> we need to stress the importance of the individual of what-
> ever color. At best, race is a superstition. There will be no
> color war here if we will work not to have one, although some

> kind of color line there may always be, as there is elsewhere
> in the world. We do not need to share the wealth as much as
> we need to share our heritage so that all may proudly claim
> ownership in it. We need to strive to become one people in
> our resolution, determination, and achievement instead of two
> peoples, colored and white.[52]

True to his conservative principles, Schuyler extols the virtues of the individual, rightly claiming that personal responsibility will lead to group achievement. For Schuyler, the group or tribe was not a particular race—it was the nation. In this moment Schuyler reveals the possibilities of personal and collective transformation, but many of the documents that precede and succeed this idea emerge with regrettable polemics.

Schuyler's lifelong journey with conservatism reminds us of the diversity of intellectual voices in African American communities. Because black conservatism experienced a period of decline during the 1950s and 1960s—a decline due in large part to Schuyler's polemics—we have witnessed a contemporary resurgence of black conservative dialogue. Glen C. Loury offers a promising model of personal development that affirms Schuyler's conservative ideals while rejecting the unbridled ideology of Schuyler's later years:

> I no longer believe that the camaraderie engendered among
> blacks by our collective experience of racism constitutes an
> adequate basis for any person's self-definition. . . . Who am I,
> then? Foremost, I am a child of God, created in his image,
> imbued with his spirit, endowed with his gifts, set free by his
> grace. The most important challenges and opportunities that
> confront me derive not from my racial condition, but rather
> my human condition. I am a husband, a father, a son, a teacher,
> an intellectual, a Christian, a citizen. In none of these roles is
> my race irrelevant, but neither can racial identity alone provide
> much guidance for my quest to discharge my responsibilities
> adequately.[53]

Ultimately, Loury's conservative philosophy is not rooted in illogical or reactionary ideology but in the radical belief in a common humanity; political orientation notwithstanding, we can appreciate this vision of promise, as well as the manner in which these possibilities are reflected in the democratic process. In the final stage of his development as a political thinker and conservative, Schuyler lost faith in the possibilities of democratic politics.

Schuyler was indeed an iconoclast; he assumed that political ideals could be transformed into political realities, but he failed to understand the gradual nature of this process. Because of his northern roots and his family's history of freedom, he underestimated the level of emotional frustration in black communities nationwide, especially in the South. Contrary to more militant black leaders, he argued that black equality would be achieved in gradations, oblivious, however, to the reality that many of his larger conservative ideals also would come to fruition in the same manner. In his zeal to resist the excesses of liberal ideology and his desire to reveal the possibilities of racial integration, Schuyler adopted a similar form of ideological excess.

Complicated person that he was, Schuyler's satirical and ribald perspective of the world did not endear him to others. Indeed, some may argue that Schuyler's argumentative rhetoric resulted in failure. In my opinion, Schuyler did fail to accomplish certain personal and political objectives, but failure often serves as a precursor to growth. His life, then, should not be reduced to failures and successes. In a sense America may have failed Schuyler. Despite the absurdity of some of his assertions, Schuyler offered legitimate warnings concerning the ways in which liberalism could attach unrealistic and untenable expectations upon the federal government. As one of the voices of radical conservative dissent in a political culture of homogeneity, Schuyler was silenced in both mainstream black and white political circles.

In the life of George S. Schuyler, we have a fascinating example of a man who offered provocative and informative commentary on African American experience for more than forty years. By the 1960s, Schuyler confronted a twofold dilemma in his race to the right: he could not be heard, and he would not listen. This dilemma framed and revealed his precipitous downfall as intellectual and cultural critic. In the end, however, blackness and conservatism are by no means antithetical, as the title of Schuyler's autobiography and the trajectory of his life remind us.

NOTES

1. Booker T. Washington, *Up from Slavery* (1901; rpt. New York: W. W. Norton, 1996), 98.
2. Peter Eisenstadt, ed., *Black Conservatism: Essays in Intellectual and Political History* (New York: Garland, 1999), xi.
3. George Schuyler, *Black and Conservative* (New Rochelle, N.Y.: Arlington House, 1966), 2–4.
4. Claudia Tate, *Psychoanalysis and Black Novels* (New York: Oxford Univ. Press, 1998), 6.
5. Schuyler, *Black and Conservative*, 32.
6. Talalay, *Composition in Black and White*, 67.
7. Ibid., 68.
8. Schuyler, *Black and Conservative*, 113.
9. Ibid.
10. Ibid., 136.
11. Jervis Anderson, *A. Philip Randolph: A Biographical Portrait* (New York: Harcourt Brace Jovanovich, 1972), 140.
12. Schuyler, *Black and Conservative*, 115.
13. Anderson, *A. Philip Randolph*, 144.
14. Arthur P. Davis, *From the Dark Tower* (Washington, D.C.: Howard Univ. Press, 1974), 107.

15. Mark A. Sanders, ed., *A Son's Return: Selected Essays of Sterling A. Brown* (Boston: Northeastern Univ. Press, 1996), xii.
16. Schuyler, *Black and Conservative,* 138.
17. Shelby Steele, *A Dream Deferred* (New York: Harper Collins, 1998). Steele's premise is that African Americans possess the talents and abilities to achieve without special programs created for them by the white majority, and that affirmative action gives the false impression to African Americans that they are less intelligent and therefore need special assistance to realize their potential. In theory, Steele's ideas reveal a grain of truth: African Americans do possess the capacity for realizing fruitful lives. But let us apply this template to white Americans, the primary beneficiaries of "affirmative action" historically. We never hear white Americans, those of the privileged class, that is, bemoaning the fact that they have inherited money, property, and thus political power. They do not express feelings of guilt or frustration for having certain benefits because of their economic and racial status. Why does Steele believe only blacks will develop this kind of complex? Moreover, Steele's status as a black conservative is singed with irony: how has he become one of the primary spokespersons for black conservatism, when he is a literature professor with no formal training in political science, sociology, or economics? As an African American who has earned a doctorate, he is a beneficiary of affirmative action; and, given his background in English literature, his rise to fame as a prominent conservative is yet another example of "affirmative action."
18. Schuyler, *Black and Conservative,* 2–4.
19. Martha Hodes, *White Women, Black Men, Illicit Sex in the Nineteenth-Century South* (New Haven, Conn.: Yale Univ. Press, 1997).
20. Langston Hughes, "Negro Artist and the Racial Mountain," in *Norton Anthology of African American Literature,* ed. Henry Louis Gates Jr. (New York: W. W. Norton, 1997).
21. George S. Schuyler, *Racial Intermarriage in the United States: One of the Most Interesting Phenomena in Our National Life* (Girard, Kans.: Haldeman-Julius, 1929), 16.
22. Ibid., 164.
23. Talalay, *Composition in Black and White,* 113.
24. Ibid., 33.
25. Ibid., 12.
26. Ibid., 14.
27. Jane Kuenz, "American Racial Discourse, 1900–1930: Schuyler's Black No More," *Novel: A Forum on Fiction* 30, no. 2 (Winter 1997): 176.
28. Rudolph P. Byrd, *Jean Toomer's Years with Gurdjieff: Portrait of an Artist, 1923–1936* (Athens: Univ. of Georgia Press, 1990), 49–50.
29. Frederick L. Rusch, ed., *A Jean Toomer Reader: Selected Unpublished Writings* (New York: Oxford Univ. Press, 1993), 105.
30. Talalay, *Composition in Black and White,* 251.
31. George S. Schuyler, *Black No More: Being an Account of the Strange and Wonderful Workings of Science in the Land of the Free, a.d. 1933–1940* (1931; rpt. College Park, Md.: McGrath, 1969).
32. Davis, *From the Dark Tower,* 104.
33. Schuyler, *Black No More,* 40–41.
34. Ibid., 87–89.
35. W. E. B. Du Bois, review of *Black No More, Crisis* 39 (Mar. 1931): 100.
36. Andrew Paschal, ed., *W. E. B. DuBois Reader* (New York: Macmillan, 1971), 86.
37. Washington, *Up from Slavery,* 100.
38. Louis Harlan, *Booker T. Washington in Perspective* (Jackson: Univ. of Mississippi, 1988), 113.
39. Sandra Gunning, *Race, Rape, and Lynching: The Red Record of American Literature* (New York: Oxford Univ. Press, 1996), 5.
40. Eisenstadt, *Black Conservatism,* x.

41. Dan T. Carter, *Scottsboro: An American Tragedy* (Baton Rouge: Louisiana State Univ. Press, 1968).

42. Ibid., 139.

43. Ibid., 141.

44. Schuyler, *Black No More*, 189.

45. Ibid., 253.

46. E. Franklin Frazier to George S. Schuyler, n.d., Moorland Spingarn Library, Howard Univ., Washington, D.C.

48. Schuyler, *Black No More*, 317.

49. Eisenstadt, *Black Conservatism*, xxiii.

50. Ibid., xxi.

51. Lee Rainwater, *The Moynihan Report and the Politics of Controversy. Including the Full Text of "The Negro Family: The Case for National Action by Daniel Patrick Moynihan* (Cambridge, Mass.: MIT Press, 1967).

52. Schuyler, *Black No More*, 352.

53. Glen C. Loury, *One by One from the Inside Out* (New York: Free Press, 1995), 7–8.

Schuyler as a first lieutenant during World War I. Photographer unknown.

PART I

LEANING
TO THE
LEFT

The Negro and Nordic Civilization
(1925)

Published in A. Philip Randolph's Messenger, *the first journal of
African American socialist thought, this essay introduced readers
of the 1920s to Schuyler's satirical and critical talents. Having
joined the Socialist Party in 1922, Schuyler mocks the achievements of "Nordics"—persons of European descent in what is considered the Western world—offering evidence of their crass
materialism and political hypocrisy. During the 1920s, Schuyler
exercised a pan-Africanist world view, and this essay reveals his
early flirtation with socialism. In just a few years, however, his
conservative background would emerge forcefully in his essays.*

Although I am an American citizen of decidedly sable hue, thoroughly understanding and sympathizing with the aims and aspirations of my
motley brethren, both here and elsewhere I can no longer remain silent in the
face of the baseless allegations of irresponsible propagandists anent the equality of the Negro with the Caucasian race. I think our leaders and spokesmen
have gone too far and claimed too much. In fact, I feel that we must admit in
the face of a mountain of evidence that the modern civilization of the Caucasian far excels anything developed by the Negro in Africa or elsewhere. Even in
the New World where we have the widest contact with the incomparable society of the whites, we have failed to markedly profit by this association. True,
we have our gangsters, politicians, editorial writers and drug addicts, but these
are largely due to an infusion of white blood (although I have never seen white
blood) and the compelling forces of environment. Naturally, large numbers of
Negrophiles will violently disagree with me, but an orderly, dispassionate and
objective survey of the facts will convince even Marcus Garvey that I am right.

The proof lies properly in Africa. One can travel from one end to the other
of the Dark Continent, and save where the flaming torch of civilization, held
aloft by self-sacrificing missionaries and unselfish empire builders, has enlightened the poor natives, one will find no insane asylums, foundling hospitals or
bread lines. I seriously doubt if there is a single Rotary Club or Y.M.C.A. on the
continent, and such hall-marks of civilization as toothpick shoes, bell-bottom
trousers, French heels, derby hats and corsets are conspicuous by their absence.
No streams of Fords; no snugly packed subways; no healthy steel mills, coke

ovens or brass foundries; and no well-regulated coal mines in which to be gassed. While such refinements as the Ku Klux Klan, automats and comstockery are of course nonexistent. Aye, 'tis a dismal picture, but we must be courageous enough to face the facts. Wherever these evidences of an advanced civilization are present, we must thank the white man for them. He is solely responsible for their existence.

"But what of the celebrated African art?" my hard-pressed friends will ask. "Look at the magnificent sculpture, excellent pottery, clever ironwork and wonderful weaving!" they urge. How absurd! The idea of comparing handi-crafts with machine-made goods. What of the white man's movies, comic strips, billboards and Sunday supplements? Only a dozen people may see some excel-lent African mask in a jungle village, but a million Nordics see Mutt and Jeff every day. Nor could these black people, unassisted by white men, produce the wonders with which white Americans, for instance, are daily surrounded, for they possess neither the industry or capability. Laziness abounds. Hardly any work is done at all, save by the grim command of necessity. I understand the people just live a plain, easygoing, thriftless life. It is all the good missionaries and concessionaires can do, with the usual theological and military arguments, to get the blacks to work the ten-hour day ordained by God.

There is no eager scrambling out of bed at six o'clock in the morning, six days a week, to the melodious strains of the alarm clock; no bolting of coffee and rolls in happy anticipation of the pleasant day's work ahead; none of the com-radely banter that usually ensues when the subway guard assists one affection-ately into the airy and commodious coaches with the business end of his 10 EE. The joy of trundling trucks on the docks, mixing concrete, pounding a type-writer or operating a sewing machine is denied them. The flush of pleasure that comes with the knowledge that one has contributed something toward the production of 950 Ford runabouts or the unloading of a carload of Portland cement during the brief day of work, is something these people never experi-ence. Even the comforting thought that only two-thirds of the day's princely wage will gain the privilege of sharing a six-room flat with two other families is a joy unknown. Vast areas without landlords, credit parlors or pawn brokers. Think of it! "Better fifty years of Europe than a cycle of Cathay"; Tennyson voiced the sentiments of all right thinking people.

There has been much talk about the admirable social life of the Africans. Over enthusiastic visitors, I fear, have been responsible for the propagation of a great deal of nonsense. As a matter of fact, the social life is unspeakable. Uninformed people might ask: "Are there no well-dressed billboards in and around all the spots of great scenic beauty, as in America, extolling the virtues of certain brands of laundry soap, stomach remedies and bunion cures? Do they not prepare elaborate feasts for the local business men where slick-haired, immaculately dressed young men harangue the assembly on the methods of selling five hundred suits of Scratchem Underwear where only five were sold before?" Not at all. Those Negroes don't have laundry, nor stomach or bunion troubles, and they seldom stage large feasts except when some corpulent theologian is the pièce de résistance. In many of the tribes there is outright slavery and only the ruling classes are wholly free. Women are publicly bought by the highest bidders, and, of course, they do all the work around the home. (You see, they still have such primitive institutions as the home!) Polygamy is openly practiced and many of the prominent men have numerous women.

How different the Nordics arrange these things. Here we see men and women free, with no one controlling the life of another. And this is largely because the people rule. Here we have democracy. Love always takes precedence over riches in marriage, and no Caucasian can win a comely maid simply because of his wealth and position. Enlightened white society would tolerate no such reversion to barbarism. Strict monogamy is the rule from which there is not the slightest inclination to swerve—as proven by the existence of the Mann Act and numerous bigamy laws. Instead of the weaker sex toiling their lives out in the home, an advanced civilization allows them to spend their time profitably in well-appointed steam laundries, beautiful tiled restaurants, great clothing factories and huge office buildings. The more elderly females may even get to be scrubwomen in palatial banks and hotels. Virtue is cheap: marriages seldom cost over five dollars, so prostitution has never raised its hydra-head in Nordic lands. Love is the only thing that counts. The result is that marriages are happier and more enduring than elsewhere, as proven by the low divorce rate.

This should certainly be sufficient to silence dissenters, but I shall continue. Take housing, for instance. Here again the Africans are hopelessly behind the times. No massive modern tenements greet the eyes of the traveler in that unfortunate land. The healthy exercise of running up six flights of stairs after the day's toil is quite impossible. They are still at the primitive stage where only one family occupies a habitation. Instead of a couple toiling forty or fifty years to pay off the mortgage or meet the landlord every thirty days, I am informed that the whole tribe pitches in and erects a home for every couple on their wedding day! How can a real spirit of thrift exist in such an environment? Though I cannot place much credence in a rumor so terrible to contemplate, I have heard it reported that these people practice a crude form of communism. Of course it can hardly be true since all our college professors and editorial writers have always told us that communism is contrary to human nature. If it is true, may this not be the cause of their easy-going, indolent, thriftless life? Let the restless proletarians of advanced Nordic civilization beware of new-fangled ideas. Who knows but revolution might return us to an era of sprawling ease and worklessness?

Since the habit of dying is fairly general throughout the earth, even among Africans, one would naturally assume that in the disposal of the dead these natives would be abreast of the white man. It will come as a surprise then to learn that burials and services are free. Yes, insurance companies and undertakers are unknown. Furthermore, the death rate is disgustingly low (except where the civilizing influence of the whites has been felt), since there are no doctors, chiropractors or Christian Scientists. Is it necessary to go farther to prove the inferiority of the Negro. Long live such scientists as Lothrop Stoddard and Madison Grant!

Most of those who laud the purity of these people's lives seem to overlook their general use of intoxicating beverages. It is only natural that biased opinion should overlook such a damnable custom. I seriously doubt if there is a single branch of the W.C.T.U. [Women's Christian Temperance Union] in Africa. And even if there were Prohibition Enforcement squads, the liquor is made and handled in such small quantities that seizure would not prove as profitable to the law officers as it has in the United States. Nor have these Negroes reached the cultural stage that would enable them to enforce anti-imbibing legislation as it is enforced here. How in the world can Nordic pastimes such as bootlegging exist when drinking is permitted by those in authority? Well, what more can you expect? You can't get blood out of a turnip!

Now I fully realize that in a discussion of this kind one's zeal is apt to outstrip one's fairness. I want to guard against any injustice to my Negro kinsmen of the Old World or the New. I am willing to concede for the sake of argument that the Negroes (and anyone with one drop of "black" blood is a Negro) contributed the foundations upon which Nordic civilization rests: the level, the wheel, the cam, the pulley, mathematics, paper, iron smelting, and, to go from the sublime to the ridiculous, much of what is known as Christianity. But these were accomplishments which of course, required far less mentality than the later adoptions and improvements. I am even charitable enough to grant the Negroes such men as Antar, Pushkin, Dumas, Latino, Alexander Hamilton, Toussaint L'Overture, Booker T. Washington, Coleridge Taylor [Samuel Taylor Coleridge] and Henry O. Tanner. But who are such fellows compared to the men who are at the top of things in the white world today? Surely we have never reached the level of Warren G. Harding!

In the field of religion my African brethren exhibit amazing childishness. Praying for rain, good harvests or success in battle is still the custom—a custom, happily, from which white people long ago emancipated themselves. Idol worship, too, is general, but some tribes have no religion at all. Just think of it! The idiocy of worshipping a visible deity or none at all in preference to an invisible one must be apparent to all sound thinkers. Unlike the Christian clergy of Nordic lands, their witch doctors and medicine men play wholly upon the ignorance of the laymen with magic and incantations. The most absurd statements coming from these wily fellows are implicitly believed. Let us be not unmindful of the sacrifices and labors of the hard working missionary, who, having saved his white brethren from evil and sin, braves the dangers of foreign lands immersed in savagery to protect the benighted heathen from the wrath of God.

Not for these backward Negroes the classic strains of "The Livery Stable Blues," "You Got to See Mama Every Night," and "Barney Google," for the phonograph, player-piano and radio are unknown. Here again ignorance is a boomerang. It is truly a dull existence for any people. In some tribes, in order to enliven things, each person composes his or her own songs. Isn't that too primitive for anything?

After all this, one is naturally prepared to hear that the Africans are also politically backward. I regret to admit that such is the case. Absolute monarchy is the rule. Democracy, with all its demonstrated benefits, is unknown. You can make sure there are no such ably governed communities as Philadelphia and Chicago on the Dark Continent. With the absence of democracy, the most intelligent and capable Negroes consequently control affairs. There is no opportunity for men with the mentality of truck drivers or dish washers to become great statesmen as they continually do in the more enlightened Nordic lands. Seers like [New York Mayor] John F. Hylan or Calvin Coolidge would never reach the seats of power in the Congo. The natives would be too obtuse to elect them even if given the opportunity. Democratic political practices, i.e., ballot-box stuffing, vote buying, bribing, slandering campaigns, colonizing and gerrymandering have yet to penetrate to African communities. The burning of his capital city by the much-overrated King Karma is a good illustration of the sort of leadership the African must tolerate!

Twenty thousand or more blacks resided in the town, and, although there were no restaurants, delicatessen stores or druggists there, the loyal subjects began to hasten over the River Styx in unusually large numbers. Though unaware at first of the cause of this brisk business in grave digging, the king wagged his head, pursed his lips, wrinkled his brow and in every way attempted to look as wise and profound as any American politician under similar circumstances. Finally it was learned that either the water supply was polluted or the location of the kraal was otherwise unhealthy. Did this monarch handle the situation (and it was a grave situation) in a civilized manner, that is, convene the legislature, hold midnight sessions, make and listen to long and boresome speeches in which the situation was "deplored" and "viewed with great alarm," hold great prayer meetings, etc.? Nothing like that. He ordered a new town built on higher ground; moved the entire remaining population into it; and then with his own hand put the torch to the old capital. No regard for property rights; no appeal to God; no referendum on the question! It is characteristic of the uncivilized mind to place human rights above property rights and to act simply and directly. We have a long way to go before we can overtake the whites.

But I think our greatest failure has been marked in the science of warfare. Wherever we have remained uncivilized by the Krags and Mausers of the progressive Caucasians, we still play with spears, arrows, assegais, blowguns and other toys used in the childhood of humanity. In short, we have not advanced beyond mere retail killing. When shall we too graduate to rifles, trench mortars, tanks, poison gas, germs, airplanes and dreadnaughts? Never, I fear, without the usual assistance from the superior race. They do know the game! Ten million killed in half a decade—thirty thousand to our one. A dull report, the scream of a shell, the deafening roar of the explosion and a marvelous cathedral is razed. In a flash these canny Nordics can obliterate a hospital, orphan asylum, old ladies' home or even an entire city. One becomes speechless in admiration of such progress. What a people!

I suppose many spokesmen for the Negroes will assert and maintain that in the New World we have all the improvements unknown in the backward regions, in brief, that we are not inferior here. Even granting that we have done well in the New World, do we measure up to Nordic standards? I don't believe so. We have yet to develop such men as Fall, Denby, Billy Sunday, William H. Anderson, Daugherty, Gipsy Smith, A. Mitchell Palmer, William J. Burns, Burleson, Dr. Frank Crane or George Creel. Should we not hang our heads in shame? We are so backward and inefficient here in America that the whites won't play baseball, golf or tennis with us, and only reluctantly and protestingly compete with us in the schools, colleges and prize rings. They assume this attitude solely because they do not wish to humiliate us by continually demonstrating our inferiority. They refuse to employ our smart boys and girls in responsible positions for the same reason. Some Negro agitators of my acquaintance have been bold enough to charge the whites with taking this attitude because they feared Negro competition. But this is of course absurd, because it is contrary to all our teaching in schools and editorials concerning the generally acknowledged Caucasian spirit of fair play. And right here I might say that our failure to grasp the real spirit underlying the Nordic civilization is largely responsible for our backwardness in the midst of so much progress. We don't enter into the spirit of the thing; we are entirely alien to the social and cultural forces surrounding us. We don't join in the activities of the whites with the zest and abandon becoming of a pioneer people in America. For instance, there is seldom more than one Negro at a lynching bee and he or she is usually an unwilling participant in the fun. We even deign to go counter to the national mores by decrying anti-Semitism, although the Jews make as much money in our settlements as among the Anglo-Saxon, Protestant, native born whites. We also err by being on good terms with the Catholics, yet, I suppose, we must remain on good terms with the police! We are narrow, prejudiced and clannish. We segregate ourselves in little colonies in nearly every city although the whites make no effort to prevent us from living anywhere we choose—if we can outwit the real estate associations, dodge the bombs and win sufficient cases in the Supreme Court. If we attend the theaters we always huddle together in the balcony as if we couldn't purchase seats anywhere in the house like other citizens! In the South, we are even more clannish, for we require separate cars on every train and separate waiting rooms at every station, regardless of the fact that Japanese, Chinese, Hindu and Mexican aliens are satisfied to sit anywhere. Our young men adopt the same policy when they enlist in the Army or Navy: if they join the land forces, they never enter the higher branches such as the field artillery, signal corps, coast artillery or air service merely because there are no Negro units as in the infantry and cavalry; if they go to the naval branch they seem satisfied to remain firemen, coal passers and mess attendants, for one never sees them on deck as gunners, seamen or marines; and our college boys won't enter the Student Training Corps like other Americans, just because there are no provisions for them! It is quite useless to argue that discrimination is practiced, because government officials are too fair to stoop to such low behavior toward fellow citizens. We fail, too, to avail ourselves of our privilege and duty to participate in the government of the country. There has never been a known-to-be-Negro President, and there are no Negro Congressmen, governors or mayors, despite the fact that we also possess large numbers of unsuccessful lawyers and businessmen. And there is no need to argue that we haven't the men with ability to hold such positions—look at Hylan and Coolidge! The old charge that the attitude of the whites toward us prevents our participation in the national activities is a dangerous falsehood. Haven't they adopted our music and dancing? Don't they gush over with love for their black mammies, real and imaginary, even to the extent of proposing a monument to them? Didn't the Supreme Court decide and the Confederate Army fight to keep us down South where we would be closer to the whites than we are up North? Doesn't our four or five millions of mulattos prove that the whites are flesh of our flesh and blood of our blood? Why there is hardly a white person down South who hasn't a Negro relative! How nonsensical it is then to always prate of prejudice against us. Efforts to stigmatize the Nordic spirit of justice by calumny will never get us anywhere. We have been in the New World for five hundred years and we have nothing like the Credit Mobilier, Hog Island, the 1918 airplane frauds, or Tea Pot Dome to show for it. True, we have Marcus Garvey, Roscoe "Cacklin" Simmons, and a larger percentage of clergymen than any other group in the country, but otherwise our record is disgraceful.

In Haiti, we had our greatest opportunity to make good. What was the result? After Toussaint L'Overture cleared the white folks out of the island; instead of building macadam roads, inaugurating child labor, erecting canning factories, sawmills, insane asylums, textile mills and poor houses, the ignorant and shiftless natives worked just enough to keep themselves alive and spent the rest of their time in dancing, singing, voodism and opera bouffe revolutions. It remained for Wall Street, properly aided, as usual, by the armed forces of the United States, to rouse the people out of this sloth. Of course a few thousand of the more stubborn natives became casualties in their misguided efforts to emulate the farmers of Lexington and stay the forces of civilization. But the sacrifice of men and money poured out unstintingly by Uncle Sam for "the protection of American interests" was not in vain, so the island has been made safe for democracy. The little country is now on the upgrade; people are working all day, under the benign supervision of U.S. Marines, cheerfully constructing good roads to enable the numerous American officials to exercise their Fords, Buicks, and Packards; friendly police are cornered in every district; and plans are afoot to clear off the forests, open up stone quarries, develop the mineral resources and generally get things going in the right direction. Naturally a sizable minority of the leading spokesmen of the Haitians were not completely reconciled to this era of progress and expansion, so a large number of editors, and other lazy and troublesome fellows had to be jailed for entertaining fanciful ideas about the sacredness of treaties, independence, freedom of speech and press, and otherwise taking, the Bill of Rights, the Declaration of Independence and international law too seriously. However, it can be truthfully stated that the masses in Haiti today have as many liberties as the citizens of the United States enjoy. Ten or fifteen years hence when the thrifty Haitian leaps out of his Grand Rapids bed at 5:30 A.M. to the strains of Big Ben, and, going to the window of this flat, surveys the gorgeous panorama of smokestacks, tar roofs, fire escapes, clothes lines and cigarette advertisements, he will throw back his head, fill his lungs with the fresh morning coal dust, and thank God and the investment bankers for rescuing his people from barbarism.

Yes, we Negroes have a long way to go before we can truthfully claim to have anywhere approximated the development of the Caucasian. Our birth rate is still disgustingly high; we are only beginning to use the divorce courts; a large number of our young men and women still go to college to study; and the majority of our folks prefer the Bible to "Snappy Stories," "Whiz Bang," or "The Saturday Evening Post." Most of our people continue crowding the churches and singing spirituals on Sunday rather than recline amid the newspapers, soda bottles and cracker boxes on the spacious beach at Coney Island. The war records reveal that our young men were the most physically fit in the country. We must try to live down this poor showing. With great effort on our part, we may, in another half-century reach the Nordic level. In the meantime let us admit our backwardness and earnestly endeavor to appreciate the benefits we are undoubtedly deriving from our association with the supermen. It is clear the Nordics are ahead of us. Why not acknowledge the truth and silence our vociferous propagandists? Let us be fair and sensible!

Who knows we may yet prove our capacity for Nordic civilization? The case is not entirely hopeless. In Africa and elsewhere our people are being shaken out of their listlessness. Only recently my attention was drawn to the increasing number of suicides among our people, and at least two Negro bankers in the past ten years have absconded with the funds entrusted to their care. So the outlook is not entirely hopeless. Nearly all dependable observers returning from Africa testify to the great moral influence of white civilization on the natives. So Harry H. Johnston, the noted explorer and administrator, in his recent book, *The Story of My Life*, cites the case of a cultured and God-fearing Portuguese gentleman in Africa who took unto himself a black wife "without benefit of clergy," and produced a multicolored progeny by her, by his mulatto daughters and by his quadroon grand-daughter. How reminiscent of the chivalrous conduct of the Nordic aristocrats of our own ante-bellum South whose descendants are revolted by the very idea of social contact between the inferior and superior races—except at night! Indeed, millions of blacks are each year being awakened to the blessings of civilization. Is it too much that we also may some day burst forth in all the glory of honest graft, automobile bandits, strip poker and alimony? Stranger things have happened. Where there's a will, there's a way.

No, we should not despair of our black brothers. Remember, the Caucasians were once almost in the same boat. Tacitus said he didn't think the Germans would ever be civilized (and during the late annoyance many of our educators and statesmen said the same thing). All Europe at one time was inhabited by tribes of Nordics who did little else than lie around and enjoy life. Frivolity and indolence had Europe in their dastardly grip and there was no John H. Sumner, Lord's Day Alliance or Anti-Saloon League to say them nay. Great forests covered a large part of the continent; placid rivers wended their ways through picturesque valleys to the sea, with here and there a skiff or barge skimming their surfaces. The country wasn't developed at all. People wasted an immense amount of time on cathedrals, stained glass, poetry, music, tournaments and fairs. For a time it looked as if the white race was destined to be a failure. Jongleurs, troubadours, fat priests, hungry bandits and lean knights wandered around the country from place to place. A peaceful citizen was often held up and robbed in broad daylight. There was never the feeling of security that one experiences in cities free from outlawry, such as Memphis and Pittsburgh. The best building sites were occupied by castles, cathedrals and monasteries. In the midst of this slothfulness the white people of that day are reported to have actually been happy. What a sorry picture!

Well, thank God, a sense of responsibility to posterity was finally aroused in them through Crusades, trade with the Far East and the discovery of America. The age of laziness and vicious merriment has gone forever. The forests have been cut down and burned up; most of the people are living thrifty lives in the spacious slums of the large cities, and they are much healthier for the change since medical authorities assure us that only ninety percent have a certain social malady, merely four out of five suffer from pyorrhea and less than sixty percent wear spectacles. The erstwhile placid surfaces of the rivers are now disturbed by the hustle and bustle of thousands of tugs and barges carrying on the world's business, and the river lips once fledged by lilies and weeping willows are now fringed by soap factories, paper mills and garbage disposal plants. The Europeans of today and their American cousins are far more efficient in every way: The population is bigger (and so are the armies and jails); the bandits have also entered the cities along with the rest of the people—some going to prison or the police force, while others become bankers, brokers, or Congressmen:

fighting is done with much less frequency but with greater effectiveness—the victor losing as much as the vanquished—but the nonsensical chivalry of the Middle Ages has given way to the practicality of the twentieth century. Instead of the Jongleurs and troubadours, the modern Nordic has the "Blues" on all sorts of mechanical instruments at all hours of the day and night; the superb literature of the newsstands and the highly instructive dramatic productions of Hollywood. The old policy of each feudal lord furnishing his serfs with board and lodging has been happily discarded, and no longer is the rightful place of such business builders as real estate agents and food gamblers ignored.

This, I believe, is enough to show how far the Nordics have traveled in just a few hundred years. Is there any reason why the Negro should not do the same? We have, of course, made some gains: Our hotel proprietors, cabaret owners, insurance writers, physicians and undertakers have already developed an unusual ability to coin large profits in a small space of time. We can and must do better. It is absolutely essential that we cultivate the Nordic spirit of thrift and go-get-em. We must, therefore, in the words of Major (?) Robert "Rusty" Moton, the Sage of Tuskegee, "Be Modest and Unassuming," until such a time as we can show the world something like Amritsar, the World War, the West Virginia coal fields, the sweat shops of New York, and the Bowery. Then we shall have reached the level of Nordic civilization.

Negro-Art Hokum
(1926)

When this essay appeared in the Nation, historically a strong arm of liberal thought, Schuyler could not have imagined its impact on his personal and professional development. He argues in language that is both compelling and combative for the Americanness of the "Negro," anticipating the cultural analyses of Ralph Ellison, Albert Murray, and Toni Morrison. Despite the race consciousness associated with the New Negro movement of the 1920s, which focused less on cultural hybridity and more on racial autonomy, Schuyler insists on sifting through the interracial cultural grains of the United States. By referring to the "Aframerican" as a "lampblacked Anglo-Saxon" during one of the most important periods of black cultural production, Schuyler ensured his marginal place in African American cultural criticism. Moreover, the editorial staff of the Nation was so concerned about the repercussions of Schuyler's essay that Langston Hughes was enlisted by the journal to offer his perspective on the notion of black art in the following issue. In "Negro Artist and the Racial Mountain" (1926), Hughes would write the most important critical essay of his career. Contrary to the consensus among scholars, Hughes offers an alternative perspective on black art, but his essay is not a direct response to "Negro-Art Hokum."

Negro art "made in America" is as non-existent as the widely advertised profundity of Cal Coolidge, the "seven years of progress" of Mayor Hylan, or the reported sophistication of New Yorkers. Negro art there has been, is, and will be among the numerous black nations of Africa; but to suggest the possibility of any such development among the ten million colored people in this republic is self-evident foolishness. Eager apostles from Greenwich Village, Harlem, and environs proclaimed a great renaissance of Negro art just around the corner waiting to be ushered on the scene by those whose hobby is taking races, nations, peoples and movements under their wing. New art forms expressing the "peculiar" psychology of the Negro were about to flood the market. In short, the art of Homo Africanus was about to electrify the waiting world. Skeptics patiently waited. They still wait.

True, from dark-skinned sources have come those slave songs based on Protestant hymns and Biblical texts known as the spirituals, work songs and secular songs of sorrow and tough luck known as the blues, that outgrowth of rag time known as jazz (in the development of which whites have assisted), and the Charleston, an eccentric dance invented by the gamins around the public market-place in Charleston, S.C. No one can or does deny this. But these are contributions of a caste in a certain section of the country. They are foreign to Northern Negroes, West Indian Negroes, and African Negroes. They are no more expressive or characteristic of the Negro race than the music and dancing of the Appalachian highlanders or the Dalmatian peasantry are expressive or characteristic of the Caucasian race. If one wishes to speak of the musical contributions of the peasantry of the South, very well. Any group under similar circumstances would have produced something similar. It is merely a coincidence that this peasant class happens to be of a darker hue than the other inhabitants of the land. One recalls the remarkable likeness of the minor strains of the Russian mujiks to those of the Southern Negro.

As for the literature, painting, and sculpture of Aframericans—such as there is—it is identical in kind with the literature, painting, and sculpture of white Americans: that is, it shows more or less evidence of European influence. In the field of drama little of any merit has been written by and about Negroes that could not have been written by whites. The dean of the Aframerican literati is W. E. B. Du Bois, a product of Harvard and German universities; the foremost Aframerican sculptor is Meta Warwick Fuller, a graduate of leading American art schools and former student of Rodin; while the most noted Aframerican painter, Henry Ossawa Tanner, is dean of painters in Paris and has been decorated by the French Government. Now the work of these artists is no more "expressive of the Negro soul"—as the gushers put it—than are the scribblings of Octavus Cohen or Hugh Wiley.

This, of course, is easily understood if one stops to realize that the Aframerican is merely a lampblacked Anglo-Saxon. If the European immigrant after two or three generations of exposure to our schools, politics, advertising, moral crusades, and restaurants becomes indistinguishable from the mass of Americans of the older stock (despite the influence of the foreign-language press), how much truer must it be of the sons of Ham who have been subjected to what the uplifters call Americanism for the last three hundred years. Aside from his color, which ranges from very dark brown to pink, your American Negro is just plain American. Negroes and whites from the same localities in this country talk, think, and act about the same. Because a few writers with a paucity of themes have seized upon imbecilities of the Negro rustics and clowns and palmed them off as authentic and characteristic Aframerican behavior, the common notion that the black American is so "different" from his white neighbor has gained wide currency. The mere mention of the word "Negro" conjures up in the average white American's mind a composite stereotype of Bert

Williams, Aunt Jemima, Uncle Tom, Jack Johnson, Florian Slappey, and the various monstrosities scrawled by the cartoonists. Your average Aframerican no more resembles this stereotype than the average American resembles a composite of Andy Gump, Jim Jeffries, and a cartoon by Rube Goldberg.

Again, the Aframerican is subject to the same economic and social forces that mold the actions and thoughts of the white Americans. He is not living in a different world as some whites and a few Negroes would have us believe. When the jangling of his Connecticut alarm gets him out of his Grand Rapids bed to a breakfast similar to that eaten by his white brother across the street; when he toils at the same or similar work in mills, mines, factories, and commerce alongside the descendants of Spartacus, Robin Hood, and Erik the Red; when he wears similar clothing and speaks the same language with the same degree of perfection; when he reads the same Bible and belongs to the Baptist, Methodist, Episcopal, or Catholic church; when his fraternal affiliations also include the Elks, Masons, and Knights of Pythias; when he gets the same or similar schooling, lives in the same kind of houses, owns the same makes of cars (or rides in them), and nightly sees the same Hollywood version of life on the screen; when he smokes the same brands of tobacco and avidly peruses the same puerile periodicals; in short, when he responds to the same political, social, moral, and economic stimuli in precisely the same manner as his white neighbor, it is sheer nonsense to talk about "racial differences" as between the American black man and the American white man. Glance over a Negro newspaper (it is printed in good Americanese) and you will find the usual quota of crime news, scandal, personals, and uplift to be found in the average white newspaper—which, by the way, is more widely read by the Negroes than is the Negro press. In order to satisfy the cravings of an inferiority complex engendered by the colorphobia of the mob, the readers of the Negro newspapers are given a slight dash of racialistic seasoning. In the homes of the black and white Americans of the same cultural and economic level one finds similar furniture, literature, and conversation. How, then, can the black American be expected to produce art and literature dissimilar to that of the white American?

Consider Coleridge-Taylor [Samuel Taylor Coleridge], Edward Wilmot Blyden, and Claude McKay, the Englishmen; Pushkin, the Russian; Bridgewater, the Pole; Antar, the Arabian; Latino, the Spaniard; Dumas, père and fils, the Frenchmen; and Paul Laurence Dunbar, Charles W. Chesnutt, and James Weldon Johnson, the Americans. All Negroes; yet their work shows the impress of nationality rather than race. They all reveal the psychology and culture of their environment—their color is incidental. Why should Negro artists of America vary from the national artistic norm when Negro artists in other countries have not done so? If we can foresee what kind of white citizens will inhabit this neck of the woods in the next generation by studying the sort of education and environment the children are exposed to now, it should not be difficult to reason that the adults of today are what they are because of the education and environment they were exposed to a generation ago. And that education and environment were about the same for blacks and whites. One contemplates the popularity of the Negro-art hokum and murmurs, "How come?"

This nonsense is probably the last stand of the old myth palmed off by Negrophobists for all these many years, and recently rehashed by the sainted Harding, that there are "fundamental, eternal, and inescapable differences" between white and black Americans. That there are Negroes who will lend this myth a helping hand need occasion no surprise. It has been broadcast all over the world by the vociferous scions of slaveholders, "scientists" like Madison Grant and Lothrop Stoddard, and the patriots who flood the treasury of the Ku Klux Klan; and is believed, even today, by the majority of free, white citizens. On this baseless premise, so flattering to the white mob, that the blackamoor is inferior and fundamentally different, is erected the postulate that he must needs be peculiar; and when he attempts to portray life through the medium of art, it must of necessity be a peculiar art. While such reasoning may seem conclusive to the majority of Americans, it must be rejected with a loud guffaw by intelligent people.

Uncle Sam's Black Step-Child
(1933)

This essay appeared in the American Mercury, a conservative maga-
zine edited by the cantankerous H. L. Mencken. In 1931 the pub-
lisher, George Palmer Putnam, sent Schuyler on a covert mission to
investigate whether the Liberian government was practicing sla-
very, as alleged by the League of Nations. Unfortunately, the rumors
of government-sanctioned slavery proved to be true. Based on his
firsthand observations, Schuyler would soon publish Slaves Today:
A Story of Liberia *(1931), the first novel about Africa by an Afri-*
can American. After its publication, Schuyler wrote several articles
on the state of Liberia. Founded for former American slaves in 1822,
the country was a victim of both international and domestic exploi-
tation. In this essay, Schuyler discusses the ways in which Liberia
and other African countries that have had close ties to America have
floundered economically and politically. In other words, those Afri-
can countries vital to American economic interests have not been
able to establish the self-sufficiency required for autonomous exist-
ence. With such a Pan-African critique, Schuyler's analysis serves
as a forerunner to the contemporary analyses of Western imperial-
ism and its impact on Africa by Randall Robinson, president of
TransAfrica.

I

Liberia is at once the hope and the despair of all race-conscious
Negroes and friendly whites. In its early years it seemed a glorious vindication
of the black race's capacity for self-government, but today only the lunatic
fringe of Garveyite Aframericans remain deluded.

The Aframerican who goes there a resolute advocate of Liberian independence is more than likely to come away convinced of the necessity for American
intervention. Arriving in Monrovia, the capital, enthusiastic over being at last in
a country ruled by black men, he is shocked by the lack of common sanitation,
the unpaved, rock-strewn, meandering, weed-grown, unlighted streets, the swarm
of rats, and the general atmosphere of shiftlessness and decay.

He finds a government combining the worst corruptions of American democracy with complete incompetence and barbaric cruelty. He finds a ruling class that is lazy, shiftless and unprincipled. He finds the trade of the country in the hands of the Germans, Britishers, Frenchmen, Dutchmen and Syrians, and the only bank, controlled by the Firestone Company, an American concern. He learns that no one will employ Liberians because of their own incurable untrustworthiness. He discovers that every literate Liberian is after a job on the government payroll, while agriculture languishes and each day the jungle crowds in closer to the settlements. He finds the terrorized aborigines fleeing to the neighboring colonies of the European Powers or hiding deep in the primeval forest to escape the tax-gatherers.

He is puzzled when he is warned at the American Legation to think twice before he becomes a Liberian citizen. Is this not the Black Man's Land, the haven of colored folk eager to escape white oppression? He is reluctant to believe the story of the American Negro who arrived with $800 in cash, immediately became naturalized, a week later was defrauded of all his money by native slicksters, and left to rush back to the American Legation, begging vainly for assistance. He is amazed at the story of the colored woman who debarked with $400 and a son of twelve years—and two weeks later both were found poisoned, and their money stolen. He listens with dismay to the tales of Aframerican farmers who came out with high hopes to till farms, only to find there were no roads to bring their produce to town. He is surprised to learn that no money is to be earned in Liberia in the practice of his trade of his profession, whatever it may be, and that every time an American freighter visits the port of Monrovia, stranded Aframericans beg for an opportunity to work their way back to the United States.

Soon he hears about an Aframerican nicknamed Sweet Candy. Sweet Candy was a very race-conscious Negro who came out to Liberia to make his home and run a candy-store. At the start he did pretty well but in the course of time the Liberian soldiers took to visiting his little store and grabbing handfuls of candy. He complained to the authorities, but they only laughed at him. He warned the soldiers away but they paid no attention. Finally, enraged beyond endurance, he fired on several of them, whereupon, led by their officers, they chased him to the home of his lawyer, where he sought refuge. The house was surrounded by a yelling mob but his aim was too accurate for them to rush him. So they set fire to the place and poor Sweet Candy was incinerated.

II

Conditions in Liberia were not always so bad. The early settlers, from the United States, for all their faults, were a pretty sturdy lot, and they made up in industry, thrift and ambition what they lacked in knowledge, capital and experience. These pioneers raised large quantities of ginger, rice, cocoa, sugar and tobacco, and reared big flocks of goats, sheep and cattle. They prepared and shipped palm, oil, kola nuts and piassava fiber. Beginning in 1858 they held big fairs at Monrovia, exhibiting produce, cattle and handicrafts. At the largest fair of all, held in 1890, there was exhibited the first bale of cotton raised in the new land and yams weighing from 200 to 300 pounds. Cargoes were not only shipped in foreign bottoms but also in four Liberian ships manned by Liberians, and the Liberian flag appeared in the ports of Liverpool and New York. Many of the big planters, born in slavery in our Southern States, became wealthy. But today their plantations have disappeared in the ever-encroaching bush, and their saw-mills, sugar mills and homes have gone to ruin.

America fathered Liberia, but has failed to mother her. White Americans, including slaveholders, founded the American Colonization Society in 1816 for the repatriation of black freedmen. Bushrod Washington, nephew of the immortal George, was its first president. The northern philanthropists among its members were touched by the uncomfortable status of emancipated blacks in the United States, and the slaveholders feared their influence on the slaves, who were daily becoming more valuable with the increasing demand for cotton.

The first group of eighty-eight colonists, led by three white men—the Rev. Samuel Bacon, John Bankson and Dr. S. Crozier—reached Africa in 1820. They landed in what is now Sierra Leone, but because of the bad climate they were later transferred by the U.S.S. Alligator to Providence Island, opposite the present site of Monrovia, arriving on January 7, 1822. The following April they crossed to the mainland, and settled on a small tract of land purchased from naive kings. Glad to have the colonists as a buffer between their people and the slave raiders, the kings later presented the newcomers with a 150-mile strip of coastland.

Slave dealers along the coast incited some of the natives to attack the settlements, but in bloody battles fought in October and December 1822, the attackers were driven off. Late in 1826 a hundred colonists led by Jehudi Ashmun, an American white man, assisted by three United States brigs of war, routed the private army of two rich slavers, Theodore Canot and Don Pedro Blanco, and destroyed their base seventy miles below Monrovia. In 1839 the savage and warlike Kru tribesmen were defeated, and later in that year the colonists beat the powerful Golas in several engagements, being led by Thomas Buchanan and the first Governor of the colony. Other engagements and skirmishes were fought in 1851, 1861, 1893, 1915, 1917–18 and 1931, mostly against the Krus, Buzis and Greboes.

The colonists settled along the coast on lands acquired by treaty and purchase. One treaty with the Vai kings around Grand Cape Mount stipulated that land so acquired should not be sold to foreign subjects or governments. This stipulation was later embodied in the Liberian Constitution (Section 13, Article V):

> The great object of forming these colonies being to provide a
> home for the dispersed and oppressed children of Africa and

to regenerate and enlighten this benighted continent, none
but Negroes or persons of Negro descent shall be admitted to
citizenship in this Republic.

Unfortunately, Governor Thomas Buchanan died of the fever in 1841. At
the time he was trying to persuade the United States to purchase all the territory below Liberia down to what is now Nigeria and to develop the whole vast
area as an American colony, a home for freed Negroes. Had he lived he might
have succeeded, for his proposal should have appealed to the nervous American slaveholders who controlled the Washington administration down to 1860.
Had the United States been far-sighted enough to do as he suggested it would
have obtained very cheaply a vast African territory, at once a valuable market
for manufactured articles, a source of raw materials, and a means of solving the
vexatious problem of what to do with the emancipated Negroes before and
after the Civil War.

West Africa is richer in natural resources than the Philippines and is not so
far away. Back in 1841 the European Powers scarcely controlled any of it. But the
Americans of the time were busy ousting the Indians from their lands, settling
the West, plotting to grab Mexican territory, and rehearsing the impending conflict
between North and South, so they did nothing in Africa.

Alarmed over the rising territorial ambitions of the French, Liberia in 1842
purchased the remaining important sites on the littoral. British traders, however,
ignored its revenue laws and continued smuggling goods to the natives. The
American Colonization Society appealed to the United States, which requested
an explanation from the British government. In reply Great Britain said that she
"could not recognize the sovereign powers of Liberia, which is a mere commercial experiment of a philanthropic society." The United States then dropped the
matter, and the Colonization Society was compelled to abandon the colony. In
January 1846, it told the Liberians:

> The time has come when it is expedient for the people of the
> Commonwealth of Liberia to take into their own hands the
> whole work of self-government, including the management
> of their foreign relations.

Accordingly, on July 26, 1847, the Liberians adopted a constitution declaring Liberia a free and independent state. An American white man, James
Greenleaf, wrote this constitution, which provided for a form of government almost identical with that of the United States. Unluckily, it was wholly
unsuited to the administration of a primitive African state. Its author never
saw Liberia and knew nothing about its needs.

Great Britain, France and Prussia soon recognized the new state. The first
President, Robbers, an octoroon, journeyed to England and was received by
Queen Victoria aboard the royal yacht. She afterward made Liberia a present of

a warship, which she replaced with another when the first became unfit. The French also became friendly. Singularly enough, the United States did not recognize Liberia until 1862. Nevertheless, it spent $60,778.98 for the repatriation of some 13,000 Negroes (Congoes) taken from captured slaving vessels. Arrangements were also made for the education, training and maintenance of these unfortunates and Congress appropriated $150 apiece for their support.

This was a windfall for the settlers. They promptly divided up the Congoes among the leading Liberian families and set them to work clearing the jungle and planting crops. The money appropriated by the United States for their support was apportioned among the best people. This marked the appearance of a definite America-Liberian aristocracy, living, like their former white masters, off the labor of black serfs. The aristocracy still persists, despite Liberia's motto: "The Love of Liberty Brought Us Here."

Society soon became sharply stratified. At the top were the "old" families, often mulattos, who owned large estates and many slaves and controlled the government. Below them were the poorer free farmers, and still farther down the detribalized natives and Congoes. Back in the hinterland were some two million warlike aborigines who for nearly a century defied the authority of the coast government.

Color distinctions soon arose, based on this stratification. The ruling class, being mulattos and often the offspring of their former white masters in America, had better opportunities than the blacks, and made the most of them. But in the course of time the blacks began to agitate against this mulatto aristocracy and especially against mulatto Presidents. A white American visiting Liberia during the campaign of 1855, when President Roberts, an octoroon who had served four two-year terms, was being opposed by Stephen A. Benson, a black, was told by a Liberian:

> The folks say as how we darkies ain't fitten to take care o'oursels—ain't capable. Roberts is a very fine gentleman, but he is more white than black. Benson is colored people all over. There's no use talking government and making laws and that kind of thing if they ain't going to keep 'um up. I vote for Benson, sir, cause I want to know if we's going to stay nigger or turn monkey.

III

Few American Negroes emigrated to Liberia after the Civil War. The last considerable group of colonists, some 300 West Indian Negroes, mostly Barbadians, went out in 1865. Unreplenished by fresh blood, the "old" stock quickly lost its vigor, and the pressure of Africa made itself felt. Native girls were easily obtainable as concubines. Native boys could be induced or forced to work for nothing. It was more comfortable to loll in a hammock on a shady veranda than to labor under the relentless tropical sun.

By 1871, the government was in financial difficulties and a $500,000 loan at 7% was floated in England. The Liberians actually got but $100,000 of it, and that partly in goods, after the bankers had made their deductions. The furious citizenry, learning the facts, promptly assassinated President Edward J. Roye, whom they accused of having accepted a handsome commission for his part in arranging the loan. Liberia defaulted on this loan in 1874. In 1883, after many armed threats, the British government seized the Sherbro and Gahlinas territories in what is now Sierra Leone, and which Liberia had purchased for $100,000 thirty years before. In 1902, an effort to sell mining rights in the country to a British concern with Liberian stockholders fell through when the people heard rumors of bribery.

Money was still urgently needed. Owing to foreign competition and the failure of the local nabobs to improve the quality of the agricultural output, Liberia's trade in sugar, cocoa, coffee and palm oil declined. Leisure had taken the place of labor and it was easier to borrow money than to earn it. In 1906 a $500,000 loan at 6% was got from Erlanger & Company, London bankers, through another British concern, the Liberian Rubber Development Company, of which Sir Harry A. Johnson was president. Part of the money was spent financing a survey of the resources and peoples of the country by Johnson which later appeared in two volumes. The rubber company also borrowed a part to build a road which the torrential tropical rains promptly destroyed. Liberia really got only about one-third of the loan. The rubber company finally failed but there was enough money left in the Liberian treasury to organize a constabulary, the Liberian Frontier Force, which has ruthlessly subdued the hinterland folk opposed to taxation without visible benefits.

Soon Liberia was broke again and seeking another loan. Wary now of the British, a delegation was dispatched in 1908 to the United States. In 1909 an American commission went out to study conditions and make recommendations. The result was the $1,700,000 5% international loan of 1912 in which Great Britain, France, Germany and the United States participated. The expense of four receivers, one from each country concerned, was saddled on to the country. In 1912, the total foreign debt exceeded $2,000,000.

Then came the Fernando Poo "boy" racket. An agreement was made between the Liberians and the Spanish to furnish laborers for the cocoa and coffee plantations on Fernando Poo, a fever-ridden island 1200 miles to the southward. The Liberian politicians were overjoyed at the prospect of getting some ready cash once more. The Spaniards paid $50 a head for the "boys," and there was a golden opportunity to chisel "back taxes" from those who survived the yellow fever, yaws, elephantiasis and sleeping sickness prevalent on the island, and returned to Liberia after their two-year period of toil. Right away 260 "boys" were snatched by the Frontier Force and shipped to the Spanish planters. The civilized Powers were too busy murdering each other to be concerned about this revival of the slave trade. But while the Liberian politicians grew rich, the treasury remained empty.

When President C. D. B. King assumed office in 1919 he proceeded to negotiate a $5,000,000 "war" loan from the United States. (Liberia had also declared war against Germany!) He journeyed to the United States with three other prominent Liberians and $15,000 spending money, but after eight months returned aboard the U.S.S. Richmond, the Senate having somehow failed to ratify the loan.

Enter now Marcus Garvey and his Back-to-Africa movement. He wanted to use Liberia as the headquarters of his grandiose plan to wrest Africa from the clutches of the white nations. He sent out a commission to study conditions and make overtures to the Liberian politicians. The 1923 presidential campaign was impending and certain Liberians thirsting for office agreed with Garvey's agents to buy the election for $50,000 and install a regime favorable to his designs.

But time passed and no money was cabled. Frantic messages from the Liberian conspirators fruitlessly deluged the dingy headquarters of Garvey's Universal Negro Improvement Association in Harlem, for at this time the "Provisional President of Africa" was in the clutches of Uncle Sam for using the mails to defraud his dupes. The Liberian Redemption Fund, from which the $50,000 slush money was to come, had to be used in a vain effort to keep him from behind the bars. Immediately upon King's reelection, he had the Constitution amended to bar Garveyites from Liberia forever.

Then came Harvey S. Firestone, the rubber man. When the Liberian politicians learned he was eager to break the British rubber monopoly, they sent a former cabinet officer all the way to the United States to track him down. In return for a 1,000,000-acre concession, Firestone agreed to float a $5,000,000 loan for Liberia through the Finance Corporation of America, which he controls. The agreement was signed by the then Secretary of State, Edwin Barclay, who is now, as President, loudly denouncing it. The Liberian politicians were delighted by the prospect of some more ready money after the lean years in which their only revenue had come from selling "boys" to the Spaniards. Big times were had with the first receipts. Pompous officials bounced over the rocky streets in expensive automobiles and the din from cabarets vied with the rumble and rattle of native drums down in the native quarter.

But the celebration was short-lived. The service of the loan weighed heavily and the customs revenues grew smaller. To add insult to injury, there arose an international hue and cry over the forced labor of the natives at home and the sale of "boys" to Fernando Poo. An international commission consisting of an American, an Englishman, and a Liberian was appointed at the "invitation" of Liberia to investigate the charges. Its published findings were so shocking that President King, Vice President Yancey and several other higher officials were forced to resign.

Broke again, the Liberian government requested the help of the League of Nations. A commission was sent out to Monrovia in the summer of 1931. Upon returning to Geneva it drew up a Plan of Assistance calling for white administrative officers, sanitary improvements, the reorganization of the Frontier Force, the cessation of ruthless food requisitions in the hinterland, and an ending of forced labor and disguised slavery. The Firestone Company agreed to release $100,000 of the $2,500,000 remaining of the $5,000,000 loan to enable the plan to function. But on December 15, 1932, the Liberian Legislature, impatient at the delays and eager to pay back salaries, spoiled everything by stopping payments on the loan. The United States sent Major General Blanton Winship, Judge Advocate General of the Army, to Monrovia in March, 1933, in an effort to straighten out the financial tangle, and there the matter rests at present.

IV

Liberia is about the size and shape of Virginia, and of somewhat similar topographical arrangement, but is almost completely covered with jungles, swamps, and virgin forest. It is watered by numerous rivers and streams, any of them capable of supplying considerable hydroelectric power. Its natural resources are gold, iron, oil, diamonds, copper, zinc, and valuable woods. Its products are ginger, rice, coffee, cocoa, kola nuts, gum copal, palm oil, fan palms, coconuts, rubber, ivory, tortoise shell, goats, sheep, cattle, horses and donkeys. The forests, valleys and plateaus are teeming with elephants, bush cows, deer, chimpanzees, monkeys and leopards. Its streams and lakes swarm with fish.

The country begins to rise a few miles from the sea and the ascent continues gradually until great mountain ranges, in some places nearly 10,000 feet high, are encountered. It is not as unhealthful nor is the climate as oppressive as one might think. Even on the coast there is usually a breeze in the evenings during the hottest months of the year, and in the mountainous hinterland a fire and a blanket are not at all uncomfortable at night. Only on the coastal plain are mosquito-bars obligatory. There are many beautiful park-like plateaus, numerous forbidding miasmic swamps, and great primeval forests with enormous, vine-festooned, interlaced trees rising hundreds of feet. One can well accept the general opinion that Liberia is the most beautiful country in West Africa. Certainly the hunting is excellent.

Except on the 50,000-acre Firestone rubber plantations, which are located near the coast, there are not 100 miles of roads worthy of the name in the entire Republic. The best highway is little better than a wide trail and almost four hours are required to motor its forty-five miles. The only other means of communication is by trail or canoe, and unless one is transported in the jungles by a hammock swung from the shoulders of husky carriers one must walk. Riding in a hammock is much like journeying by camel back or going to sea in a small boat.

There are estimated to be close to 2,000,000 natives in the hinterland, divided between ten or twelve tribes or nations, each speaking a different dialect, which changes about every forty miles. Towns are ten, fifteen or twenty miles apart, each one surrounded by a circle of agricultural settlements buried in the jungle within a radius of three or four miles. The natives are of a fine type, physically and morally, save where they have been corrupted by misguided missionaries and their Liberian masters.

In striking contrast to the towns of the "civilized" coast folk, the native villages are well-drained by ditches around the huts, always well swept, and noticeably free from refuse. The huts are built of hardened clay from the anthills laid on a sturdy framework of post interlaced with vines. The walls are very thick and the interiors are cool by day and warm by night. The roofs of palm thatch are conical and steep. Many of the larger huts have three and four rooms.

Unlike their masters, the natives are self-sufficient economically and socially. They cultivate rice, cotton, cassava, coffee, vegetables and grain; they spin, dye and weave their own cloth; they keep cattle, build sturdy canoes and ingenious suspension bridges, make nets and baskets, mine and smelt iron, make pottery and ornaments, collect ivory and tan leather. Their religion is mainly animistic, although the Vais and Mandingoes are Mohammedans, and their educational system adequately fits the children for adulthood.

The Liberian politicians control the aborigines by appointing their paramount chiefs or kings. These rulers were in the old days selected by the people, but the Liberians learned by experience that sometimes an unpliable fellow got into power that way. In deposing a paramount chief reported to be friendly to the opposition party, the Secretary of Interior informed him in quaint Africanese: "A log has fallen across your path. Until you can remove that log, you cannot become paramount chief."

Through control of the paramount chiefs, the politicians also control the witch doctors and the Leopard Society or Native Ku Klux Klan. The former are a combination of clergymen and physician; the latter is a savage fraternal order whose members prowl at night draped in leopard skins and armed with iron claws to lacerate unpopular natives. In one district in 1930 a score of men were carried off within a month and their mutilated bodies found afterward in the jungle. In several instances officers sent out by the internal revenue collector (white) have been scared away from villages by "devils" sent out by the witch doctors at the instigation of Americo-Liberian officials who desired themselves to collect the taxes and appropriate them. From these witch doctors the Liberians have learned so much about the art of poisoning that they bid fair to outdo the Borgias.

The natives are systematically fined, overtaxed, robbed of their produce and cattle, and beaten up or shot down if they resist. They run pell-mell from their villages when a party of Liberians approaches. Labor is impressed for "road work"—and sent to work on the farms of officials. Soldiers debauch the native girls without restraint, requisition carriers without compensation and commit other atrocities at will. The writer has been begged by many a town chief in the back-country to ask the America Man (the American Minister) in Monrovia to save his people from the vengeance of the soldiers. One chief, with tears of humiliation in his eyes, told of soldiers carrying off his men and then coming back and breaking down some of his huts when he sent a messenger to the Secretary of War complaining against the outrage. In 1931 an expedition was sent down the Kru coast to punish the natives for alleged non-payment of taxes. Over 600 men, women and children were murdered and their huts burned.

The hut tax is five shillings annually but it is collected often as many as three or for times a year. Since it must be paid in British silver, which is difficult to get in exchange for produce because of the lack of transportation facilities to the traders on the coast, the natives are frequently unable to pay it. This invites reprisals in the form of heavy fines, increased food requisitions, and the whipping of the chiefs in the presence of their people.

The answer of many natives is flight. They desert their villages, hide in the deep bush or go into the French colonies of Guinea and the Ivory Coast. I have entered villages of 200 huts absolutely deserted, though in good physical condition. On one occasion, pledged to secrecy, I was taken many miles through the matted jungle along the bed of a stream to a remote settlement of fugitives.

V

Christian missionaries have been in Liberia from the first. They constitute three-fourths of the foreign white population of 200. There are about sixty missions now: Episcopal, Baptist, Methodist, Lutheran and Catholic. The Liberians, of course, are Fundamentalists, even though they have adopted many of the superstitions of the natives, such as the use of witch doctors when ill. They fill their churches every Sunday, rain or shine.

The numerous mission schools teach about 4000 children. All but a half dozen of these stations are located in the coast region and are mostly headed and staffed by whites and colored assistants. A few are supported by American Negro denominations and run by colored missionaries sent from the States. All in all, these disciples of the Lord are a callous, muddle-headed, incompetent lot; patronizing, pitying, and despising the natives, teaching them to sing hymns and parrot prayers in various dialects, and closing their eyes to Americo-Liberian atrocities. Their books are filled with pictures of white angels and supposed likenesses of Jesus making Him resemble a Norse deity. Thus the native children exposed to their training soon come to look down upon the simple, communistic life of their parents and to glorify everything white. The graduates of these schools are among the most untrustworthy natives in Liberia.

The missionary business, indeed, appears to be just another racket, with the gentlemen and ladies of the Lord living easy lives and commanding swarms of barefoot black boys to wait upon them and carry their hammocks. People who could not earn $30 a week in the States live at the mission stations like little kings. According to them, the natives are benighted children whose manner of living is all wrong, despite its survival through several thousands of years. They denounce the superstitions of the aborigines but teach them that the Hebrew children walked into the fiery furnace and emerged unscathed, and the multitude was fed on a basket of fish and bread, that Jonah was swallowed by a big fish and lived to tell the story, and that the dead will rise. It is not strange that the natives, whose beliefs are no more absurd, generally cling to their animism.

While these missionary schools are supposed to include some industrial training in their curricula, it is next to impossible to find a competent artisan in Liberia. Carpenters and masons have to be imported from Sierra Leone. Several missionaries admitted to me confidentially that the Firestone Company had taught the natives more along this line in five years than they had in seventy-five. There are missionary "colleges" in Cape Palmas and Monrovia, but they are really second-rate high-schools.

The forty or fifty public schools in Liberia enroll some 2000 children when they are open, and seldom go beyond the fourth grade. The Liberia College busily grinds out lawyers, though the legal gentry in Liberia are numerous and generally briefless. The Department of Public Instruction is a political machine. Little is known there about the school system and even the examination papers that come in are not graded. There are bales of them in closets, succumbing to the appetites of rats and termites.

The Liberians are past masters at the art of extortion. Kru seamen who formerly resided in Monrovia now choose to live in Freetown, Accra and Lagos rather than submit to payment of "back taxes" every time they return from a trip with a pocket full of wages. It is a common thing for native towns to be "fined" £100 or £200 by officials short of funds. A white motorist was once arrested for speeding in Monrovia. How this was possible in view of the condition of the streets is a mystery, but arrested he was. He was fined $25. The judge accepted the testimony of a barefoot traffic policeman who had determined the speed of the car by a device which he had borrowed from a man named Joe. Neither Joe nor the device was presented in court.

Another white motorist was arrested for killing a female dog about to have pups. The judge fined him $10 for killing the dog and twelve shillings each for killing the six puppies she would have had. It was assumed that she would have had six puppies because she had two the first time. It is a common practice to fine black clerks the exact amount of their monthly salaries for alleged disturbances of the peace.

Public officials seldom turn in any money they collect. In one year only $1400 was received from $15,000 consular fees due the Treasury. The government had to close its customs houses on the boundary because so little money came from them. Customs officials threatening to fine ships' captains are mollified with provisions from the refrigerator, a phonograph, or a cheap firearm. A Negro bishop from the United States could get no official to release his baggage from the customs, but when he presented the right man with ten shillings the trunks were released without an inspection whatever.

Ever since 1924 there has been an opposition political group, the People's Party, headed by Thomas J. R. Faulkner, a naturalized Americo-Liberian who came from the United States over thirty years ago. Many of the more progressive young Liberians belong to it and if it could gain power there might be considerable hope for Liberia. Unfortunately, overthrowing the reigning True Whig party, which has been in power for over thirty years and is dominated by an oligarchy of six or seven families, is almost impossible. In comparison to Liberian practices, the political thuggery of Tammany and the Southern oligarchies pales into puerility.

Although there are but 15,000 qualified voters in Liberia, in the 1927 elections President King received 243,000 votes and Faulkner received 9000. In Sinoe, a town of scarcely 4000 population, the registrar submitted a bill for $948 for registering supposedly qualified voters at two cents each. During the 1931 campaign President Barclay was accused by Faulkner of distributing thousands of blank deeds to property among his party henchmen. These deeds were presented to the registrars by the True Whigs actually propertyless and thus ineligible to vote, but were accepted nonetheless. In only one of the five counties did anything go wrong: Maryland. There the People's party garnered 1669 votes while the True Whigs got but 367. The accident was promptly remedied by the Secretary of State, who declared the captured legislative seats vacant and arrested the People's party leaders on charges of sedition before calling for another election.

Sensing the probability of armed revolt in the near future, the Barclay regime has recently passed a Sedition Act establishing penalties of seven years' imprisonment for criticizing the President. One editor who dared do so was promptly thrown into a filthy jail. Dr. F. M. Morais, a representative of the Grebo nation who went to Geneva to protest to the League of Nations against Liberian terror, now languishes in a prison far in the jungle. Others have suffered a similar fate. Whether these steps will stave off a revolution remains to be seen. It is the consensus of opinion among the Americans in Liberia that the thing most necessary there now is American intervention and benevolent supervision for a few years, with perhaps intelligently directed immigration of Aframerican farmers and artisans later on to fuse some new life into our African step-child.

Rise of the Black Internationale
(1938)

By 1938 Schuyler had made a significant move to the political right, primarily as a result of the communist manipulation of the Scottsboro case of 1931. In this essay, Schuyler suggests that as the African diaspora becomes more self-sufficient, it will resist eventually the imperialist racism of Western countries. Before the publication of this essay, which originally appeared in the NAACP's Crisis, *this revolutionary sentiment emerged only in Schuyler's serial fiction, published in the* Pittsburgh Courier, *which is now collected in one volume:* Black Empire *(1991). Moreover, Schuyler used pen names such as Samuel I. Brooks and Rachel Call when publishing his serial stories on black liberation. The anti-establishment sentiment of this particular essay demonstrates Schuyler's intellectual abilities, but these abilities would soon be replaced by a relentless conservative ideology.*

The three generations since Lincoln signed the Emancipation Proclamation (which a quarter million black Union soldiers rescued from oblivion as a mere scrap of paper) have been the most momentous in the history of the world. They have seen unprecedented shifts and incredible alignments. They have seen miraculous inventions fantastic in their potentialities. They have seen such cruelty, such conquests, such persecution and oppression, such exploitation as humanity never dreamed before.

More important to colored people, these 75 years have seen the steady decline in the power and prestige of people of color the world over, thanks to the improvement in European firearms, the amazing technological advance of the West and the shattering of distance and isolation by modern transportation and communication. And most important of all, these years have seen the resultant rise of the White Internationale and the gradual rise of the Black Internationale in opposition; not powerful opposition as yet, perhaps, but containing vast potentialities of which the white world is all too painfully cognizant.

So far as the colored world is concerned, one might refer to these three generations as the period of fluctuating inferiority complexes. The decline in the fortunes of the darker races was quickly reflected in the attitude of the white world toward them and the colored people's attitude toward themselves. An important factor in the racial equation, this self-opinion, for there is a human tendency to become what we think we are. Status largely determines hope or hopelessness. Coupled with white control of colored education through control of government and missionary schools, the colored races were put on the defensive psychologically and so remained until the World War. It is important to trace the politico-economic changes that altered the world without and so altered the world within.

In 1863 Africa with the exception of South Africa, Sierra Leone, Senegal, the Boer Republics, various stations and forts on the West Coast and the Barbary States on the fringes of the South Mediterranean was virtually unknown territory to Europeans. Europe had not yet been sufficiently prodded by circumstances or implemented by armaments to effect the conquest of Africa.

In the 7th century the dusky Moslems had conquered all northern Africa. They had planted colonies at Mombasa, Malindi and Sofala which developed into powerful commercial states. They had swept into Spain and Portugal, ruled the former for 700 years and threatened the freedom of white Europe. In 1453 the Turks had conquered Constantinople. From 1517 to 1551 they extended their rule over Egypt, Algeria, Tunisia and Tripoli, and at one time rolled up to the gates of Vienna. Beginning with the European "Age of Discovery" in the 15th Century the fortunes of the darker races began to decline, but the trend was slow until 1875. As late as the beginning of the 19th century the dusky Barbary States held tens of thousands of whites captive and flaunted their banners in the faces of Europe's navies.

While the slave trade had undermined the excellent, monarchocommunistic economy of Africa, black men still ruled it (and often profited from the traffic). Europe had first to defeat the "Infidel," to end its disastrous nationalistic wars, to down Napoleon and to start the age of steam before it could know Africa. Prior to that it was only interested in slaves and tall stories from the Dark Continent.

Interest in Africa revived with the explorations beginning in 1788. Interestingly enough this was also the age of Watt and Eli Whitney, of the Declaration of Independence and the Rights of Man. France occupied Egypt in 1793–1803 and Britain followed her. But an almost independent state was formed there under Mehemet Ali which extended its rule deep into the Sudan from 1820 onward. The first recorded crossing of Africa was accomplished between the years 1802 and 1811 by two Portuguese Negro traders, Pedro Baptista and A. Jose, who passed from Angola eastward to Zambezi. In 1814 England formally annexed Cape Colony, over 150 years after the first permanent white settlement by the Dutch on April 6, 1652.

WATERLOO FOR AFRICA

Waterloo in Europe spelled Waterloo for Africa. But the end was still a long way off. There was still the ages old struggle between Christianity and

Mohammedanism for trade rights and political supremacy disguised as Holy War and suppression of slavery. The Moslems were accused of continuing the slave trade and stripping Africa of manpower. The Christians with their developing power economy needed raw materials furnished by enslaved black workers at the source of supply. So the rush of "Christian" explorers, traders and missionaries descended upon Africa.

In 1863 Livingstone was exploring the Zambezi and Lake Nyasa, and making mulattoes the while. Speke was "solving the riddle of the Nile," Baker was "discovering" Lake Albert Nyanza, Stanley was yet to "find" Livingstone and solve the "mysteries" of Victoria Nyanza, Tanganyika and the Congo River. It was the age of Schweinfurth and du Chaillu, of stirring tales of rich and powerful black kingdoms with swarms of stalwart black warriors, of mysterious cities like Timbuktu, of strange religious rites deep in the heart of steaming jungles.

As late as 1875 Great Britain controlled but 250,000 square miles, France 170,000 square miles, Portugal 40,000 square miles, Spain 1,000 square miles and the Dutch Republics of Transvaal and Orange Free but 150,000 square miles of Africa. Turkey held sway very loosely over Egypt; the Egyptian Sudan, Tripoli and Tunis, Morocco, Abyssinia, Zanzibar and Liberia were independent. The great kingdoms of Ashanti, Dahomey, Benin, Uganda, Cazembe, Musta Yanvo and countless other Mohammedan sultanates and pagan countries still enjoyed their freedom. The Boers paid yearly tribute to the warlike Zulus and it was not until England's successful campaign against the Ethiopians in 1867–1868 that that mountain kingdom learned what to expect from the white world.

In 1869 the richest diamond fields on earth were discovered in the Vaal River valley and the Suez Canal was opened to traffic: two events that focused added attention on Africa. Two years later England completed acquisition of the Gold Coast littoral. Already France had grabbed Senegal (1854) and Obok (1862) at the entrance to the Red Sea. In 1873 England worsted the Ashantis and two years later lifted the Union Jack over Delagoa Bay. Events were happening faster than anyone imagined, and yet on the eve of the biggest land-grab in history a House of Commons committee considering West Africa affairs could recommend "that all further extension of territory or assumption of government, or new treaty offering any protection to native tribes, would be inexpedient." Thick-witted Britons!

Now economic rivalry, political necessity and rapid flow of invention were forcing the issue. The South beaten, the U.S. government forced withdrawal of France from Mexico and compelled other European powers to relinquish hopes of snatching territory in South America. Prussia defeated France in 1870 and the land-hungry German Empire was born late on the colonial scene. Italy became a nation instead of a conglomeration of Caribbean-like dukedoms and baronies and began looking for real estate abroad to add to her prestige.

Defeated France perforce switched her ambitions from Europe to Africa. The ambitions of young Germany and the grasping Leopold of Belgium set the pace for the imperialistic-minded world. These two countries had only Africa and the South Seas in which to seek exploitable territory. England, France, the Netherlands, Spain and Portugal had grabbed everything else. Leopold's 1876 conference grew into the International African Association which afterward snatched the rich Congo "Free" State, with the United States the first to recognize the robbery. In 1879 the Zulu military power was broken. The Germans called the 1884–1885 imperialistic conference for the "proper" regulation of all stolen lands in Africa, but even while the criminals were conferring German agents planted the Kaiser's emblem in Southwest Africa, Togoland, Cameroons and Southeast Africa. Alarmed by these precipitous and typically Teutonic methods, the British, French and Portuguese redoubled their efforts. By means of bullets, chicanery, gin and Christianity the white nations by 1900 had conquered or annexed all the rest of Africa and native kings who opposed them were either in exile or gathered to their fathers.

THE AMERICAS

The period from 1863 to 1876 which saw the African kingdoms drop into the European sack, also saw the emancipated Americans rise to the full promise of Appomatox [sic], the 13th, 14th and 15th Amendments and the political power inaugurated by Reconstruction. There was hope in their breasts that the darkest era was behind them; that they were on the threshold of full citizenship rights and privileges in the Union, and destined to march arm in arm with their white fellow men to the creation of a truly great civilization.

Southward in Mexico chaos reigned. In Spanish America dictator followed dictator and black men played their part in nation-building. In Brazil and Cuba slavery still obtained. Unhappy Haiti was torn with the usual strife and tyranny. In the Orient Britain had just emerged from a serious Indian rebellion. The Malay Peninsula, Indo-China and the Spice Islands, asleep in the azure seas, were still under their native rulers. China was still powerful, despite the aggressions of Britain, Russia and France, and lording it over Korea, Manchuria, Mongolia, Tibet, Formosa and adjacent lands. Little Japan, forced out of her voluntary isolation by Admiral Perry, was hastening to make up for lost time with the classic policy stated by one of her diplomats as "We adopt, we adapt and so we become adept."

Railroads and steamships were in their infancy. Electric lights, telephones, bicycles, automobiles, the airplane, motion pictures, vulcanizing rubber, the phonograph, the radio, television and countless other inventions and processes that have revolutionized industry and commerce and are now taken for granted were still in the future. The use of oil was confined to kerosene lamps and lubrication. Production and distribution of foodstuffs was yet to be revolutionized. Neither the repeating rifle, the machine gun or the submarine had made its appearance. The new world economy that, by a combination of purely fortuitous circumstances, was already making the white nations the world rulers of colored nations was still in its infancy and the needs of national industry could still be served by the nation.

The scramble for colonies was not only a scramble for robber prestige but also a scramble for raw materials (or war materials) necessary to meet the essential demands of the new power economy without which no nation could or can become or remain a great power. The astounding technological mutation in the West in the century preceding and the years following 1875 also firmly established the international color line which until recently was only challenged by the sturdy and canny Nipponese. Black, brown and yellow alike were maligned and jim-crowed on every side and in every place. Everywhere white people took precedence over darker people. "Science" justified the stealing, exploitation and oppression by "proving" to white satisfaction the "inferiority" of colored folk. History was rewritten in the light of the Aryan race theory. The so-called social sciences were yoked to the chariot of imperialism. The whole thing was blessed by the Church which undermined the psychology of colored peoples under the guise of teaching "morality."

AMERICAN NEGROES GROPING

Betrayed by the Great Compromise of 1876 when Northern Republicans blessed their virtual re-enslavement in exchange for white southern recognition of the crooked Hayes election, the colored freemen progressively lost power and prestige in the face of the Ku Klux Klan persecution and public indifference. By 1900 only one Negro's voice was heard in the halls of Congress and he was soon gone. The loudly hailed rapprochement between the white South and the white North was well under way.

Nevertheless there was a tremendous store of hopefulness, optimism and naivete in colored America. All you needed was education, religion and thrift to succeed. You must pioneer and build something. Let down your bucket where you are. The Republican Party is the ship, all else the sea. The name of Lincoln made hearts leap under dusky hides and whatever white folks said was gospel.

Perhaps there was something to what they said about our having no history! Perhaps, after all, colored folks were inferior. Where, pray, was our background? What had our forefathers done except hew wood and haul water for Marse John? Mightn't it be true that we had never built a civilization? Wasn't that what our "education" taught us? Was there anything for us to be proud of—even our smooth dark skins and soft krinkly hair? Wasn't there some logic to the white contention that the lighter we were, the better we were? Didn't that put us nearer to perfection? So let's ridicule anything and everything Negro and eulogize everything white per se. Let's insist that black be comic and yellow refined but of course not as refined as no color at all! Let's make wallflowers out of our dusky-hued maidens and yell "Did you order any coal?" when a black man appears. True, Negroes had ruled under Reconstruction, but weren't they corrupt like white folks said and too ignorant to be entrusted with responsibility of office?

Thus some of the gropings of the Aframerican mind: fearful, uncertain, ignorant and yet hopeful withal. Elsewhere in India, China, Malaya and Africa the products of mission training were similarly groping.

Then something else happened. World population, especially in Europe, was taking a tremendous spurt as forecast by Malthus. World area had not expanded an inch. Indeed, excessive and ignorant cultivation had contracted the arable surface. As competition in international trade grew, capitalism turned to more intensive exploitation of homelands and there also competition grew more fierce. Panics came, unemployment grew, talk of a workers' revolution grew. There were insufficient markets for the goods produced in an ever endless stream. Fewer markets mean fewer jobs. Fewer jobs made emigration imperative. The United States became the great labor market for white alien workers. The lower middle class of the white colonial powers sent their sons to Africa and Asia as clerks, army officers and petty administrators. In America the growing emigration pushed Negroes farther and farther out to the economic fringes.

The period of 1900–1920 saw the social consequences of the politico-economic imperialism. Color discrimination and segregation grew apace as job competition intensified and imperialism became solidified. The lynching wave reached its peak. The Grandfather Clauses and the Springfield Race Riot were straws in the wind. Then the triumph of Japan over Russia in 1904 roused hope among colored people that the balance of power might again shift to their side. The Pan-African Conference in Paris in 1899, the Niagara Movement in 1904 and the organization of the National Association for the Advancement of Colored People in 1909 marked a turning point in the mentality of the Negro. Elsewhere, brown, black and yellow men were coldly appraising this enforced white ideology and inaugurating a renaissance in opinion of self.

Beginning of Revolt

The World War came. The migration of black southerners to the industrial North, the transportation of millions of brown and yellow and black workers and soldiers to the docks and battlefields of Europe gave new impetus to Negro thought; brought up new ideas of solidarity in the world of color. A quarter million dusky Americans in uniform went to France to be insulted and maligned and returned to be shot down. The Wilsonian slogans stirred the hearts and minds of the oppressed Africa and Asia. Dark colonial emitters schemed and planned in the salons and cellars of London, New York, Paris, Bombay, Batavia, Singapore and Cairo. Mahatma Gandhi electrified the world with Non-cooperation. White people were not united, the colored world learned, and there were flaws in the armor of imperialism. Spengler and Stoddard wrote gloomily of the decline of the West and the rising tide of color. Soviet Russia, emerging from the slime of Czarism, tossed her bloodstained cap into the international arena professing love for all the oppressed the better to win concessions from their oppressors. Race riots swept over America and occurred elsewhere. American Negroes fought back with the white man's weapons in Chicago, Washington, Longview and Tulsa. Thousands of Indians defied the British Raj and went to jail. In South Africa Clements Kadalie threw down the challenge of organized black workers to the brutal Boers. Four Pan-African Congresses under DuBois brought together many bright minds of the Negro world.

Black scholars turned to piecing together the Negro's background. Negro newspapers, once mere pamphlets, challenged the best in America and unified the thinking of their people as never before. Black magazines seriously discussed the Negro's place in the world and his relation to other colored peoples. Black lawyers thundered at the bar of white justice. Marcus Garvey stirred the imagination of the ignorant and romantic; fostered pride of color where before there had too often been shame. Dusky surgeons headed hospitals. Businesses sprang up throughout Aframerica attesting to Negroes increasing belief in themselves if nothing more. Again men of color sat in a dozen State legislatures and even returned to the halls of Congress. Black agitators spouted the jargon of socialism and communism and openly plotted the overthrow of the capitalist system.

In America, in Asia, in the islands of the sea the darker men became critical and condemnatory of white civilization where once they had been worshipful and almost grateful for shoddy castoffs. Today the colored worker strikes in Trinidad and Jamaica, in Bathurst and Cape Town, in Nigeria and the Gold Coast. He sits down in Detroit and Chicago and pickets in New York and Pittsburgh. He sees whites relinquishing extraterritoriality in China and Egypt and giving Burmah and India self-government. He sees erstwhile haughty whites cowering in the shell-holes of Shanghai, a British ambassador machine gunned on the road to Nanking and an American gunboat bombed to the bottom of the Yangtse River without reprisal from a Caucasia become panic-stricken and paralyzed.

THE NEW NEGRO ARRIVES

The New Negro is here. Perhaps no more courageous than the Old Negro who dropped his shackles in 1863, and fought against ignorance, propaganda, lethargy and persecution, but better informed, privy to his past, understanding of the present, unafraid of the future. No longer blindly worshipful of his rulers, he yet has learned to respect and study the intelligence and accumulation of power that has put them where they are. He has fewer illusions about his world.

He is aware that the balance of power is shifting in the world and so are his cousins in Africa, in India, in Malaysia, the Caribbean and China. He is rightly suspicious of white labor even when it is sincere. He has seen white labor forget the Marxist divisions of proletariat and bourgeoisie and join the White Internationale with the capitalists. He has seen both the 2nd and 3rd Internationales abandon the colored peoples to the mercies of their masters in order to perpetuate the industrial system of Europe which is based on colonial slave labor. He sees Russia abandon its revolutionary role and with French and British workingmen back Deladier and Chamberlain. And, as crowning infamy, he has seen the ruthless rape of defenseless Ethiopia with the Pope applauding on the sidelines.

He knows that the fear of losing the colonial peoples and their resources is all that prevents another World War. He believes that to combat this White Internationale of oppression a Black Internationale of liberation is necessary. He sees and welcomes a community of interest of all colored peoples. No longer ignorant, terrorized or lacking confidence, he waits, and schemes and plans. He is the Damoclean sword dangling over the white world. Everywhere he is on the march, he cannot be stopped, and he knows it.

The Caucasian Problem
(1944)

This essay appeared in What the Negro Wants *(1944), a collection of essays edited by Rayford Logan. Mary McLeoud Bethune, Langston Hughes, and Sterling A. Brown, among others, contributed to the volume. Focusing on the struggle against racial apartheid in World War II America, Schuyler continues his pan-Africanist criticism, delineating the history of Western imperialism and its calamitous effects on the African diaspora. In a rhetorical form that reminds us of W. E. B. Du Bois and with a clarity of thought comparable to Ralph Ellison, Schuyler asserts that white Americans are the most debilitating problem in America. With prescient historical and cultural observations, he forces whites to process the way in which their economic and political power emerge from perverted notions of racial superiority. Having begun his shift to the far right, this is one of Schuyler's final liberal salvos, censuring Euro-Americans without equivocation.*

By a peculiar logical inversion the Anglo-Saxon ruling class, its imitators, accomplices and victims have come to believe in a Negro problem. With great zeal and industry those controlling the media of information and instruction have succeeded in indoctrinating the whole world with this fiction. It is written into the laws, accepted by organized religion; it permeates our literature, distorts our thinking and is deeply imbedded in our customs and institutions. So successful has been this propaganda that even its unfortunate victims often speak of it with the same conviction with which many people talk of guardian angels, ghosts and malignant spirits. It is the "stop thief" technique at its best—a great testimonial to the ingenuity of exploiters with a bad conscience; for while there is actually no Negro problem, there is definitely a Caucasian problem.

Continual reference to a Negro problem assumes that some profound difficulty has been or is being created for the human race by the so-called Negroes. This is typical ruling class arrogance, and, like most of the faiths circulating in our civilization, has no basis in fact. It has been centuries since any Negro nation has menaced the rest of humanity. The last of the Moors withdrew from Europe in 1492. Since that time not one of the numerous industrially retarded but socially complex African states has molested the rest of the world with the possible exception of pirates of the Barbary Coast. They have neither possessed the means nor the inclination to do so, and they lived more or less happily in isolation until the coming of the European with his Bibles and bullets.

The so-called Negroes did not inaugurate the trans-Atlantic slave traffic, although some profited from it. They have not invaded anybody's territory for almost a millennium. They have passed few if any Jim Crow laws, established no Jim Crow customs, set up few white ghettos, carried on no discriminatory practices against whites and have not devoted centuries to propaganda attempting to prove the superiority of blacks over whites. The last Negro writing with that slant was in the Tenth Century. We seek in vain during modern times for any record of Negroes having destroyed any white cultures, having ravished and debauched white women wholesale, or having stolen white manhood. On the other hand the history of the world since 1815 is crowded with references to wars, campaigns and expeditions by Caucasian Powers against almost every African and Asiatic nation.

Of the international capitalists who control the lives of over a billion colored people practically all are white, and so, also, are the technicians, brokers, lawyers, generals, admirals, artists and writers who serve them. Colored people are largely excluded from this select group and relegated to the economic fringes of society where labor is long and hard and pay is short and seldom. The occasional exception here and there only emphasizes the point. The only sense in which there is or has been a Negro problem is in the colored folk's natural human aversion and opposition to conquest, enslavement, exploitation and debasement during the long and bloody period of Caucasian military ascendancy.

With the exception of such camouflaged colonies as Haiti, Ethiopia, Liberia and Egypt, all the Negro countries have been overrun long since, their rulers killed or exiled and their peoples chained and exploited like those of the European lands currently under Nazi rule. The colored countries in Latin America and Asia are either directly the victims of aggression and occupation by Caucasian powers—chiefly Anglo-Saxon and their imperialist satellites—or they are controlled indirectly by native dictatorships backed by white international bankers and their tax-supported armed services. Where and when the opportunity presented itself, the other Caucasian countries did likewise or to the extent of their abilities. Thus, Russia subjugated the people of Siberia, Spain slaughtered her way to empire in the Americas and the Philippines, Germany and Italy grabbed remnants in Africa and Asia, and Denmark gathered a few islands in the Caribbean. Portugal, Holland and Belgium have assembled valuable real estate and subject peoples in Asia and Africa, although the Japanese have rudely relieved these British satellites of some of their ill-gotten gains.

The only nation that has become a problem to the Caucasians is Japan which was the hired gunman of Anglo-Saxondom until the beginning of this decade, checkmating Russia and helping to weaken, undermine and debauch

China. Only when the Nipponese bandit went into business for himself and practiced what he had been taught, equipped and financed to do so by erstwhile employers, did he become a problem.

While we may dismiss the concept of a Negro problem as a valuable dividend-paying fiction, it is clear that the Caucasian problem is painfully real and practically universal. Stated briefly, the problem confronting the colored peoples of the world is how to live in freedom, peace and security without being invaded, subjugated, expropriated, exploited, persecuted and humiliated by Caucasians justifying their actions by the myth of white racial superiority. Put bluntly, that is the concern uppermost in the minds of all intelligent and sensitive colored people whether they live in Birmingham, Boma or Bonares. They are nauseated by the fictions and hypocrisy cloaking military aggression and crass materialism, and everywhere today their dream is to rid themselves of the whole Caucasian problem which is basically the same throughout the colored world.

Whether he be as wise as Einstein or as saintly as Jesus, the colored man must everywhere accept a subordinate position. There are restrictions on where he may live, on what work he may do, with whom he may associate, how and where he may travel, on his right to choose his rulers, on his education, on whom he may marry, and, in many places, on where his last remains may be interred. The problem is worse in Kenya or Australia than in Mississippi or Sierra Leone, but the general pattern is similar. It is no easier for him to get bed and board in London than it is in Washington, D.C. Whether in the Transvaal or in Texas, he is at the bottom of the industrial hierarchy—except in war time when the system is imperiled and every man is expected to do his bit for democracy. He observes that the press, radio, and cinema are primarily for the entertainment and benefit of white people and almost never for colored people. He has become painfully aware that generally throughout the world he is treated by white people as a pariah. Whether in Fiji or Florida, the black man's burden is this vicious color caste system which makes his world a cultured hell. On the other hand, the white man's burden is his guilty conscience which he sublimates with racial fictions to which he laboriously accommodates his morals and ethics.

The term Negro itself is as fictitious as the theory of white racial superiority on which Anglo-Saxon civilization is based, but it is nevertheless one of the most effective smear devices developed since the Crusades. It totally disregards national, linguistic, cultural and physical differences between those unable to boast a porcine skin, and ignores the findings of advanced sociologists and ethnologists. Avoiding the consideration of such obvious differences between colored people, it facilitates acceptance of the fiction of similarity and identity which is easily translated into a policy of treating all colored people everywhere the same way.

The once-popular American ditty "All Coons Look Alike," was a musical statement of the Anglo-American color philosophy already embodied in the law and hallowed by custom and tradition. So likewise was the thought expressed in that other popular American song of the turn of the century, "I'd Rather Be a White Man Than a Coon, Coon, Coon." In the word "nigger" (the overall-and-jumper version of "Negro") we have a term conveying this thought throughout the Caucasian—and especially the Anglo-Saxon—world. To a lesser extent it circulates also among the satellite Belgian, Dutch and French ruling classes, and among the other white aristocracies. Almost everywhere the colored people are "niggers" or they are called by the less biting synonyms: "native," "kaffir," "fellah," "boy" or "coolie," which serve the same purpose. In the United States the childish device of attempting to make "Negro" respectable by using a capital "N" seems to have deceived everyone except a realistic, and therefore insignificant, minority of thinkers.

Of course "white" and "Caucasian" are equally barren of scientific meaning but are similarly useful for propaganda purposes. There are actually no white people except albinos who are a very pale pink in color. A white skin would be a diseased or dead skin. If the name "Caucasian" is meant to imply racial purity or unusual paleness, it is certainly fallacious because the original home of the Caucasians, from which some romantic scientist assumed the present Europeans migrated, contains some 150 to 300 different "races" or types, and, as Ruth Benedict points out: "Caucasians have no characteristic cephalic index or body height, no specific hair color or eye color; their noses may be Roman or concave; even the color of their skin is extremely variable." Aryan, of course, is a language designation, and anybody using an Indo-Iranian tongue is an Aryan regardless of appearance; while Nordic, as a description of the Northern European blondes presumed to be a pure race is somewhat invalidated by the belief of some anthropologists that they are bleached Bantu who originally came north out of Africa and followed the receding glaciers.

However, the point is that these general terms "Negro" and "Caucasian," "black" and "white" are convenient propaganda devices to emphasize the great gulf which we are taught to believe exists between these groups of people. It is significant that these divisions very conveniently follow the line of colonial subjugation and exploitation, with the Asiatics and Africans lumped together smugly as "backward peoples," "savages," "barbarians" or "primitives": i.e., fair prey for fleecing and enslavement under the camouflage of "civilization."

Prior to the rise of the present imperialist Powers on the wings of piracy and conquest, and during the period when the African states were still intact and powerful, colored people were generally known as Saracens, Moors, Ethiopians, Africans or by other nationalistic names which conjured visions of pomp, tradition, glory and might, or they referred to some specific locality. Before the inauguration of the slave traffic, Europe knew these people as warriors, merchants, physicians, sailors and artists; but afterward they ceased being Mandingoes, Yorubas, Fulanis or Vais and, merged in common servitude, they became "niggers," or the more dignified "Negroes." These terms became in time synonymous with servitude and debasement, and still are.

The slave was a piece of property, a thing. Learned clerks argued long and heatedly over whether or not he was a human being and possessed a soul. The term Negro or "nigger" implies that he is still a thing, a member of a robot-like mass of inherently inferior beings essentially the same regardless of intelligence, education, skill, profession or locality, and in any case of lower status than any white person though the latter be a criminal or imbecile. Thus the so-called Negro race is a melange representing every known variety of human being with nothing whatever in common except a common bondage and a common resentment against enforced poverty and pariahdom, and an increasing determination to rid the world of the Caucasian problem which hampers its progress and development.

The racial fiction has been industriously spread over the world with the extension of white hegemony. The Anglo-American immigration policies excluding Orientals from the United States, Canada and Australia, have been part of the white supremacy doctrine introduced to Asiatics. It is noteworthy that while these colored peoples are excluded from white lands, the Caucasian missionaries, soldiers, sailors, racketeers, merchants, salesmen and investors have swarmed over the South Seas and Asia carrying the torch of civilization which, as René Maran has well said, "consumes everything it touches."

Wherever they landed, they insisted upon and got special privileges, thanks to superior arms. Soon there were special Caucasian concessions, courts, and "spheres of influence" throughout Japan and China backed by ubiquitous detachments of troops and occasional cruisers. India fell to the British adventurers. The former Chinese imperial provinces of Tibet, Manchuria, Burma, Malaya, Cochin-China, Annam, Cambodia, Tonkin and Laos got white overlords. The erstwhile independent kingdoms of the East Indies languished under the heels of Dutch freebooters whose regime became so cruel and corrupt that it shocked Sir Stamford Raffles, founder of Singapore, when he took over as governor during a temporary transfer to the Union Jack in 1811. The numerous paradises of the Pacific, those lovely, languorous emeralds set in the azure seas, became sugar and pineapple plantations or mining concessions of absentee owners and worked by peons.

The white man became the sahib, tuan or master, living aloof in luxury with the prettiest "native" women (whom he abandoned when he returned home). The "native" saw his land taken, his crops appropriated, his labor stolen, his leaders debauched or imprisoned, his culture undermined and destroyed, his family and friends debased by alcohol and opium, and their lives shortened by malnutrition and disease. Along with this imperialism went various forms of Jim Crowism and humiliation. It is not singular that these Asiatic colored folk are in revolt against white rule. To them the Caucasian problem means the same thing that it does to the serfs of Georgia, of Trinidad and of South Africa.

Turning to Latin America we see basically the same problem. There is to be found the same white economic and financial ownership and control of natural resources and public utilities administered by white or mestizo politicians

financed and maintained by foreign loans and subsidies. As an inevitable cor-
ollary we find the Indio-African masses impoverished and degraded, with the
little islands of whites living in affluence and looking down upon them as
"spigs." Significantly enough the more highly colored Latin American countries are regarded as having failed to live up to the democratic ideal whereas
the "white" lands like Argentina, Chile and Costa Rica—equally torn at inter-
vals by internal revolts and bossed by alien-supported dictators—are hailed as
successes. A more sinister aspect of this economic domination is the spread
among the white and near-white Quislings of the Nordic-superiority nonsense
prevalent elsewhere. Both Waldo Frank and Donald Pierson have recently noticed
this development in Brazil, although so far it is happily restricted to only a few.

It is noteworthy that most Latin American nations are careful to send only
white or near-white diplomatic and consular representatives to England and
the United States. The experience of Haiti on this point is very illuminating.
From 1804 to June 5, 1862, the United States refused to recognize Haiti although
there were American legations in twenty-one countries of less commercial importance to America, and although many other nations, including Great Britain,
had done so. The reason was clear. Senator Thomas Hart Benton of Missouri
very succinctly stated the case for the opponents of recognition:

> Our policy towards . . . Haiti has been fixed . . . for three and
> thirty years. We trade with her, but no diplomatic relations
> have been established between us. . . . We receive no mulatto
> consuls, or black ambassadors from her. And why? Because
> the peace of eleven states will not permit the fruits of a suc-
> cessful Negro insurrection to be exhibited among them. It
> will not permit black ambassadors and consuls to . . . give
> their fellow blacks in the United States proof in hand of the
> honors that await them for a like successful effort on their
> part. It will not permit the fact to be seen, and told, that for
> the murder of their masters and mistresses, they are to find
> friends among the white people of these United States.[1]

President John Quincy Adams quickly concurred in this view.

Later in 1852 when a system of "partial recognition" was prepared, the
Emperor Soulouque upset the apple cart by appointing an American to be a
Haitian consul at Boston. Secretary of State Daniel Webster refused to accept
an appointee bearing that title, implying recognition, but stated that any person "not of African extraction"[2] would be welcomed as a commercial agent.
Even when the Haitians promised to send a diplomatic representative to Washington so light that he would be indistinguishable from the other members of

---

1. [Schuyler's original note] *Congressional Debates*, 19th Congress, 1st Session, Cols. 330–332.

the diplomatic corps, the United States was adamant—until the slaveholding South seceded and thus lost its grip on American foreign policy. The lesson has not been lost on other countries.

In the Caribbean area where American "penetration" is most marked the color line has kept pace with Yankee imperialism. Cuba, Panama, and Puerto Rico have become well acquainted with this phase of the Caucasian problem. Since the taking over of naval and air bases in the British West Indies, American missionaries of Negrophobia have alarmed the "natives" by insistence upon Jim Crow set-ups and practices formerly unknown even in those English colonies.

Only when we understand the universal character and international ramifications of this Caucasian problem are we able to see how faithfully it follows the pattern in the United States, with important differences and variations. Here the so-called Negroes are a small minority living in the midst of a great majority. They use the same language and have the identical culture. They arrived with the whites—and before most of them. Both peoples have made important contributions to the development of this civilization which both regard as their own. The colored Americans are perhaps more American than most of the whites since they have practically no foreign connections. The ruling class here encourages the white generality to believe they control the government, but it does not permit the colored minority to share this illusion. The thousand and one devices and artifices used to prevent the colored people's full enjoyment of citizenship rights and privileges fully attest to that.

The position of the colored subject in England, although born to the soil, is equally unenviable, and in some ways is worse. Neither ruling class, unlike the rest of the Europeans, is willing to accept the colored person for what he may be as an individual, perhaps because such exceptions are regarded as undermining the color caste system. There are exceptions but their paucity only emphasizes the rule. Maintaining this international biracialism in the face of the growing demand of colored people everywhere for justice, equality and opportunity is what white spokesmen mean by "the Negro problem." It is the same problem which confronted the French in Indo-China and Africa, the Dutch in the East and West Indies, and the British in Burma, Malaya, India, Africa and the Caribbean.

Students of the Caucasian problem will admit that Negrophobia has spread far beyond the upper and middle classes and has penetrated the lowest stratum of white society. But they are aware that the ruling class and its intellectual gendarmerie set the fashion in prejudices as they do in clothing, habitations and hair-do. The uncannily accurate polls of public opinion have proved that these few shape the thought of the masses, rather than the other way around. There is much evidence that the color prejudice of the masses is not too deeply

2. Ludwell Lee Montague, *Haiti and the United States* (Durham, 1940), p. 59

rooted. For one thing there has always been a natural trend toward fraternization between the common folk, regardless of skin color, as shown by the strenu-
ous efforts throughout American history to prevent it and by the progressive
lightening of the color of American Negroes.

It is clear that the numerous laws and regulations enacted to halt association between the colored and white people on a plane of equality have been
written and passed by the few and not by the many. It was the "pillars of society" who insisted upon racial segregation. Jim Crow schools, railroad coaches,
bus compartments and waiting rooms would not exist if those who are influential
in American society had opposed them. They have not frowned upon the self-
appointed missionaries of racial purity. Wherever permitted, the common people
have established the democratic relations that should exist in a free country.

Even after three centuries of Negrophobic indoctrination, no deep-seated
revulsion or antagonism has prevented 15,000 interracial marriages and countless clandestine relations in all parts of the country. It would be extremely
difficult to find a community in the United States where members of the two
groups reside and where no intimate interracial relationship between both sexes
of both "races" exists. It is well known that white people from the most Negrophobic areas will move to other and more liberal communities and speedily
adjust themselves to eating with, riding alongside, working and living with
colored people with extremely little friction and scarcely a murmur of protest.
The growth of Negro ghettos in large cities can be traced chiefly to avaricious
realtors eager to roll up bigger profits through artificial scarcity of habitations.
The fact that almost every one of these ghettos has been permitted to expand
with increased Negro migration indicates that profits rather than principles
were behind the original restrictions.

The United States government has bowed without exception to the will of
the ruling class in these matters. No one seriously contends that it is a government of the people. Although colored and white soldiers served side by side in
the early wars of the Colonies and the Republic, the federal government segregated them in separate units during and after the Civil War. Following the
First World War it restricted colored sailors to service only in the mess departments of its warships. It is not hard to guess why Negroes have had such
difficulty in gaining admission to the military and naval academies, or to the
citizens' training camps. It is no accident that at least nine-tenths of the colored soldiers and even a large percentage of colored sailors serve as stevedores,
laborers and in other "service" branches. It has remained for the French General Henri Giraud to state bluntly the reason for this policy in the case of the
Jews. The same reasoning is doubtless behind the American and British restrictions, but inherent hypocrisy militates against such frank statement. Ordered
General Giraud: "Jewish commissioned and non-commissioned officers and
men in the reserve will generally be assigned to special non-combatant and

work units. This measure appears necessary in order to avoid having the entire Jewish population gain the title of war veteran, which might prejudice the status given these people after the war."

The Panama Canal Zone, built largely with Negro labor and run autocratically by the War Department, is a strictly Jim-Crow set-up operating under "silver" and "gold" euphemisms, with the whites naturally coming under the name of the more valuable metal. In practice this means the operation of two sets of public places, separate housing and a double standard of pay and promotion. The American people did not insist that this be done. Nor did they demand that the War Department divide the Puerto Rican National Guard regiment so that light islanders served in one branch and dark folk in the other, with the result that brother was often separated from brother.

Segregation and discrimination have been systematically practiced in the United States Civil Service, and although identifying photographs on applications (as Negro traps) are no longer required, it just happens that colored workers seldom seem to occupy certain positions, especially those of the white collar variety where they might have to meet the general public. The student of these tortuous artifices must ever wonder how much time and effort is spent by tax-paid officials on working out these schemes devised to prevent just treatment of fellow citizens. The same meticulous care in protecting white supremacy is to be observed in all other departments of the government, and this is not done at the insistence of the white masses. It is also significant that such public positions as Negroes held fifty years ago are in many instances unobtainable today.

The United States Supreme Court is certainly far removed from the pressure of the masses of white Americans, and yet it has distorted and twisted out of all semblance to the originals those Constitutional amendments guaranteeing full rights of citizenship to all citizens regardless of creed or color. By its interpretations of the Constitution, colored citizens have been systematically reduced to the status of half-men. It has consistently supported segregation as a genuflection to State's Rights while denouncing discrimination—knowing full well that the two are inseparable when applied to a weak minority. No mob has as yet stood at the doors of the Justices' chambers compelling them to concoct unjust decisions blessing the anti-intermarriage laws of two-thirds of the states which Hitler so slavishly copied. They did these things in obedience to the Negrophobic philosophy of our dominant class.

Congress, which has always faithfully represented the American propertied interests, administers the District of Columbia. In this, the capital of the world's allegedly greatest democracy, a colored citizen is and always has been a pariah. No mass upheaval has prevented the District Committee from ending this shameful situation, and thus making it possible for Negroes to be free in at least one place in the Republic. The District could certainly have as liberal civil rights laws as New York, Illinois, Connecticut and New Jersey where the masses of white people actually vote and, in the main, are no more liberal and tolerant than the inhabitants of the nation's capital, who do not vote and thus exercise no control over their civic administration.

The students of the Caucasian problem do not find it surprising that those who control the government are no more liberal than those who operate it. This small minority of financiers, industrialists and merchants made perhaps the greatest contribution to the problem by barring Negroes from the mechanical trade and technical professions, from commerce and finance. This "cold pogrom" has caused more bitterness among colored people than any other American racial policy. It is not a policy which can be blamed on organized white labor, as American business is wont to do, because only a few industries and businesses, up until a decade ago, were organized by the unions. The rest were open shop, free to hire and fire whom they chose without interference. Invariably they chose the racially chauvinistic course, and then declared it was done because their unorganized hands objected to working alongside Negroes. The successful interracial employment policy of Henry Ford, the greatest industrialist, gave the lie to these excuses.

Unquestionably a score or more of unions of skilled workers have made the Caucasian problem more difficult by adopting constitutional or ritualistic provisions barring colored workers from membership, and thus from earning a living. But here they have been upheld and encouraged by the courts of justice (?) and by the overwhelming majority of the employers. If there had been any solid front of business and financial interests against color discrimination in industry, it would have never found a foothold. The fact that under war time stress thousands of employers have lowered the color bar with little protest and no decrease in production shows that it could have been done years ago.

While numerous labor unions have been and are guilty of color discrimination, and have contributed much to keeping the colored people hanging on the economic fringes of society, it is seldom recognized that organized labor as a whole has been more liberal than organized business, organized religion or organized education. If there are a score of labor unions from which Negroes are barred there are thousands of churches and schools which do not accept them, and an equal number of business and professional organizations where, to say the least, colored members are not welcome.

However, there can be no question about the increasing public aversion of the white masses to Negro equality. Fundamentally, racial relations have worsened as the propaganda of white supremacy has sunk deeper and deeper; and the Aryan policies of government, the courts and business have become more wide-spread while national leaders denounced Hitler, Goebbels and Rosenberg. Biracialism has become the accepted practice in America as in South Africa at the time when the shouts are loudest in praise of freedom and democracy. In most instances this has meant the exclusion of Negroes, legally and in practice, because even the United States is not rich enough to maintain two sets of facilities of equal quality and quantity, even if the desire were there.

Thus, on a little higher scale, America is following the African and Asiatic practice. The basic philosophy of the white rulers here is the same as that elsewhere. It is not a national problem but a world problem. But curiously enough, as the Caucasian problem has grown worse, there has been an increasing denial of the white supremacy philosophy and of the whole racial mysticism by more and more authorities on the subject. Not only is the superiority of one race being vigorously denied but the whole concept of race is being effectively challenged. This phenomenon dates chiefly from the First World War. Numerous books and articles disproving the racial basis of supremacy have been written and circulated. Anti-discrimination clauses in state and federal laws and regulations have increased yearly. Even some of the sternest Negrophobes deny that they are prejudiced against colored people and state their opposition to color discrimination. A few school and college textbooks have been written and adopted which attempt a rational approach. It is becoming infrequent for newspapers to wave the red shirt of racial antagonism as was the wont of so many in the not-so-distant past. All of the leading magazines are "right" on the race question—or at least they do not now flaunt their phobia. All unions of the Congress of Industrial Organizations have anti-discrimination clauses in their constitutions. Several A.F. of L. unions have become more liberal on the question. Official pronouncements of the various Christian church groups begin to breathe the spirit of Jesus on the matter of color—although practice falls far, far short of the ideal. Three times in the past twenty years the House of Representatives has passed anti-lynching bills and it recently voted against the poll tax. Interracial committees have grown and flourished all over the country. It has become not uncommon to see news items in Southern papers about Negroes who have committed rape, robbery or arson.

But unhappily this dramatically sudden change has come too late. The die has been cast. The snowball has reached such proportions and velocity that only some determined and revolutionary program can stop it. A small but growing number of white people in the United States and elsewhere realize that this is a Caucasian rather than a Negro problem and have been trying to do something about it. But the process of indoctrination has gone much too far for all the ordinary remedies. A few books, articles and pamphlets, a few polite committees, occasional radio speeches and sonorous pronouncements from politicians—these will not suffice to re-condition the public mind. We cannot teach racial fictions from 1619 to 1919, and then expect people to change overnight to brotherly love and neighborly justice.

In the early days there was fraternization, intermixture and intermarriage between the masses of Negroes, whites and Indians in all the colonies. Had this process been permitted to continue publicly and unhampered, there would now be no Caucasian problem. But those in authority insisted on all sorts of legal and extra-legal devices to enforce biracialism. Through the years it became a social distinction and an economic advantage to be non-colored. Despite this advantage of being white, the masses gradually lost their freedom and their hopes in a progressively regimented machine of feudalism draped in the habiliments of democracy. As they sank lower and lower into a proletarian status, they clung the more desperately to the one possession that could not be taken from their superior status as whites. This lifted them a notch higher than somebody else; and to a drowning man, an inch is as good as a mile. By virtue of their absence of color, they can go wherever they please—if they have the money; marry whom they wish—if they have the money; live where they choose—if they have the money. The problem, of course, is to get the money. Nevertheless it is comforting to know that nature has put Utopia within reach.

Having become used to this situation by long conditioning, the people are more reluctant to change their habits, even if it can be demonstrated beyond doubt that those habits are wrong. People are not motivated by what is right but by what they believe to be right—and the general white public believes that discrimination and biracialism are right because they have always been told so. So the white supremacy propaganda has become a Frankenstein's monster which, having largely served its purpose, the more intelligent members of the ruling class would fain destroy but now are terrorized by their creation. Of course it must be admitted that they are not as eager for change as they were when the Afrika Corps was pounding toward Alexandria, when the panzers were on the outskirts of Moscow and half our Pacific fleet lay on the bottom of Pearl Harbor.

On the other hand, while a few whites have realized that the so-called Negro problem is actually a Caucasian problem, millions of colored people have arrived at the same conclusion. For some years after emancipation there was a general belief among American colored people that they were responsible for their lowly status, and that all they had to do was to measure up to the requirements of Anglo-Saxon society and they would be accepted as individuals on their merits. Similar views were held by bright and ambitious colored folk in other parts of the world before they discovered the difference between Caucasian professions and practices. To be sure there was a skeptical minority which had so little faith in the big white brother that it urged emigration. But these fellows were shouted down by the chorus of optimists.

However, as Negro literacy increased, and the true nature of the problem was brought home by reading, travel and experience, disillusionment and pessimism took possession. This great awakening came shortly after the realization that the war for democracy had been a war for white democracy—and little of that. When the deluge of propaganda died down, they discovered that they had been carried "back to normalcy." This increasing disillusionment has driven the Negroes within themselves, bringing about a group solidarity as basically unhealthy as that of the whites, but just as real. It has developed a racial chauvinism countering that of the whites which has dangerously deepened the gulf between the two peoples who are actually one people. The study of African history and civilization, the fostering of Negro business, the support and growth of the Negro press, the power of the Negro church, and the general development of anti-white thinking is a reaction to social ostracism and economic discrimination. Race, which began as an anthropological fiction, has become a sociological fact. Socio-economic biracialism advanced as a "solution" for the color question has brought about a psychological biracialism which may bring about an entirely different "solution."

An antagonism has developed on both sides which is increasingly similar to that between two Balkan nations. From being regarded as something present in and yet apart from American life and institutions, the Negro is coming to regard himself in the same way. He is thinking about solving the Caucasian Problem by his own actions rather than by healthy cooperation. He can scarcely be blamed for feeling this way, being a product of his environment. This reaction is not confined to the colored people in the United States, but exists wherever they have been the victims of white subjugation, exploitation and humiliation. It is a development which can only end tragically unless some way can now be found to re-condition colored and white people everywhere so that they will think of themselves as the same.

What chance is there of doing this? It would require a revolutionary program of re-education calling not only for wholesale destruction of the accumulated mass of racialistic propaganda in books, magazines, newspapers, motion pictures and all the present laws and regulations which recognize the racial fiction and are based upon it, but for a complete reorganization of our social system. It would have to include the complete abolition of Jim Crow laws and institutions; the rescinding of all racial pollution laws barring marriage because of so-called race; a complete enforcement of the letter and the spirit of the federal constitution, and the ending of every vestige of the color bar in industry, commerce and the professions. The words "Negro," "white," "Caucasian," "Nordic" and "Aryan" would have to be permanently taken out of circulation except among scholars and scientists. There would have to be an end of gathering population statistics by so-called race. Government service in all its branches, state and federal, would have to be thrown open to all on the basis solely of merit, and promotions made accordingly. It would probably be necessary to have drastic laws against manifestations of color prejudice and discrimination, just as we have legislated against kidnapping, arson and murder which are certainly no more serious from the viewpoint of national welfare.

It is extremely doubtful if the colored people here or anywhere else will accept anything less than this, and if they do it is very likely to prove unsatisfactory. The alternative is to drift toward an international color war. Already there is a dangerous feeling abroad among colored people that they have been treated so badly that they want nothing more to do with white people. This mood is circulating rapidly as science shatters distance in the modern world.

This is a time of mass action and mass thinking. While privately white and colored persons still get on fairly well, it is the public attitudes which will

Schuyler's wife, Josephine, in the 1940s. Photograph by C. B. Grace.

more and more prevail until the leavening influence of the former is eventually destroyed; and those who once were and still could be friends stand against each other as enemies. If there is sincerity and determination in the hearts of the mighty, there is still time to make a new world where tolerance, under-standing, mutual respect and justice will prevail to a greater degree than men have ever dared dream. True, this means a complete about face on the part of the white world, but this is only right since the race problem is of its own making. The alternative here and abroad is conflict and chaos. We shall have to make a choice very soon.

PART II

MOVING
TO THE
RIGHT

Jim Crow in the North
(1949)

Published in the American Mercury, *this essay is another example of Schuyler's capacity to be evenhanded in his racial and cultural criticism. As a northerner, Schuyler often found the race rituals of the Jim Crow South especially exasperating, but in this essay, he reminds the rather complacent whites of the North of their own policies of racial segregation. Racial conflict, in other words, is not confined to the former states of the Confederacy. Politically speaking, most of Schuyler's essays from this point forward celebrate American capitalism and reject outright all movements associated with communism.*

I

People in the North tend to look down on Southerners in the matter of discrimination against the Negro, and to pride themselves upon the civilized treatment accorded to him in communities north of Mason and Dixon's Line. The facts, unfortunately, give little cause for condescension or pride. The Negro is still pretty much a second-class citizen all over the country, and the whole concept of civil rights continues to be largely a dream to men and women who are colored. Much progress has been made in the past twenty-five years—and this progress has by no means been confined to the North. Nevertheless, conditions in the North are still, as we shall see, very far from ideal. I am reporting on these conditions, not out of any desire to aggravate racial feelings, but only to set the record straight. What I have to say is directed primarily at the millions of complacent white folk in the big Northern cities who are totally unaware of any color problem in their midst. The Southerners, at least, know they have a problem.

A survey of Jim Crow in the North might logically begin with New York. No state of the union draws Southern migrants more magnetically than New York. The Southern Negro has heard of the state's civil-rights laws, of its cosmopolitanism, of its reputation for being liberal. He knows that when he gets to New York he will be putting the hated Jim Crow laws and "For Colored" signs behind him. What he finds, however, are other forms of discrimination—more subtle, not sanctified by state law, but nevertheless almost inescapable.

In New York City, the supposed center of American enlightenment, he will find his choice of living quarters restricted to those in the "black ghetto." He will find that open racial discrimination is practiced in two of the major housing developments—both of which, incidentally, enjoy considerable tax exemption. Liberals asked that they be granted the exemption only on the condition that they practice "the policy of non-discrimination," but so far the courts have not held this to be necessary.

In November 1948 he would have noted bitterly that a veterans housing project a short distance from New York City was charged with forcing "upon unwilling tenants and purchasers a racial restrictive clause" requiring them to "subscribe to a denial of fundamental democratic principles." The clause in question reads: "No dwelling shall be used or occupied except by members of the Caucasian race, but the employment and maintenance of other than Caucasian domestic servants shall be permitted." Thus, the only Negro veterans who will be allowed in the development will be maids and janitors.

This particular development happens to be insured by the Federal Housing Authority. However, protests to FHA Commissioner Franklin D. Richards have been futile. In February 1949, Walter White, secretary of the National Association for the Advancement of Colored People, addressed a strong protest to President Truman, and in an accompanying 4000-word brief charged that the FHA "has continued to lend full support to the perpetuation of ghettos," and that, moreover, it has stated that, "it would continue to give its support to such [racially restrictive] projects." Mr. Truman did not reply. In March 1949, Thomas G. Grace, the New York State FHA Director, told a protesting group of liberals that the agency did not have the power to bring builders to terms with Negro buyers. He said that Federal approval of a mortgage could not be withdrawn if the owner wrote into a lease or deed a clause barring occupancy to any racial, religious or national group.

Jim Crow in the North exists in the unlikeliest places. In New York City a special fact-finding committee of the National Conference of Christians and Jews reported to the mayor, not long ago, that the Brooklyn-Queens YMCA had some units which refused membership to Negroes, even though Negroes predominated in the neighborhoods of those units, and even though the need of Negroes for such facilities was desperate. The same committee reported that, despite New York's civil-rights laws, "some hotels, cabarets and eating places still find methods of preventing full use of their facilities by Negroes." The committee concluded that the discrimination "can in almost every instance, be traced back to segregation or apathy."

It is difficult to assess the practical effectiveness of New York's civil-rights laws. In December 1948 two groups investigating the city's race relations reported that one out of five New Yorkers interviewed had personally experienced job discrimination. Most experts believe that the state FEPC law is easy to circumvent, and these particular investigators reported: "Discrimination is believed to exist in all branches of industry and occupations in New York City, especially in heavy industry, public utilities and finance."

So much for New York City. In the rest of the state the situation is generally worse. It is practically impossible to find a colored clerk in a department store in Albany, and Negroes in that city are pretty well restricted in job opportunities. Negroes have also learned not to expect too much from Syracuse—not long ago a colored woman filed suit against a hotel there for turning her away. In the main, the pattern of segregation and employment discrimination is solidly fixed all throughout upper New York State, in both the urban and rural areas. It is abetted even by many labor unions,[1] and it extends even to the use of recreational facilities.

This latter question is becoming a real sore point with Negroes, many of whom live in slums and so have special need of places where they can relax. At least 95 percent of the privately owned resorts, bathing beaches, bowling alleys and other places of public recreation in New York State do their best to keep out Negroes. The White Plains YWCA is "solving" its Negro problem by letting Negro women use its swimming pool one evening a week.

II

Historically, New England has always been regarded as the most liberal section of the country in its treatment of Negro citizens. It was the stern Puritan conscience of this area that produced the Abolitionist movement in the early nineteenth century. Today there is little open discrimination in New England, especially in Maine, New Hampshire and Vermont, where Negroes are few in numbers. However, Negroes are not wanted at most resorts in these states, and where there is any question of competition, employment opportunities for Negroes are sharply limited.

In Massachusetts, Rhode Island and Connecticut, where there are more Negroes, the color bar is camouflaged but quite potent. It is only since 1940 that Negroes in these states have been able to breach the employment barrier to the extent of getting white-collar and skilled jobs. The enactment of fair-employment-practice laws in Massachusetts and Connecticut has helped appreciably.

It is easier for Negroes in New England to live where they choose than in any other section of the country, but even here there are some formidable barriers. The ghetto situation in New Haven is notorious. In Providence there are "understandings" which discourage purchases and rentals by Negroes in white areas. Some Providence realtors maintain special lists of sub-standard houses to be kept open for Negro occupancy; this procedure ensures that the colored areas will always have the worst slums.

A similar situation exists in Hartford, where it is virtually impossible for a Negro to rent a home outside the colored area. It is somewhat easier for a

---

1. For a detailed discussion of this touchy problem, see "Race Discrimination in Unions," by Herbert R. Northrup, in the July 1945 *Mercury*.——The Editors

Negro to buy a home outright, but if word gets around that such a purchase is contemplated, pressure is often placed on bankers to withhold loans. Some Negroes find that they can buy property only if they have a white friend who is willing to act as a "front man" for them.

The pattern of Jim Crow in the North begins to emerge more clearly when we leave the comparatively enlightened regions of the Northeast and begin to consider facts and figures for the country as a whole. There is hardly a state in the whole North that can take pride in its treatment of our most abused minority.

The problem of obtaining decent housing is becoming a desperate one for Negroes all through the North and the West. The decision of the U.S. Supreme Court last year to outlaw restrictive covenants was an immense help. But the battle is far from won. In Kansas, where John Brown once risked his life to help colored men, the state legislature recently passed an act specifically authorizing certain types of restrictive agreements. In Southern California, the regional office of the Anti-Defamation League has been fighting the attempts of real estate organizations in the Los Angeles area to circumvent the Supreme Court decision. The League reported recently that "a campaign of terrorism, vandalism and discrimination has begun to prevent Southern California families from enjoying [their] rights." Among the Negro victims of this campaign have been Nat ("King") Cole, the musician, who bought an $85,000 residence; Paul R. Williams, an eminent architect; Dr. Carl A. Dent, a Santa Monica physician who is reportedly afraid to occupy his new home; Dr. Pauline O. Roberts, who had a cross burned in her elegant new residence by some local patriots; and Mr. and Mrs. Ben Eustus, who were driven from their house when it was fired by vandals.

These cases are admittedly extreme, but of 55 cities outside the South reporting on residential restrictions for Negroes, there were only a few where purchases might be made with any freedom. Among these were Massillon and Columbus, in Ohio, Sacramento and San Francisco, in California, Morristown, New Jersey, and Albany and White Plains in New York. Even in these cities the privilege was almost always qualified, and purchases were usually much easier to arrange than rentals. In most other cities the black ghettos are expanding rather than disintegrating.

The school situation is also appalling in the North, where, contrary to the popular conception, there are plenty of racially segregated public schools. New Jersey and Indiana have recently abolished Jim Crow schools, but they still exist in Delaware, Pennsylvania, Kansas, Arizona, New Mexico, Maryland, Missouri and the District of Columbia. Actually, because of the expansion of solid Negro urban districts, there are more segregated schools in the North than ever before.

Naturally, there is a tendency to assign Negro schoolteachers to Negro schools, which often have sub-standard equipment and inferior curricula. In several Northern, Eastern, and Western cities, no Negro teachers at all are hired. In Lansing, Michigan, the mayor answered a criticism on this score by saying that the city's schools had Negro janitors and that that was enough.

On the college level, most schools have fairly rigid Negro quotas, and Negroes who are admitted are subjected to various forms of segregation. An Amherst chapter of a student fraternity was expelled from the national organization last year for admitting a Negro to membership. When the National Interfraternity Conference met in New York City last December it postponed taking any stand on this issue for another year.

III

Things have improved somewhat since the day when Booker T. Washington commented that "in the North the Negro can spend a dollar but cannot earn it, while in the South he can earn a dollar but cannot spend it." But the employment situation is still bad in the North. A survey of 55 cities showed that in only 19 of them were Negroes employed as clerks or store salesmen. (The prejudice in this connection was least in New York City, but even here the number of such Negro employees was usually held carefully to a token half dozen or so.) The rise of closed labor unions has aggravated the problem considerably. The same survey showed that only 10 of the 55 cities were without discriminatory unions. The worst offenders are the unions of skilled workers, but inconsistencies, evasions, and run-arounds are practiced by all types.

Finding a hotel to stop at is another of the Northern Negro's considerable problems. In about half the cities of the North, Negroes are never accepted. In the others they are accepted but made to feel that they are unwelcome. As a general rule, the only a way a Negro can get a hotel room is to make an advance reservation. Sometimes even this is not enough. In Springfield, Lincoln's home, it is reported that five colored state legislators cannot get accommodations at any decent hotel. In Olympia, the capital of Washington, the famous "Wings over Jordan" choir members were barred from both of the city's hotels.

All hotels in Washington, D.C., now have a rigid color bar. There is a rather unusual history to this story. In 1872 the popularly-elected District Assembly passed a stiff civil-rights law, and until past the turn of the century, Negroes were welcome in all the capital's public places. But around 1904, this law "mysteriously disappeared from the compiled statutes of the district, and cannot be found in the present codes." There is no record that it was ever repealed, but it is certainly not enforced today.

Buying a meal in the North is almost as difficult as getting a hotel room. There are probably fewer than twenty cities in the country where Negroes are not completely barred from white-owned restaurants. Refusal is usually bold and callous; even where civil-rights laws exist, restaurant owners know that custom is with them. Negro legislators were not admitted to the Capitol Building lunchroom in Springfield until 1947, and, unless there has been a very recent change, the sixty-odd colored employees of the state of Illinois are still kept out. At the five-and-ten cent stores in Topeka, white customers sit down to eat at the lunch counters, but Negroes must stand. At some soda fountains in that city, Negroes cannot get service whether they sit or stand.

To the widely publicized Four Freedoms, American Negroes would like to add a fifth—Freedom of Recreation. In the event of another war, black boys may have to fight on the beaches, but neither in war nor peace are they allowed to bathe on them. Along the Atlantic and Gulf coasts, from New Jersey to Mexico, there are less than half a dozen spots where Negroes may enjoy bathing privileges. Almost everywhere, mountain resorts are closed to colored people. The same applies to bowling alleys and even, in some cases, to motion-picture theaters. At this late date there are upwards of a dozen Northern cities in which Negroes are either barred from theaters or segregated in them. (The national capital, of course, is included in this list.)

An especially ugly situation developed in the Palisades Amusement Park, which is right across the Hudson River from New York's Harlem. For the last three summers a non-violent direct-action group called New York's Committee on Racial Equality has been campaigning to break down the banning of Negroes from the swimming pool at Palisades. The committee's pickets were rebuffed, insulted, and finally beaten up by police and jailed. In February 1948 a Federal judge ruled that the anti-discrimination provisions of the Federal Civil Rights Law did not apply to privately owned amusement parks. But finally, at the end of 1948, the New Jersey Supreme Court ruled that the discrimination was illegal. It remains to be seen whether New Jersey's new laws, outlawing Jim Crow completely throughout the state, will be enforced and obeyed.

New Jersey's new civil-rights law forbids segregation in the state's National Guard units. New York and Connecticut have also taken this step recently, but there are still segregated units in Massachusetts, the District of Columbia, Ohio, Illinois and California. The U.S. Army controls the various State Guards, but the present administration, like its predecessors, stands solidly behind the tradition of Jim Crow in uniform.

Since the bulk of Christian churches are Jim Crow institutions, it is not surprising that the YMCA and YWCA should also be guilty of discrimination. The YWCA's record is much better than that of the YMCA, only half of whose branches accept Negro members. And even these memberships rarely include the use of swimming pools, cafeterias or dormitories. Whenever possible, colored applicants are sweetly referred to the special Negro branches.

IV

Rabelais and Swift would have been convulsed by the prodigious effort expended in their country to prevent citizens of opposite sexes and colors from legally consummating their affection. Inasmuch as 80 percent of American Negroes have some white blood, the reasons given for the restrictions are rather hypocritical. To prove the alleged aversion of the two races to intimate association, 29 states of the union (16 of them outside the South) have illegalized mixed marriages. The most savage penalties, as a matter of fact, are in the north. Georgia hands out a maximum sentence of one year for the offense, and Tennessee and Texas five years, but in Indiana, North Dakota and South Dakota, the rap is ten years. All twenty-nine states refuse to recognize even those interracial marriages which have been consummated elsewhere.

Another bitter pill for the Northern Negro is the hospital situation. In general, hospitalized Negroes are segregated. In San Francisco, Los Angeles, and Wilmington, Negroes are not permitted to enter hospitals unless they are prepared to pay for private rooms. In other cities the pattern of discrimination works differently. Trenton, Columbus, and Harrisburg insist that Negroes go into the wards; they are not allowed private rooms. Kansas City, Missouri, bars Negroes from all hospitals except two: One a municipally-owned Jim Crow Institution, the other a private hospital owned by Negroes. St. Louis bars them from some hospitals and segregates them in others. Fort Wayne segregates them in all hospitals but one. Even in large cities like New York and Chicago, there are various forms of subtle and exasperating bias.

Three winters ago, a Washington, D.C., colored woman in the throes of childbirth and unable to reach a city hospital was rushed to a church-supported institution. She was refused admission with firm Christian resolution, and her baby was delivered on the sidewalk. The somewhat contrite staff then made partial amends by supplying the mother and child with a covering sheet until the city ambulance took them away.

In this respect, as in others, the Negro from Washington, D.C. is heavily penalized. He must either accept space in segregated ward or travel to Philadelphia or New York. Aside from Freeman's Hospital, a Negro institution, the nation's capital has only two private or semi-private rooms available to colored people. It is ironical to recall that sixty years ago the eleven hospitals in Washington served all races equally. Today three of the twelve private institutions totally exclude Negroes, and the remainder segregates them.

The Negro who wants to be a doctor finds difficulties in his way all along the line. He will have difficulty finding a school that will accept him and more difficulty finding a hospital in which he can gain intern experience. (However, Negro nurses are freely accepted in most hospitals.)

The crowning indignity to the northern Negro is the treatment he receives from the proprietors of snooty cemeteries and mortuaries; even in death he cannot escape Jim Crow. However, it remained for Washington, D.C., to reach the depths of indecency. There, according to report, "a dog cemetery has erected a color bar against the burial of dogs belonging to colored people. In announcing this policy, the owner stated that he assumed the dogs would not object, but he was afraid his white customers would."

Apparently even a white dog is barred if its owner is black!

The Negro Question without Propaganda
(1950)

In 1950 Schuyler was invited to serve as a U.S. delegate to the Congress of Cultural Freedom in Berlin. As Schuyler remarks in his autobiography, Black and Conservative *(1966), "This conference was to be the largest and most important of its kind in the long history of anti-Communism." In this speech Schuyler focused on the numerous possibilities for individual advancement inherent to capitalism and the ways in which African Americans have flourished, racism notwithstanding, in this context. For Schuyler's liberal critics, these kind of remarks were troubling, because, in their view, they reflected a perspective that failed to address the moral injustices of American democracy. This speech, in various forms, appeared in the* Freeman, Christian Science Monitor, *and* Reader's Digest. *This version appeared in the* Congressional Quarterly, *Thursday, August 31, 1950.*

In the vicious propaganda campaign of lies and distortions to which ungrateful totalitarian slave states have subjected the United States of America (which saved them from Hitler), the treatment of its Negro citizens has been held up as a horrible illustration of the weakness and failure of democracy.

The prostitute press and radio of the Communist camorra [an Italian secret society organized ostensibly for political purposes] have presented a picture of Negro existence in America so fantastic, so false, so contrary to the facts of his everyday life in the 48 states as to be unrecognizable by anyone familiar with the Nation. This stereotype is so grotesque as to be at once amusing and deplorable. One must question the intelligence and integrity of those who so readily believe it.

Actually, the progressive improvement of interracial relations in the United States is the most flattering of the many examples of the superiority of the free American civilization over the soul-shackling reactionism of totalitarian regimes. It is this capacity for change and adjustment inherent in the system of individual initiative and decentralized authority to which we must attribute the unprecedented economic, social, and educational progress of the Negroes of the United States.

The chattel slave system, or any slave system, is not inherent in capitalism which for growth directly depends upon pleasing the consumer and increasing his purchasing power: whatever its flaws, the history of capitalism is one of constant mass improvement that everyone can see.

During America's 225 years of legalized chattel slavery 10,000,000 Africans were brought to the plantations of the Western Hemisphere. Because they represented economic value to their masters, every effort was made to preserve their health and productivity as long as possible. This should be contrasted with the slave system of Soviet Russia which from 1930 onward continually has held from fifteen to twenty million victims in servitude under conditions so savage and heartless that millions have died from mistreatment. Having no individual economic value, these unfortunates have been and are being worked to death with calculated ruthlessness. Whereas today the slave system of Soviet Russia has become so essential to its economy that it grows more extensive year by year, the chattel slave system of capitalism has been long since abolished. Soviet Russia after 30 years has twice as many slaves as were brought to all the Americas in 225 years. Even war prisoners have been forced into slavery and so many have died in Soviet labor camps that 1,000,000 Germans and 400,000 Japanese are "missing"; and up-to-date the Soviet government, unable to produce them, has been forced into the ridiculous denial that they ever existed! By contrast, the United States has repatriated all of its war prisoners and the prisons of America contain only 141,000 inmates—among them no political prisoners.

From 1861 to 1865 the United States fought a bloody civil war in which 200,000 Negroes joined to settle the issue of chattel slavery. By the thirteenth amendment to the Constitution, 5,000,000 Negro slaves were emancipated. By the fourteenth and fifteenth amendments, they became full-fledged citizens of the Republic, along with the half-million already free. During the Civil War, there was no uprising of the Negro slaves nor molestation of the white women and children left behind by their men. One can well imagine what conditions would be in Soviet Russia and its satellites if their enslaved millions were suddenly free.

In 1865 over ninety per cent of the Negroes were totally illiterate. Today practically all can read and write except in remote rural areas. In some places, like New York City, the percentage of Negro literates is higher than that of whites.

In 1865, not over a score of Negroes had graduated from colleges and universities. Today over 7,000 Negroes graduate from colleges and universities each year. The total graduated since 1912 is 80,000. The total which has attended college is 650,000.

All of the private institutions of higher learning for Negroes in the States of the former Confederacy were established by white people who taught in them and financially supported them. Alongside these are the colleges and universities controlled and supported by public taxation. It is inconceivable that this could have happened in the South if the racial hatred which has been represented as characteristic there had obtained in any marked degree.

Today there are 70,000 Negroes in American colleges, or proportionately a greater number than in the United Kingdom which has 82,500 out of the population of 50,000,000.

Fifty years ago it was almost hopefully prophesied that the American Negro would soon become extinct because of disease. In 1950 the life expectancy is 60 years, or only seven years less than the whites. This amazing health progress would not have been possible had race hatred been as prevalent as reported.

During the 1930s the Federal Government constructed 150,000 dwelling units; and although Negroes were only 10 percent of the population, they got 50,000 of these units.

In 1900 only 17 percent of Negro non-farm homes were owned. In 1947, the figure was over 34 percent. In 1940, Negroes dwelling in cities (half their population) owned over 500,000 homes. In 1930 these homes had a median value of $6,377.

Over 2,500 Negro dwellings in New York, Chicago, and Washington alone were worth from $10,000 to $15,000; while 850 were valued from $15,000 to $20,000 or over. Such well-being could scarcely obtain in an atmosphere of terror.

Evidence of the eagerness of the American nation to bring the Negro population up to the national level of enlightenment was the establishment in 1867 of the Freedman's Bureau which soon had 623 schools with 15,248 Negro pupils. By 1900, there were 1,539,507 Negro pupils in public elementary schools— 51.4 percent of the total Negro population of school-age. By 1920, this enrollment was 2,000,000 and today it is two and one-quarter million.

In 1910 there were 5000 Negro high school students; in 1950 there are 300,000, and the annual total of Negro high school graduates is 40,000. In 1910 there were 42 public high schools in the South and by 1950 this had grown to 2,500.

In 1900 daily attendance was 33 percent, where today it is 80 percent.

A Jewish philanthropist, Julius Rosenwald, established the Julius Rosenwald Fund in 1912. By 1932 this fund had spent a total of $28,500,000 and helped erect 5,000 school buildings in the South. Negroes themselves contributed $4,725,871.

The total value of Negro school property in the South was, in 1940, $79,250. The total value in 1948 was 129,000,000.

In 1900 total expenditure per pupil was $4.50 for whites and $1.50 for Negroes; in 1948 it was $139.49 for whites and $76.45 for Negroes. In 1904 for each dollar whites received, Negroes got 50 cents. In 1948 for each dollar whites received Negroes got 71 cents.

While southern Negro teachers generally do not get as much pay as Southern white teachers, salaries have been equalized in very many states and communities, thanks to legal action on the part of the Negroes and to the unprejudiced attitude of the courts.

In 1947 13 percent of all Negroes in the United States had completed secondary school while 5 percent or 650,000 had attended college.

Much of the stimulus for the drive to educate the American Negro came from white capitalists like the aforementioned Julius Rosenwald. Following the end of the Civil War there were few Negroes capable of teaching school so northern white missionaries and officers of the victorious Union Army set up schools and did the teaching.

The Slater fund was established by capitalists and from 1910 to 1930 contributed $250,000 for salaries for teachers in county training schools in the Southern states. This fund was administered by James H. Dillard, a Southern white man.

The Jeannes Fund was established by American capitalists and was also used to pay Negro teachers in southern rural areas beginning in 1908. It was also aided by a Southern white man, Dr. Jackson Davis of Virginia. This pattern of rural education was later copied for white rural schools and for similar schools in foreign lands. There are now 800 teachers in as many counties. Since 1908, a total of 12,407 Jeannes teachers have served in 808 counties. In 1937 these teachers started a fund as an expression of appreciation to Miss Virginia Randolph, the first Jeannes teacher. It now totals $50,000. Here, too, we have evidence of the progress of liberalism of America in the fact than in 1912 the Jeannes fund paid 92 percent of the Jeannes teachers whereas 95 percent are now paid out of the public treasuries.

Further evidence of the interest of much maligned whites in aiding these backward people, was the establishment in 1898 of the Conference for Education in the South. Then in 1902 the Rockefellers set up the General Education Board which has expended 40 percent of its money to advance Negro education.

Following that, in 1915 to 1916, came the Phelps Stokes Fund headed by Thomas Jesse Jones. Many other organizations have been extremely helpful, such as the Southern Sociological Congress, the Southern University Race Commission, the Carnegie Corporation which provides libraries, the YMCA and the YWCA, and for the last quarter century the United States Office of Education. Without the help of all these groups it would not have been possible for us to make the progress that has been made in Negro education.

The stereotype of the poverty-stricken American Negro is also paraded by totalitarian propagandists as an illustration of the failure of democracy. The facts are so at variance with this fiction as to be laughable. There are, it is true, millions of poor Negroes as there are millions of poor whites, but what is regarded as poverty in the United States is called prosperity by workers elsewhere. Steadily, for the last 50 years, the educational, cultural, and economic gulf between the Negroes and whites has been narrowing. While white Americans generally have greater income than their colored brethren, it is cause for reflection that 12.9 percent of whites and 14 percent of Negroes make from $1000 to $1,500 a year: that 1.1 percent of whites and 0.2 percent of the Negroes make from $5,000 to $6,000 a year, while only 0.8 percent of the whites and 0.2 percent of the Negroes make from $6,000 to $10,000 annually. It is not only a tribute to the Negroes that they have in such a short space of time achieved such economic well-being but it also indicates a willingness on the part of the white majority to enable them to do so. Compared to the economic condition of minorities else-where in the world, that of the American Negro is enviable. It is worth noting that 1,000,000 are members of American labor unions, receive identical wages, allowances, work conditions, job security, and paid vacations with their white fellow workers, depending on skill and seniority. Two-thirds of the American Negroes being agricultural and domestic workers, this is a very high percent-age of Negro workers in industry. It is lamentably true that a score of promi-nent labor unions in the United States still exclude Negroes or in several ways discriminate against them. However, it is also true that in the last three years six of these unions have adjusted their attitude and admit colored workers to their membership. This is just another example of the growing racial liberalism.

Wherever Negro and white workers belong to the same unions, they meet together, strike together, whether North or South, and this occasion is no sur-prise whatever to those familiar with American life. Many of these unions, predominantly white, have elected Negro officers. This could scarcely happen in an atmosphere of terror and repression. Parenthetically, only in democratic countries are labor unions free. Despite the horrors to which workers in the Soviet Union are subjected no one ever hears of a strike there or even a public disagreement, which is certainly ominous.

American Negroes own 13 banks, 74 credit unions, and scores of coopera-tive societies. They own over 50,000 retail business establishments, 20 savings and loans associations, and 204 insurance companies. In 1947, 52 leading Negro insurance companies had total assets of $94,639,376 and about $1,000,000,000 in 27 states and the District of Columbia.

In addition to this, American Negroes (mostly in the Southern states where the overwhelming majority resides) own 12,336,794 acres of farmland which represents 19,000 square miles or an area much larger than the Netherlands. There are 180,215 Negro farm owners, the farms averaging 78.3 acres. Last year some Negro farmers in the South grossed as much as $175,000.

As of today, American Negroes own nearly 800,000 homes and this pro-portion of homeowners approximates that of the American whites. Indeed, American Negroes themselves through their own builders, architects, and financial institutions have erected over 25,000 housing units.

In a free federation such as the United States, with 48 separate and inde-pendent sovereignties, communication and travel have been so easy that the population has been extremely mobile. The mobility of the Negroes has equaled that of the whites, and today the Negro population is scattered over the entire country, although 77 percent still live in the 16 Southern states. It is commen-tary on the reported terrorism prevailing in the South that the proportion of the Negro population living there has undergone no change.

There is no desire to minimize the segregational and discriminatory laws in the Southern states which are indeed a disgrace to American civilization. However, the Negroes have always been free to move where they chose without asking anyone's permission. Thus between 1930 and 1940 the Negro population increased 15.8 percent in the north, 41.8 percent in the West, and 5.8 percent in the South. The figures on white mobility are similar.

Because of this ability to move from one state to another within the nation, no Negroes have emigrated from the United States to nearby lands. As a matter of fact, there are more Negroes in the South than ever, although there are less in the rural areas than the cities, which is also true of the whites.

A commentary on the American system and what the Negroes think of it is the fact that they have born arms in every war in which the nation has been engaged. They were nearly 4,000 Negroes serving in the War for Independence, and in World War II over 1,150,000 enrolled. One-fourth of a million served in the Civil War and one-half a million in World War I. There is no evidence that any of these men or women ever deserted to the enemy or were convicted of treason. This is in contrast to the desertion of the whole First Ukrainian Army under General Vlasov, to the Germans, plus the wholesale desertion from numerous other units of the Russian armies. The attitude of the Negroes in this regard is conclusive evidence that they do not regard America as the propagandists would have us to believe.

The changes that have taken place in the structure of the American Armed Forces is further evidence of the progressive improvement of race relations. Where 30 years ago complete racial segregation prevailed in the Army, Navy, and Marine Corps, command orders from above and their implementation have resulted in wide-agreed mixing of Negro and white personnel in all branches, notably the United States Navy and to a lesser extent the Air Corp. Today, Negroes are serving in all branches of the American Armed Forces and the remaining segregation is being rapidly broken down.

Contrary to the propaganda from totalitarian slave states, American Negroes not only move freely, worship freely, and work freely, but they also speak freely. For example, where there is only one Jewish newspaper in Russia and that one controlled by the government, the Negro minority in the United States operates over 200 newspapers and has boasted a press since 1827. The majority of these newspapers are published in the "terror-stricken" South. They are individually owned; they have a combined weekly circulation of 3,000,000 copies and the value of their printing plants runs into the millions of dollars. It is largely through these newspapers and organizations which they support and publicize that the Negro population has been welded into a militant force against reactionary racism. Not a single Negro newspaper has been suppressed, North or South, although they have been unsparing in their criticism of the Jim Crow system. Obviously such oppression can only exist in an atmosphere of freedom.

Similarly, the Negro church whose 40,000 structures serve as meeting places for the colored people could not have carried on or grown except in a tolerant environment. Serving nearly one-half of the Negro population, the total of value of these church properties is around $250,000,000. It spends well over $30,000,000 annually. There are few instances in modern times of Negroes having been prevented from asserting their spiritual rights even in the most backward rural areas. These churches have been in the forefront of all movements for the economic, political, and social benefit of their people, especially in the support of the racially radical programs for the National Association for the Advancement of Colored people. The memberships of certain individual Negro churches are the largest in the United States. Many have thousands of members and budgets ranging from $25,000 to $60,000 a year. Clearly no such extensive organization can exist except in a free country. This is in contrast to the treatment of the church behind the iron curtain.

All fair-minded Americans admit that the disenfranchisement of the Negroes in the South was a crime. For 10 years, the Negro minority in the Southern states, protected by the bayonets of the Union Army, exercised full rights of citizenship including the ballot, but progressively from 1876 onward they were disenfranchised by various legal devices and by force until by 1900 they had almost completely lost the right to vote. It might be added, however, that Negroes have voted since the Civil War in the 33 states outside the south, and in some places they voted even before the Civil War. In many of these states today, the Negroes are an increasingly important factor in elections.

But the greatest development which illustrates the ability of a free society to change is evidenced by the increasing number of Negro voters in the south in the last decade. In many Southern states, where 10 years ago a Negro did not dare to approach the polls, they are now voting in the scores of thousands, and soon will be voting in the hundreds of thousands. This remarkable change has been brought about solely through legal action and instances in which force has been used to prevent the exercise of the right to vote have been rare. There is no single state in the South today where some Negroes are not voting, and less than one-half of these states require payment of poll tax as a qualification to exercise the right to exercise the right of suffrage.

Of course the greatest blots on the American record have been mob murder, usually called lynching and race riots. The record is most grim, and yet inexcusable though these crimes be, it is gratifying to point out that the problem has been practically solved. Whereas in 1900 there were 115 lynchings, in 1949 there were three; and this was more than in the two previous years. From 1934 to 1949, inclusive, the total number of mob murders was less than in the single year of 1900. Along with this decrease in lynchings, there has been a marked increase in the alertness of police which prevented these crimes. There was a time when so-called officers of the law rarely interfered, but today it is quite different.

This gratifying evidence of increasing law and order in the United States simply indicates that the country which was still largely frontier 50 years ago and had only recently emerged from a long and sanguinary Civil War over the Negro is becoming more settled and tolerant.

In essence the Negro problem (which has been as much white as Negro) has been one of integrating a previously enslaved and ostracized group of divergent color and culture into the national social structure with due respect for, and with the acquiescence of, the white majority and in accordance with the principles of American federalism, local sovereignty, and majority rule. The speed with which this revolution developed was too slow for some and too fast for many more: too fast indeed, for the Southern states where the white majority was smallest, and where there were deep-seated fears, tensions, and resentments on both sides arising from slavery and its aftermath. The intrasectional racial adjustment was attended often by physical violence and repression, social ostracism and legal proscription which still obtain, although markedly lessening. The record of these inhumanities while deplorable and regrettable, is amazing not by virtue of these occurrences but because, in spite of them there has been such unprecedented progress toward social homogeneity and justice in every direction, and within the memory of living man.

Progressively the color bar has been lowered here and there, either voluntarily by general agreement in the localities or through legal action in the courts. Although much maligned by malicious propaganda, these American courts have almost invariably decided in favor of full citizenship rights for Negro citizens in education, housing, transportation, suffrage, and legal defense: but always and necessarily with due respect for the principles of American Republicanism as laid down in the federal Constitution. Overruling lagging justice within the forty-eight sovereign states, the Supreme Court of the nation has removed one obstacle after another from the Negro's path.

The cumulative effect of these broad, continued, and statesmen like efforts has been improvement of racial relations in geometrical progression. Thus the gains in the past 10 years have far surpassed those made in previous decades. This explains not only the social, economic, and educational well-being of the colored minority, but the latter's continued and unsurpassed loyalty. American Negroes understand, far better than Soviet propagandists, that in the American system lies the hope of all submerged peoples who have the ability and determination to rise to the full stature of free men.

Do Negroes Want to Be White?
(1956)

Published in the American Mercury, *this essay revolves around the notion that "Negroes want to be white." Culling together significant facts regarding the evolution of the black struggle for freedom, as well as anecdotal stories about racial identity, Schuyler refuses to concede that the majority of blacks desire to be white. Much to his disappointment, he contends that white racism has caused blacks to view interracial interaction with much skepticism.*

No generalization about Negroes is apt to be true, and the one that they all want to be white is not an exception. At any rate, it is far less true than it is thought to be, or ever will be. The current widespread militancy of American Negroes is symptomatic of something more serious.

Whatever dreams or ambitions Negroes may have had once in this direction have been long since dissipated by their painfully disillusioning experiences, and by their observations of the lofty Aryan both at home and abroad.

The general literacy, the influential Negro press and church, increasing knowledge of the African background and advances despite handicaps in every field of endeavor have made the Darker Tenth much less naive. The studied and encompassing complex of persecution, prescription, ostracism and insult has considerably disillusioned the dusky brethren about white superiority.

In consequence of their progress, black has lost a tremendous amount of its unpopularity among blacks. Once ruled by those with light skins and "good" (that is to say Caucasian) hair and features, colored society has undergone a change. Its present leaders can not "pass" for anything but Negroes, and none seems unhappy about it.

To be sure the national Negro addiction to straightening hair and lightening complexions by generous use of cosmetics still persists. Understandably, it has given rise to the not illogical assumption that Negroes are trying to become like white folks. Started a half-century ago, this lucrative endeavor has enriched numerous colored and white businesses and enhanced self-respect by "improving" appearances, especially of colored women. A light skin and naturally straight hair remain social assets.

With Spartan courage those pioneers, eager to approach the national standards of pulchritude glaring at them from every magazine and billboard, underwent unflinchingly the rigors of primitive chemistry. The original crude compounds, caustic and necessarily powerful, often turned kinks a bright red, scarred scalps at the hairline and marred dark skins.

One irate Chicagoan sued his barber for damages when the hair came off with the hot towel. Some extremists took mild doses of arsenic in the hope of thus attaining the "right" color. Many a flat nose was hopefully pinched in infancy that the features might grow to be "regular." Huge advertisements in the otherwise race-proud Negro newspapers praised a magic elixir guaranteed to turn a black person white in "Three minutes by the Clock." Today, similar but less harsh compounds are advertised more circumspectly in deference to the greater sophistication of the clientele. With the Negro press no longer solely dependent upon this type of copy, it does not dominate the pages as it once did.

In his recent "The Color Curtain," the Negro author Richard Wright relates a hilarious anecdote in his report on the Bandung Conference indicating that these rites are not extinct. A white woman writer sharing a bedroom with a colored Bostonian reporter mistook her acquaintance for a voodoo priestess because each night in the darkened room she heated her straightening comb over the eerie blue flame from a Sterno can. When Wright had allayed the woman's fears by explaining this circumstance, she recalled that her roommate spent an hour each morning locked in the bathroom, finally emerging two or three shades lighter.

For fear erroneous conclusions may be drawn, it should be mentioned, on the other hand, that the huge white cosmetic industry is based largely on American female efforts to approach nearer to the wavy-haired fair goddess ideal of gentlemen who prefer blondes, but no one has cited these practices as evidence of an inferiority complex of white females.

Nor is the avidity with which sun tanning, real or artificial, is practiced by millions any indication that American whites desire to be Negroes. At the beginning of the sun tan craze, one large Washington department-store posted signs warning clerks to watch their manners since some of its best customers had been south and acquired deep tans. Those were the days before colored patronage was encouraged and before dusky diplomats' wives had joined the capital's social set.

In Negro society today, the acquirement of a wife indistinguishable from a Nordic is no longer a mark of social arrival. The black girls at dances are no longer wallflowers and the appearance of an ebon lass in a chorus line no longer fetches gales of derisive Negro laughter. There are few, if any, churches remaining where black members are conspicuously absent. However, Negro society here has always been ahead of the East Indian, Latin American and Caribbean peoples among whom a rigid color cast system remains intact.

Gone is the one-time boast of Negro dandies of their preference for "yellow taxis, yellow money and yellow women." Taxis are now multicolored and available to all, gold certificates disappeared with Roosevelt's New Deal, and black women with voice, education and money have risen high in the social scale. As a visiting black Brazilian recently exclaimed, admiringly, "Where else in the world will you see a black woman driving a Cadillac?"

Apprehensive white America itself is responsible for the brown-skin militancy and solidarity it now deplores, a solidarity transcending petty divisions and appealing to pride of race. In law and practice it imposed the "one drop" theory, according to which pseudo-science, everyone with one drop of the potent "Negro blood" is dubbed a Negro while one drop of "white blood" is too weak to make a Negro a Caucasian! This is science. When the United States Supreme Court invokes a far more valid sociology in its desegregation decree, it enraged the Southerns.

The precise colored gradations obtaining in other multiracial countries fostered division within non-white groups. American "one drop" perfectionists forced all non-whites together without distinction into one pariah class. This unique American practice was summed up in the popular song of fifty years ago, "All Coons Look Alike."

Those with light skins, better manners and a little literacy (mostly gained as house servants for white planters who were not infrequently their relatives) cannot escape to the white groups as in Latin America. They were compelled to identify themselves with the swarm of black field hands and proletarians. They supplied the early Negro leadership, trained and uplifted the masses and instilled them with race pride and resentment of their lot. Thus, the hobgoblin of black unity which still excites many Negrophobes is a white creation.

It was in the South, where social relationships have always been on a more personal plane that this liaison of mulatto kinfolk somewhat tempered the post-bellum savagery of the emergent Cracker element, itself emancipated by the surrender.

In addition to these light Negroes, free and slave, there was a considerable number of mixed Europeans shanghaied into chattel servitude and sold as Negroes by grasping slave dealers. These latter regularly curled the hair of hapless Nordic bondsmen to still the qualms of prospective buyers alarmed by the white skins and blue eyes. It was then widely believed by Southern racial experts, still addicted to fingernail evidence of Negro ancestry, that curly hair was indicative of African blood. Many of these whites intermixed with their black fellow chattels.

As a commentary on the post-bellum practices of the South's new rulers, it is interesting that the pre–Civil War freedman, though enjoying few citizenship rights, was generally unmolested in the slave states. He rode with free whites on trains, in stage coaches and on steam boats, often was a slaveholder, and was not infrequently married to a white woman. One such ran a private school for the sons of wealthy whites. An entire regiment of mulattos, free and supplying their own equipment, offered their services to the Confederacy in New Orleans when the war broke out. While many Negroes fought in the Confederate armies, it is significant that they are today barred from all National Guard units in Dixie.

Jim Crowism and anti-intermarriage, the much trumpeted Southern "way of life," came largely after the magnoliaed mansions had Gone With the Wind and the piney woods denizens had risen to power. In retrospect it is ironical that the first antislavery movements originated in the South and that the book which most enraged the planter oligarchy was not Stowe's *Uncle Tom's Cabin* but Helper's *The Impending Crisis*. Had the author not fled to the north, he would have been burned along with his books.

Is the current drive of Negroes for immediate realization of full citizenship an indication that they want to be white? Do they wish to barge into the privacy of white homes and clubs? Do they hanker inordinately for Nordic spouses? Some of the louder Negrophobes profess to believe so. Having themselves made heroic contributions to the "mongrelization" of the Senegambian, they are understandably hysterical lest the tables, or the couches, be turned. If "mongrelization" in truth be a threat to the white "way of life," it would seem too late to do anything much about it.

Seriously, there is little evidence that most Negroes want to be white. If, as their detractors allege, they have not attained full social and intellectual maturity, their experience in what Claude McKay called this "cultured hell" has not left them panting for intimate association with whites. All they say they want is the freedom and opportunity others enjoy.

No group could easily forget more than a century of unbridled vilification in pulpit, press, literature and politics by spokesmen for the dominant group, as diseased, ignorant, amoral and brutish. Like others who have come to these shores, Negroes readily adapted themselves to their new environment but could never have changed their pigment, even with chemicals. So they have made a virtue out of necessity and developed an exclusiveness which is more ominous than any alleged yearning to be white.

For good or ill, a black nation has been developed in the midst of a white one. It is increasingly self-centered, suspicious, hypersensitive, and proud. Its solidarity now painfully surprises many whites who once boasted that they "knew" the Negro.

This solidarity is no sudden growth stimulated by Communists, although Reds have sought to exploit it. Over a century and a quarter ago Negroes held their first conference in Philadelphia with delegates from distant places. In 1827, two educated colored men, one a college graduate, founded the first Negro newspaper, "Freedom's Journal." The unvarying theme of all subsequent gatherings has been full immediate citizenship rights under the Constitution. There was lively controversy between those who wished despondently to emigrate to some black Zion and those opposed to leaving what they regarded as their native land. Emancipation put an end to that debate.

The powerful campaign to terrorize and virtually re-enslave the Negro after the Civil War reached its peak between 1890 and 1910, when lynching, contract labor, Jim Crow laws, job bias and disfranchisement did not ennoble the white folks in the Negroes' opinion. This opinion solidified and centered on a common goal and a strategy to achieve it.

Early in the century when mentioning lynchings occurred thrice weekly, the Niagara movement was formed to do something about it. In rapid succession their followed the Negro Business League, the National Association for the Advancement of Colored People, the National Urban League, Negro Health Week, and the Association for the Study of Negro Life and history which published the *Journal of Negro History*.

Before this, the Negro Church, now boasting ten million members, grew out of a revolt against racial segregation in white churches. It was literally born with the Republic since the first church was launched by Richard Allen in Philadelphia and 1787. As early as 1820, the African Methodist Episcopal Church had missions in Christophe's Haiti and in West Africa. The early churches provided Negroes with a meeting place and forum. They established schools. Every group is based on the institutions it has established, and there's no desire among Negroes to abandon so noble a tradition. They have pride in what they have wrought.

The goal is not to be white but to be free in a white world. The Negro does not regard himself as an alien after over three centuries of residence and sacrifice. This supposition that the Negro is eager for liquidation as a group is groundless. He is not panting to associate intimately with whites as such, nor is he avid to submerge himself through inter-marriage. Even where laws do not prevent them, it is difficult to find "mixed" couples. In the entire country there are less than 25,000.

In a multiracial nation there will always be clandestine and extra-legal sex relations, and if the greatest romances are those fraught with the greatest dangers, then there is a much untapped literary material in the United States. There are more Madam Butterflies here than in Japan.

For better or for worse, centripetal and endogamous societies have evolved in America. They seem to be as mutually exclusive as the Walloons and Flemings in Belgium, the Moslems and Hindus in India or the Jews and Arabs in Morocco.

Both now have a vested interest in their integrity. Few whites want to be black and few Negroes yearn to be white. There will always be a necessary measure of cooperation and liaison between them for the common good of all, but the idealists' vision of an ultimate racial Melting Pot is, to say the least, dim and remote.

The Black Muslims in America
An Interview with George S. Schuyler, Malcolm X, C. Eric Lincoln, and James Baldwin
(1961)

During my research on Schuyler, I located the cassette version of "The Black Muslims in America," a radio discussion featuring black religion scholar C. Eric Lincoln, novelist James Baldwin, Nation of Islam disciple Malcolm X, and Schuyler, moderated by Eric F. Goldman, author of *Rendezvous with Destiny: A History of Modern American Reform* (1961) and professor of history at Princeton University. After hearing the sociological observations of Lincoln, the black nationalist ideology of Malcolm X, the patriotic assertions of Schuyler, and the cultural insights of Baldwin, I began transcribing the text. From their heated but respectful discussion, one can discern the searing questions concerning race, citizenship, and nationhood, issues which continue to bedevil our Republic. In terms of cultural criticism, Baldwin's is clearly the superior intellect, refusing to allow Schuyler and Malcolm X to reduce human experience to a particular ideological formula.

GOLDMAN: The census of 1960 indicated that about 18 million of our citizens or some 10.5 percent of the total population are Negroes. Since World War II, the struggle of equality for these members of American society has been simply the most spectacular and probably the most significant feature of domestic American life. All the while the Negro has struggled for this equality, observers have been noting something of a change in his tactics and something in the change of the mood of millions of members of that people. The general question has been that there is a growing militancy, a growing impatience with gradualism, a growing unwillingness to wait. Among the militant movements which Negroes have founded and built during this period, perhaps the most publicized and certainly one of the most important is the Black Muslims. They are our subject today: where they came from, what they are, and where, perhaps, they are going.

Our panel here to my right: Mr. Malcolm X, Minister of the Temple of Islam Number 7, in New York City, and generally acknowledged to be the number two leader in the national Black Muslim movement, Mr. C. Eric Lincoln, professor of social philosophy at Clark college in Atlanta, and author of the new volume *The Black Muslims in America,* the first serious scholarly study of this movement, and a book which has been called by the authoritative Gordon Alpart one of the best technical case studies in the whole literature of the social sciences; the distinguished American writer Mr. James Baldwin, author of the novel *Go Tell It on the Mountain* (1952) and a book of commentary, *Notes of a Native Son* (1940); and George S. Schuyler, associate editor of the powerful newspaper the *Pittsburgh Courier,* and a man who has long enjoyed an international reputation as a journalist.

GOLDMAN: Mr. Lincoln, may I ask you to start us—you, as the author of this scholarly study, with a comment on what you consider to be the nub of the Black Muslim program.

LINCOLN: It would be difficult in a few words to set out the nub of the Black Muslim movement because it is very many things, but I think for our purposes today one could say that the Black Muslim movement is essentially a movement of social protest which moves upon a kind of religious vehicle. It's a movement among many thousands of America's Negroes, principally those Negroes who belong to the lower economic class, and a kind of a struggle to find their way and to find their place in the nation's society, or perhaps I should better say in an attempt to set up their own society, a black Nation of Islam.

GOLDMAN: That would be its general approach. Could we get a little more specific, Mr. Schuyler?

SCHUYLER: Well, yes, of course, I have read this very excellent book by Mr. Lincoln, and I have been following the movement of Muslimism, and particularly as expounded by Mr. X, for some time. I think that one of the bases, of course, for the anti-Christian, anti-white view is that white Christians were responsible for slavery in the world, and that for this reason they are to be cast into the outer pale. Now that is one of the many falsehoods upon which this movement is founded. As a matter of fact, the Moslems carried on slavery for something like twelve or thirteen hundred years before the white European Christians started it. I think one of the outstanding slave traders in Africa, and there's a monument to him in Zanzibar, is Tip Bu Tip, who devastated all central and eastern Africa—

GOLDMAN: Mr. Schuyler, before we get into criticisms of the movement, couldn't we at first get out on the table what precisely it stands for? Mr. X, would you like to comment?

X: First of all, I would like to point out we who are Muslims who follow the Honorable Elijah Muhammad don't accept the term "Negro"; we stand against that, and I would like to clear myself. I am not the number two leader of the Muslim movement because we don't think of ourselves in that light. We have one God, whose proper name is Allah; we have one leader, who in America here is the Honorable Elijah Muhammad; we are one people; and we have one aim, and that's the upliftment and betterment of our people here in America who are called Negroes. And where the objectives and program of the Honorable Elijah Muhammad differ from the objectives, programs, and methods of these other groups that represent the so-called Negro, most of the other groups, their method of operation has a tendency to lead us to believe that it will take us another thousand years if we follow their tactics. Whereas we who are Muslims, we're not willing to wait another hundred years.

GOLDMAN: In this uplift of the black man and unwillingness to wait, what specifically do you want to do?

X: Number one, I think it should be pointed out clearly that as Muslims, we are not a political group, nor are we a civic group, but rather we are a religious group. When I say that we are not a political group, it's being made plain there that we are not relying on the politicians for a political solution, because experience has taught us that in the past the politicians have promised but never delivered, and if we rely on a politician we feel we'll be going right around in circles like our people have been doing here in America a hundred years since Lincoln issued the so-called Emancipation Proclamation.

GOLDMAN: Well, not relying on politicians, Mr. X, is it not correct that the Muslims seek to completely separate the black and the white man in America and to win and establish for the Negro their own homeland in several states of America?

X: That's religion with us. If it was religion for Moses four thousand years ago to be missioned by God to separate the slaves in that day from the slave master of that day—complete separation, not integration—and still the Christians and Jews both today regard Moses not as a politician but as a religious leader and a religious man, motivated by religion completely, we feel that what the Honorable Elijah Muhammad is doing here in America today in demanding a complete separation of this slave from his slave master [is imperative] and as Moses asked for a land of his own flowing with milk and honey, the Honorable Elijah Muhammad is likewise asking for a land for us, flowing with the sweet milk and honey of freedom, justice, and equality.

SCHUYLER: Just wait a minute now. At the risk of going into politics, I would like to know how any group in the United States is going to separate part of the United States for them to live in without having something to do with politics. Do you plan to do this through warfare?

X: Sir, I don't think that it's necessary to bring about any warfare. If the ex-slave in America has to go to war with his former slave master to get what is his by right, then that in itself is a condemnation of the former master. If Lincoln issued the Emancipation Proclamation a hundred years ago—which means we're supposed to be free, we're supposed to be citizens, we're supposed to be protected by the Constitution that we fight and die for—and yet at the same time today, the so-called Negro is knocking at the White House door still begging his master to pass legislation that will give him recognition or protection by the Constitution that is supposed to represent him, I think, sir, that the man who is depriving him of these rights cannot open up his mouth and say that it would be wrong to go to war against him to get these things.

GOLDMAN: Gentlemen, before we go further, I would still like to get out here the full program of the Muslim religion in America. We now have the desire for a separate grouping in some states of America. Mr. Baldwin, would you comment on your understanding of other purposes of the movement?

BALDWIN: It's very difficult to talk about it in these terms, I think. I think that the Muslim movement is involved with power. I know about power. It's involved also with morality and identity. This is the argument I have for Mr. X. Actually, he's got a very good thing going for him, the Muslim movement does, because after all, what they are asking for is also what the country is on the record in asking for: a whole separation of the races is what Mississippi wants and what Georgia wants and on the basis of the record what the country wants. That isn't what I want.

GOLDMAN: Pardon me, doesn't Mr. X and the Muslim movement call for the separation of the races by having the Negroes all in certain states of America?

BALDWIN: Yes.

GOLDMAN: Which is different from what the Mississippians want.

BALDWIN: Well, what the Mississippians want is to have the Negroes separated in the same state. This is why we're talking about the nature of power, and I think one has to make this clear: what the Mississippians have or think they have is power; what the Muslim movement wants is power. And I don't think we can talk about it unless we're aware of this distinction, because of this reality, because again, what the Muslim movement is doing is simply taking the equipment or the history really of white people with Negroes and turning it against white people. Now, in this country today and yesterday—it is terribly difficult to believe—Americans have never really proven that they really consider Negroes to be men. Now, from my point of view, this has done more to destroy white men in this country than it has done, quite apart from all the things we know about, the oppression and the ghettoes and the lynchings and so forth, it has done much more to destroy the country than it has done to destroy the Negro.

What I am suing for, what I myself am personally suing for, is not a separation of the races. I don't believe in the first place in races, and especially in this country. Again, when one is in the situation of the Congolese fighting the Belgians, when one is in the situation, whether white men or black men want to admit it, of fighting one's brothers and one's ancestors—and this is a reality which, no matter how hidden, will sooner or later come to light—when one takes the road to power, it seems to me that the white world proves this, one ends up where the white world is. What has happened in the country since World War II has not been because white people have suddenly changed their minds or have become more generous or any of those things; what has happened is that power is beginning to shift.

My concern is what will happen when I, a Negro, no longer have you as my oppressor but am responsible, altogether responsible, for what is happening to me, for what kind of world I want. Now, I don't want to see the history of Europe, the history of Western nations, repeated for another thousand years with the shoe on the other foot. The handicap one has in talking this way is that there is no way to use the record, the American record, or the record of Western nations, to prove this point. All the evidence really is on the side of the Muslim movement. What one can and must quarrel about is the issue and where this will lead and what this means in terms of human beings who are finally neither white nor black.

GOLDMAN: Well, now, staying on that issue, if I may, and establishing here in a way that we can all agree upon how the Muslim intends to solve that issue, is it not correct that he stands not only for the separation of the races in separate states but is opposed to integration, opposed to the sit-down movement?

SCHUYLER: There are two things here with which I differ violently. One is that all evidence is on the side of the Muslim movement; that is justification for this campaign of hate against white people. Now, I would like to offer that these 18 million-some-odd Negroes that you're talking about in the United States are the healthiest, the wealthiest, have the most property, the best educated, and best informed group of Negroes in the world, and that includes all those in the Muslim countries. Now, we ought to get that thing straight. Now this is a matter of record; there's no guess work about it. And the next thing is where is there anything in the Constitution or anything that Lincoln said or wrote that says that a group has a right to part of the United States to take it off by itself? I thought that issue was settled a hundred years ago.

LINCOLN: I'd like to respond to one of the remarks made by Mr. Schuyler. In researching the Black Muslim movement and talking with hundreds of people across the country, one of the things I found consistently was the fact that since Negroes in this country are among the best educated nonwhite people in the world, since they have the leisure time, to some extent, to read and to study, and since they live in a society where there are all of these plus values available to the white man, I found that this is one of the things that is most productive of the kind of anxiety that makes for a Muslim movement. For example, we found that the fact that the Negro is so well educated produces a kind of chaffing at the bit because he cannot a be a full-class citizen in terms of his education and in terms of his preparation. We find that with the emergence of black states in Africa and other nonwhite peoples in Asia and other parts of the world that the American Negro has a subtle, sinking feeling that if he isn't careful, he might be the last person in the world to obtain the kind of status that would be equal with his education and preparation. It is upon this kind of anxiety that the Black Muslim movement feeds.

GOLDMAN: Mr. Lincoln, before we argue the point, the first thing I think we should do is to get clear what the Muslims stand for. Now, Mr. Lincoln, you were explaining why people turn to the Muslim movement, which is important, but as I understand reading your book, you say, flatly, the Black Muslims are "emphatically opposed" to passive resistance as expressed by Martin Luther King. Or another quote: "Muslims have only contempt for the Negro sit-in movement." Now, Mr. X, is that correct or not correct?

X: America itself is opposed to passive resistance. When the Japanese attacked Pearl Harbor, America did not resort to passive resistance.

GOLDMAN: Pardon me, I'm not talking about America at the moment. I'm talking about you, Mr. X, and your movement.

X: Yes sir, I want to clarify that, because when they refer to us as nonpassive, they make it look like we're committing a crime to be nonpassive.

GOLDMAN: I'm simply asking is Mr. Lincoln, a scholar on this subject, wrong or right when he says that you and your movement have only contempt for the Negro sit-in movement?

X: We have never voiced any contempt for the so-called Negro sit-in movement, because we don't voice contempt for movements.

GOLDMAN: Are you "emphatically opposed"?

X: We are opposed to forcing our way into a white restaurant where we are not wanted and forcing that man to serve us—we're opposed to that. The Honorable Elijah Muhammad, who is our religious leader and teacher, teaches us that it would be wiser for the black people of America, instead of begging the white man for what he has and forcing themselves upon him, to try and get something for ourselves. And, for instance, if I force my way into a restaurant in Georgia, and force the white man to serve me, I would be insane to let him go back into his kitchen and prepare my food—and then I sit down and eat it, after he has prepared it out of my sight.

GOLDMAN: Perhaps I am being stupid, but it seems to me you are not answering my question.

X: What is your question?

GOLDMAN: My question is—

X: Maybe I'm not giving you the answer that you want.

GOLDMAN: Is Mr. Lincoln correct when he says that you and your movement are emphatically opposed to the sit-in movement?

X: I say this: We are emphatically opposed to the methods.

GOLDMAN: How about the objectives?

X: Sir, if an objective is to sit down in another man's restaurant and drink a cup of coffee when you don't yet have a restaurant of your own, then we have to be against that type of objective, because after that Negro comes out of the restaurant having drunk the coffee, where will he work, where is his job?

GOLDMAN: Now, you are opposed to the means, you say, and I gather you're also opposed to the end, because you are opposed to an integrated society. Is that correct?

X: The sit-in movement, to us, represents the intense degree of dissatisfaction that exists among the new generations of so-called Negroes in America. As such, it is important, because it shows that the present generation of students has lost its fear of the white man that was in the parent. Twenty years ago, the average so-called Negro in America, if he resented Jim Crow segregation, he would only manifest that resentment to the degree that he thought the white man would allow him to, or to the degree that he thought he could do it without offending the white man.

GOLDMAN: Gentlemen, I have taken too much of the table's time. Mr. Baldwin?

BALDWIN: I'm afraid that this argument about integration versus segregation is just as unreal in terms of the Muslim movement as it is in terms of the deep South or in terms of the country. In fact, one of the things in the record is this has been an integrated country, in spite of the fact that it has been illegal or sub rosa. Integration is not something new. Again, the aim of the sit-in movement is not to get a cup of coffee; it is not even to force on the white restaurant something that is unwanted; it seems to me that if it has any aim at all, the aim is to liberate this country—when I say this country, I mean for blacks and whites.

GOLDMAN: Mr. Baldwin, now you confuse me. One can have two aims in life if one is a Negro: one can be to integrate black and white society and make it one society; the other can be to create two separate societies, one all white, one all black. If I understand Mr. Lincoln's scholarly study of the Black Muslim movement, it is for the division into an all-white and all-black society.

SCHUYLER: I would like to say that another thing that the Muslim movement stands for and with which I'm in complete agreement is the greater interest in Negroes acquiring an economic stake in this civilization. Also, in the fine work of rehabilitation they've done in some of their young members who have been juvenile delinquents and criminals—and they have come out, and by virtue of the teaching they receive, have changed their way of life. Now, that's been done by other movements; the Moslem movement has no monopoly on it, but they have done it, and you have to give credit for that.

GOLDMAN: So there is this economic problem? To clarify the economic program, would you add whether you believe the Black Muslim movement wants the economic uplift of the Negro or wants two separate economies.

SCHUYLER: Well, I don't know. They may want two separate economies, but they are interested in economic uplift of the Negro, and I think that they deserve great credit for that.

GOLDMAN: Mr. Lincoln, would you answer that question please, so we can get it clear?

LINCOLN: My experience has been, in talking with the Muslim leaders about the country, that perhaps the separate economy for which the Muslims seem to be working is a means to an end, whether the ultimate end is a reintegrated society, I doubt rather much, but nevertheless, the Muslims seem to feel that in our social structure as it now stands that it is highly unlikely, if not altogether impossible, for them to have any real economic gains. Therefore, as I interpret the movement, they prefer to withdraw from a society in which they cannot move upward to establish a society of their own in which there will be black men at all levels, and then, as I understand the movement, to enter into the same kind of political negotiations with the United States as exists between various other states at the present time.

GOLDMAN: As separate entities?

LINCOLN: Yes, as separate entities.

GOLDMAN: What about this issue of force which we have got to get out here. One of the most discussed things about the Black Muslim movement is the frequent charge that it's going to resort to force because it believes in black supremacy. And Mr. X you are always quoted as having said, "There is no white man a Muslim can trust." Mr. Muhammad is always quoted as having said, "We must take things into our own hands, we must return to the Mosaic law of an eye for an eye, and a tooth for a tooth. What does it matter if ten million of us die, there will be seven million of us left and they will enjoy justice and freedom." It sounds like the language of force. Is it?

X: Before you ask me to clarify that, I wish you would allow me to comment on Mr. Lincoln's last statement concerning the separate economy.

GOLDMAN: Go right ahead.

X: Although, as you say, he studied it, by me being a Muslim myself I think I can make it more clear than a scholar.

GOLDMAN: Some of us scholars doubt that proposition, Mr. X, but go ahead.

X: Yes, well, I don't doubt that myself. I think you'll agree with me, though, sir, that a separate economy already exists between the so-called Negro and the white man in America, because there is a certain category in which black people can get jobs and a certain category in which they can't get jobs. The economies are already separate. There's only so high they can go in business fields. Some business fields are shut out to them completely. Even when a black man goes into business, and he is in the selling business, usually if he has a successful business, every sale he makes is a resale, because in order to have a commodity or goods to sell, he has to buy it from a white man, another white man, which means that no matter how large his store is, still all of the goods that are being sold are actually being sold for the white man because the black man who's in business is not a producer. He doesn't produce that which he sells. Now, we who follow the Honorable Elijah Muhammad are taught that the black man, even though he goes into business, will still be a dependent person economically because he must produce. As long as the white man is the producer, then the white man is setting the price for the goods the black man has to sell in his own neighborhood. Usually, when a black man goes into business, he doesn't go into business in a white neighborhood, he goes to business in a black neighborhood. And since he can only buy his goods from a wholesaler who is white, who gets it from a producer who is also white, he has to come back into his neighborhood and jack the prices up to get back the money that the white man has already taken from him.

GOLDMAN: This is your explanation?

X: I'm explaining it clear, so it won't be misunderstood. So Mr. Muhammad teaches us that in order for us to be economically independent, we have to have some land, where we can be producers, just like the white man is a producer for his kind.

GOLDMAN: Mr. Schuyler, you seem unhappy.

SCHUYLER: Well, of course I'm unhappy, because I want to get back to the field of reality. There's something like two hundred thousand individual Negro farmers in the United States. They raise cotton, corn. They sell milk and all of that, but they are selling it to white people, and the white people would be very hard put if they didn't have this cotton, corn, meat, and other things that Negro farmers raise to buy from them. So it seems to me that it's inherent in trade that you buy and sell. Nobody's stopping Negroes from either buying or selling in the United States. Many of them are doing it all the time, and I think it's a perversion of the fact to say the Negro has no part in the economy—that's ridiculous. They must have some part in it, when fifteen thousand of them are in labor unions throughout the country and some of them in the highest categories that I know of—it would be too long to list here. Now, if Negroes have been unable to devise ways and means of getting more of these jobs, that is partially their own fault.

X: But sir, even though they're in these labor unions, they're yet the last ones hired, first ones fired.

SCHUYLER: Not necessarily.

X: And the greater percentage of the unemployed right here in America, according to Secretary Goldberg's statement, are the so-called Negroes, despite the fact that they belong to these unions and whatnot.

SCHUYLER: That isn't entirely due to the fact that they are Negroes.

BALDWIN: I think there are some extremes in trying to talk about the economy in this way. In fact, as far as I can tell, the black economy and the white economy are interdependent, and it is quite true that Negroes are the first to be fired and the last to be hired. These details obscure the point at the moment. My question here is, How? I think we can take it for granted that the United States is not about to give away six or ten states. Therefore, in one way or another, the only way this will be achieved is that they will not be able to hold on to them. Now, the question is what happens, then, to this economy in which Negroes have, I think you say, twenty million or billion dollars at their disposal? The system under which it's obtained no longer exists, which is the only way these states can be achieved. Then what will the economy be? What will be the future of these hypothetical states? What will be their relationship not only to the United States— because by this time, as far as we can tell, there won't be anything resembling the United States as we know it now? It will be at least another country, it will be a very different country and obviously a much less powerful country.

GOLDMAN: It will be a black America and a white America, won't it?

BALDWIN: Well, it is already on this continent. If I can say one more thing. This is rather hard for me. The root of the irreality here, the illusion of white people in this country is that they're living in a white country, and I think that is a very dangerous illusion. You don't have a white country, with as many Negroes as we have had in it all these years, to say nothing of the effect on white people, and the interaction between white and black people, of this terrible history. One has to really face the facts of what really happened. I know about the oppression, the lynchings, and so forth. I know about that situation now; I'm not trying to minimize it. This is not all that happened. A great many other things happened, too; a great many other things were achieved. I'm not talking about white good will, but the point is that history is also immoral, just as immoral as power is, but what history has produced in terms of one's own personality and in terms of the present facts has to be dealt with. For example, one doesn't have to accuse the Muslim movement of being a hate movement, you know? I do realize, from my own vantage point—I'm a boy from Harlem, too—how desperately and how deeply Negroes hate white people. Now, white people don't want to know this and have spent all of my lifetime anyway protecting themselves against this knowledge. Negroes do not tell them this, either.

GOLDMAN: Mr. Baldwin, what I'm trying to find out is whether the Muslim movement does hate me or not, and whether it proposes to use force to satisfy its hatred. I don't seem to be able to get any place in finding it out.

X: I'll clear that up.

BALDWIN: It is not important to know whether the Muslim movement hates you or not; that is not at all the question. They may or they may not—that's irrelevant. But the point is that most Negroes, most black people, do not trust white people, and most Negroes hate white people, and as long as this country and the white people in this country use all the fantastic measures they do use to protect themselves against this knowledge, there's one thing every white man in this country knows: he knows he would not be black here, no matter what else he doesn't know. And all the liberal movements that I have been associated with, and all liberals, almost all the liberals—and the exceptions only prove the rule—all the liberals I have ever known are working day and night not only in terms of letting Negroes live next door to them but in terms of their own minds, their own consciences, their own way of life, to protect themselves against the crimes for which they know they are responsible. Now, I cannot—this is what is important about this I think, the future of the country depends on it—if I, as a black man, must be responsible every day of my life for something I did not do, if I must pay for the history written in the color of my skin, so must white people. The great pain about being a Negro here is that you can never get across to a white person the fact that you are as human as he is, and that he is losing his humanity in so far as he denies you yours. This is the great advantage of the Muslim movement; it doesn't matter whether they hate you or not, for one's got to deal with the record.

SCHUYLER: I marvel sometimes. If, as is said by the Muslim speakers, the white man has hated the Negro since he has been on earth, why has the white man done so much to help the Negro? For example, I notice they abolished the slave trade in Africa and from here to Africa, and I don't know whether any Moslem states have done that. They've set up schools and clinics and hospitals and asylums and colleges throughout all black Africa. I don't know that anybody can point out one Moslem college or university south of Egypt and Morocco in Africa for the education of black people. Now, these things have been done, and it doesn't seem to me that this is the action of a people that hate a whole people. Of course there are white people who hate Negroes, but I don't see any reason or justification for exaggerating the situation.

GOLDMAN: Mr. Baldwin, may I come back, just for the purposes of clarification, to try to get Mr. X's comment on the statements: first, that his movement stands for black supremacy; second, that it intends to bring it about by the use of force.

X: If by supremacy you mean rule, the fact that the white man has been ruling for so long, which is white supremacy—and most of your white historians and even your current politicians and diplomats admit that—it's losing out all over the world. Britain used to rule an empire so large she bragged the sun would never set on it.

GOLDMAN: We're talking about what you want to happen. And your leader is quoted in Mr. Lincoln's book as saying that he wants to use an eye for an eye, a tooth for a tooth, and he wants to end white rule in the U.S. He wants to "overthrow it," to use the quotation.

X: If Mr. Lincoln said that, Mr. Lincoln is one thousand percent wrong.

LINCOLN: What does he mean by the quotation "We must take things into our own hands. . . . What does it matter if ten million of us die, there will be seven million of us left"?

X: If you have men, if you have crimes such as those that were committed against Emmett Till, and the government itself could go into Mississippi and find the exact culprits who committed the crime, or the type of crime that was committed against Mack Parker, and again the government agents go in there and find the culprits who were guilty of murdering Mack Parker, and then turn around and the government admits that it is not able to bring those murderers to justice, I think that it would be insane on the part of any man to deny the family of Mack Parker or the family of Emmett Till the right to come together and defend themselves, since the government admits that it is helpless to defend them.

GOLDMAN: I take that to be your justification of the use of violence by Negroes.

X: If America is justified in retaliating against Japan when Japan strikes her, or retaliating against Germany when Germany strikes her, or retaliating against any other country to defend herself from attack, I think America has reached the point of insanity to think that the world would look upon the black here in America as being wrong if they took a stand to defend themselves against a crime that the white man is committing against us here day and night.

SCHUYLER: I don't see why you don't answer the man's questions: Are you for force or are you against force? If you're for force and use of force, then that's sedition. Why don't you level on the thing, instead of curving all around Robin Hood's barn?

X: You can't put words in my mouth. I want to get that point right there straight. Since it is Islam and the Muslims who are being discussed here, and it is Islam and the Muslims who are under fire, I think that it is only right to expect me to give you my answer—not someone else's answer—because this is what primarily has been done in America. Everyone else speaks for the Muslims, and they're not allowed to speak for themselves. Now you don't put a yes or no answer today in the mouth of any black man, other, perhaps, than Mr. Schuyler.

GOLDMAN: Mr. Lincoln, would you like to comment on this or any other related point as to what the real program is? Is it a program of force or not?

LINCOLN: From what I have been able to determine, the Muslims are very careful not to talk about the use of force. Now, in the early days of my research on the movement it was stated among Muslims that they looked forward to a sort of day of Armageddon that was to take place around 1970, when the white man in America would be overthrown and when the black man would come into what was considered to be—

X: I challenge this. And I think you're a thousand percent wrong.

GOLDMAN: Pardon me, Mr. X, let him finish, then you can comment on it.

LINCOLN: But at the same time, Mr. X, it is true that the Muslims have avoided any direct reference to the use of force.

X: No, you're wrong in the first part, and you're right in the last part. The Honorable Elijah Muhammad has never taught us that we ourselves are going to fight the white man, but he has taught us that there will come a day when God will destroy evil from the face of this Earth. God will do it; proof of the matter is we never carry arms. We're probably the only black group in America as large as we are who could absolutely say at a meeting that we have that not one man in that audience has arms in his pocket or alcohol in his head, and I think that it's absurd to stand around and accuse the Black Muslims of advocating violence, when we've never been during the entire thirty years that the Honorable Elijah Muhammad has been teaching here in America, we have never been involved in any aggressive acts against any white people. And anytime that violence has occurred—and even the newspapers have to admit this and the police—whenever we have been involved with any violence, it has always been at a time when we ourselves were attacked. Because we one thousand percent don't believe that a man should turn the other cheek when there's knots on his cheek already and the man is going to put some more knots on his cheek—we can't see that.

LINCOLN: May I respond to Mr. X's statement. We're talking about putting words in people's mouths. I have pointed out very clearly in my book that the Muslims do not initiate aggression, I have pointed out very clearly that they do not carry arms, I have pointed out clearly that they are taught not to initiate aggression, that they must not even have so much as a finger nail file in their pocket.

X: Correct, and always obey the law.

LINCOLN: Always obey the law.

GOLDMAN: Mr. Lincoln, you're confusing me. It's you who wrote that the Fruit of Islam, the secret army, saying, "They receive training in Judo, military drill and the use of knives and blackjacks. The fruit of Islam looks forward to playing a heroic role in the impending battle of Armageddon." I refer Mr. Lincoln to page 201.

LINCOLN: Let me finish. I said that they do not commit aggression—so far. What they want to do in the future nobody knows except the Muslims themselves.

X: Where do the blackjacks and the knives come in with Muslims?

SCHUYLER: They search for them.

X: Everyone who comes into the mosques that are set up here in America under the spiritual guidance of the Honorable Elijah Muhammad is checked thoroughly because we're absolutely against any kind of aggression or weapons that one could use in aggression.

SCHUYLER: Well, if they are such peace lovers, then why do you have to search them? That's the question that comes to my mind.

X: Mr. Schuyler, the thing that I can't understand on this violence and hate business—this Rockwell, this so-called Nazi who wanted to give a speech down in the village, he was stoned by the Jews, and the Jews were never accused of violence or hate. He was stoned in Boston by the Jews, and the Jews never were accused of violence and hate. The man hadn't done anything, but he wanted to make a speech. Yet anytime a Muslim or a black man—he doesn't have to be a Muslim—stands up here in America and mentions that it's time for him to try and defend himself, not from someone's doctrine but from the actual violence that is committed against him, then that black man is accused of being violent. And just because we remind the public of the crimes that were committed against our people in America during slavery, we're accused of advocating a hate campaign, but right now you turn on your television, your radio, and all of your press, and you'll see nothing on there about Eichmann and what the Germans did to the Jews a thousand years ago. And yet the Jews aren't accused of carrying on a hate campaign.

SCHUYLER: Mr. X, you talk at great length and monopolize a considerable amount of time. However, I would like to say that one of the things that was in Mr. Lincoln's book that intrigued me was the fact that this Muslim movement is run as a kind of dictatorship itself. There haven't been any elections; people are tried without having anything to say about it and cast into the outer limbo; women are subordinated and have no voice within the movement. Now, that doesn't seem to me like something new in the world; it seems to me to be pretty reactionary.

X: You wrote in the *Pittsburgh Courier,* Mr. Schuyler, about the Muslim movement yourself on May 30, 1959, at which time you said, "From what I have seen and heard about the program of the Black Muslims in this country and the past few years, I conclude that there is much to commend it to other sects and religious groups, many of whom seem to be distressingly unwitting in their way."

SCHUYLER: I just said that.

X: You also pointed out that not only do the Muslims believe in it, meaning this economic progress, but they are doing it. They are not only preparing and serving their food, but they are growing it. This is what you wrote. You also said we are alone in doing this, in regards to setting up economic enterprises for ourselves, so we are not always rattling the tin cup and begging for succor.

SCHUYLER: You see, that's what you get for trying to be nice. Now, I just told Mr. X here a little while ago that this was a part of the Muslim movement which I commended very highly. You don't have to go back to what I wrote a year or so ago. I said that this afternoon, and I say it again. But you haven't dealt with the issue that I raised about the Moslem movement being dictatorial itself.

X: Sir, it's because we have unity? It's because we have complete unity and, again, the worst critics of the Honorable Elijah Muhammad give him credit for establishing better discipline and unity among his followers than has ever been established among any so-called Negroes in America. Anytime there is unity in any country that has a philosophy or a doctrine or an aim that is in opposition to the power-existing block.

GOLDMAN: Mr. X, Mr. Schuyler wants to come in, and we have to move on to another point. Mr. Schuyler, do you want to drop this point now? I don't think you men are going to agree.

SCHUYLER: Of course we'll never agree. I won't drop it, but I do not want to monopolize the time.

X: Mr. Schuyler has noted issues about our religion, and about Muslims being the ones who create all this. He made the point, and I think I want to clear it up. He has made an issue about our religion.

GOLDMAN: I must call you to order here. Mr. Schuyler has dropped the point so that we could move to something else. I want to bring Mr. Baldwin in here, if I may, because I've been very much interested in your articles in *Harpers* and in the *Times* and so forth in which you explain the whole Negro mood, part of which is expressed through the Black Muslims, as part of your reaction to world events, particularly [in] Africa. And this is a New Negro, you say. Now, in these terms it is quite interesting to me to read of the alleged connections [between] the Black Muslims and the Muslims in Africa and between the Black Muslims and the Castro movement in Cuba. Do you know anything about this?

BALDWIN: No, I don't know anything about that in detail. I don't know anything about the Muslim movement in Africa at all, so I can't talk about that.

GOLDMAN: Well, of course it is making great progress in Africa, as you know.

BALDWIN: Yes, I know that.

GOLDMAN: Do you see this as a worldwide movement at all which would appeal to the Negro?

BALDWIN: Well, how can I put it? It seems to me to be arguing, in a way, almost after the fact. If you're talking about power, it is very clear that the Western nations, the white nations, that power is broken. The connection between Cuba and American Negroes I can see very well, because the United States' role in Cuba is exactly analogous in the mind of any Negro living in this country to the situation he finds himself in here. Again, I have to come back to this point. We are really talking about power, and we can't argue about the Muslim movement in those terms, because, I repeat this, they are only imitating. They're simply doing the same thing that the white world has done for all these years. Now, that is my objection to the Muslim movement. It seems to me what we in this country do not know and have not faced is that we can very well isolate ourselves on this continent. Because the world is no longer white at all, we do not know what to do. In the first place, I don't agree with Mr. X and I don't entirely agree with Mr. Schuyler, either, or white Americans. I don't know what white men have, in the first place, which is so desirable. I don't know why it's so important to be white anymore. It seems to me that civilization, which we are now witnessing if not the end of then the great transformation of, can only be saved by us in this country if we are willing to do something which we have not done.

GOLDMAN: What would we do, Mr. Baldwin, in your opinion? Do you favor the Black Muslim program, or do you favor the program of, let us say, the NAACP?

BALDWIN: Well, I think the NAACP program is probably outmoded because when you have a situation where the legality of a country is in question—one does not know what is legal anymore—one has got to revise the entire system.

GOLDMAN: But the NAACP says that what is legal is the integration of American life.

BALDWIN: What is legal, then, in Mississippi?

GOLDMAN: The integration of American life.

BALDWIN: How does one achieve it, then, in Mississippi?

GOLDMAN: The NAACP says you keep trying until you achieve it.

BALDWIN: Mr. X's response is that he will not wait a hundred years.

GOLDMAN: He says something else. He says he doesn't want it, either.

X: I said—wait a moment. Don't say what I say. I say that the black masses themselves in America are impatient, and that the white man does not know how the black masses think any more than he knew how the peasants in Cuba thought when he went in there and thought they would rise up and side with him.

GOLDMAN: Now, you said the white man does not know, and I'm sure I don't know.

X: He doesn't know, because he's not being told by his so-called Negro advisors, or the ones that he has set up as spokesmen for the so-called Negro.

GOLDMAN: Pardon me. These so-called advisors, I thought, were men of some knowledge about the Negro community.

X: They never live in the Negro community.

GOLDMAN: Ralph Bunche has denounced you as a totally escapist movement; Roy Wilkins, executive secretary of the NAACP, says you are preaching pure hatred; Thurgood Marshall called you such violent names I won't repeat them here; and Reverend Martin Luther King Jr. says you're simply one of the hate groups arising in our midst.

X: Wait a moment, sir. I think that in fairness, since these things that you read to your audience—in order for you to be fair, I have to make my comment. Number one, these so-called Negro leaders that made these statements, it's contrary to our policy to ever attack anyone personally, only in defense, and I think that each one you read off, you couldn't find them in Harlem. The only time you ever see any one of those that are made spokesmen by you, parrots by the white man, you never find them in Harlem. You find them at the Waldorf-Astoria. And so far as them knowing how the black men out there in the street think, all you have to do is do like John Griffin, this white man who posed as a Negro did for six weeks—he was pseudo-Negro—and yet he comes back today and he's an expert on how a Negro's supposed to feel. And we've been black all of our lives, and when we step up and try to tell you how a black man who is born black feels, you think that we are hatists, racists, or something of that sort.

GOLDMAN: Mr. Baldwin, you wanted to comment.

BALDWIN: Yes, I'm from Harlem, too. I was born in the streets and raised in them, and I think I know something about them, too. All the condemnations from Mr. Bunche, et ceteras, et ceteras, are all far too simple. The challenge that this movement represents—and I think it's very easy to think about simply as a movement—the challenge this movement represents has nothing to do with what they call themselves, or even what their aims are, whether or not Mr. X is willing to say what their aims are or whether or not we know. The challenge this movement represents is finally whether this country moves to be what it says it is. Are we free or are we not? And we can only decide this one way. If the country wants to be free, then it has got to do something to prove it; and as long as we're not willing to do it, the Muslim movement will gain more and more ground, and not only here but all over the world. If we mean what we say, I think we should put the government of Mississippi in jail, as opposed to putting harmless people who challenge the House un-American Activities Committee in jail.

GOLDMAN: Mr. Baldwin, I still don't have clear whether you favor the Black Muslim program or the NAACP program—two different approaches.

BALDWIN: I will not answer it that way. I cannot—

GOLDMAN: You can see why it came about?

BALDWIN: I can see very well why it came about.

GOLDMAN: I think Mr. Lincoln in his book has explained very well why it came about.

X: I don't think he has explained very well why it came about or how it exists. For instance, in there where it was said in the book that I spent two hours in a secret conversation with Castro, that wasn't done on any research—that was through a local New York paper who we're suing right now for $3 million for libel. We have a $3 million libel suit against a New York paper for saying that I spent two hours in a secret conference with Castro. Now, if that's an authentic statement and that's representative of the other statements in the book, then I can't say that the book is representative of Muslims.

GOLDMAN: Mr. Lincoln.

LINCOLN: I must respond to that. Mr. X, it was from you yourself.

X: Then you're wrong.

LINCOLN: I am not wrong on this case. It was from you yourself and not the lead in any New York paper that I found that you had had an appointment which you kept with Mr. Castro. These words are from your mouth.

X: No, wait a minute now. Clarify that: two of us, and I thank Allah that there were two, in a conversation with you explained about this highly publicized incident with Castro, and we told you exactly how it came about—that I was representing the mayor's office and the police department and half of the civic groups in Harlem.

[At this point Goldman interjects because it appears that Lincoln and Malcolm are going to monopolize the final five minutes. Lincoln, Goldman, Malcolm, and Schuyler are all talking. Finally, Schuyler wins this verbal joust.]

SCHUYLER: This particular sect of the movement is just one of a succession of such movements that have been in American life for the last three centuries. Among Negroes they began around 1815, when the American Colonization movement began to grow and Negroes went to Sierra Leone. They went to

Liberia, and since then these movements have been recurring. On the eve of the Civil War, Maj. Martin R. Delany had gone to the West Coast of Africa and signed treaties with African chiefs, assuring that he had a considerable following, and this thought has been in people's minds for a long time. It isn't anything new.

GOLDMAN: But Mr. Schuyler, I take it to be Mr. Baldwin's point, and Mr. Lincoln's point in his book, that there is a new situation.

BALDWIN: I think that it is misleading to talk about even Garvey—any of these movements—in the twenties. There is one great difference between them, if only one. The difference is Africa. I really want to repeat this point. I think the only way to challenge this movement or undercut it is for this country to do something it does not seem prepared to do: which is to become, really overnight, a radical country. When I say radical, I mean to reexamine and overhaul the entire social fabric, to ask—everyone in this country should ask himself— why it's so important in this country to be white, and what they would lose if

Schuyler shaking hands with Richard M. Nixon, then candidate for vice president of the United States, at the Theresa Hotel in Harlem, 1956. Photographer unknown.

they admit [that] to themselves. I, personally speaking, I cannot imagine any-thing this country can offer me, and what has happened to me, it seems to me, has happened to every Negro in this country. And the only way this can be redeemed and we can prevent a reversal, a repetition of this history, with the roles reversed, is to decide, and to decide right now: either everyone in this country is free, either I'm a man or I am not. It's up to the country to decide it; it is not really any longer up to me.

GOLDMAN: Mr. Lincoln, I don't think you agree with that.

LINCOLN: Well, I certainly agree with it in part. Whether it's the Black Muslim movement or the NAACP or the sit-ins, or the Southern Christian Leadership Conference under Mr. King, one of the objectives that certainly is identical to all of these various expressions—and that is the essential freedom and dignification of the Negro. Now, whether he goes about it in the way of the Muslims or whether he goes about it in some other way, I believe that this has to come about in this country, and it has to come rather soon. This I do say, in my book. This country cannot continue to exist black and white. Either we have to be Americans or we're going to continue to be plagued with all kinds of organizations. If the Black Muslims did not exist, then some other group would exist in their place.

GOLDMAN: Mr. Schuyler, I think you disagree even more sharply with Mr. Baldwin.

SCHUYLER: Well, I just simply think that there's a lot of wishful thinking in many of these statements. I see no statistical evidence of all this. I've been all over the country. I don't know that the masses of Negroes are panting to join the Black Muslims, just like they weren't panting to join Garvey. There are certainly ele-ments that will because you have all kinds of people in any group; the Negro group is like any other group—you have everything in it. And there's never going to be any unity with all the Negroes, and I think it would be a catastro-phe if [there] were.

LINCOLN: Perhaps there will never be complete unanimity among Negroes; it would be most anomalous if this should come about. But there is, I think, with Mr. Baldwin, a sharpening of the Negro mood, a kind of insistence that he must—

GOLDMAN: Pardon me, Mr. Lincoln, I want Mr. X to have a word here before we have to close, just a word.

X: Yes, I don't think all of the Muslims who follow Mr. Muhammad read the book—that is, those who are leaders—and we actually don't think that it rightly represents us. Mr. Muhammad's aim is this: He was raised by God to separate the black men in America from the white men, because the white men will not give us freedom, justice, and equality on his own. And he also teaches us that if white America can't give the black man in America complete recognition as a human being immediately, right here, then we have to separate and God will give it to us. He also teaches us that all of the trouble that America is having— just like Pharaoh had trouble in the Bible because he mistreated the slaves— every trouble, political and otherwise—

[X is cut off.]

GOLDMAN: I have the cut-off signal. I'm sorry. For this discussion, thank you, Mr. X, Mr. Eric Lincoln, Mr. James Baldwin, and Mr. George Schuyler.

PART III

RACE, CONSERVATISM, AND CIVIL RIGHTS

The Case against the Civil Rights Bill (1963)

This speech was delivered at the State University of New York's Rockland Community College in Suffern, New York, on Monday, November 11, 1963. Schuyler was arguing against the Civil Rights Act that would be passed in 1964. According to Professor John Hope Franklin, the act comprised the "most far-reaching and comprehensive laws in support of racial equality ever enacted by congress." Schuyler believed, however, that it would foster white resentment rather than racial equality. Although unpopular, Schuyler's argument was in the main balanced, absent of the conservative polemics that would characterize most of his civil rights essays. As a conservative, Schuyler resisted the notion that government should assume such a pivotal role in matters of conscience. If America were to embrace such a position, it would constitute, according to Schuyler, a "blow at the very basis of American society which is founded on state sovereignty and individual liberty and preference."

A proliferation of largely unenforceable legislation has everywhere been characteristic of political immaturity. As a young nation, the United States has in this regard been a particularly great offender with a decided penchant for enacting laws regulating social conduct. Moral indignation coupled with a passion for social reform has induced us to pass laws without too much attention to consideration of how and at what cost they are to be enforced, and with more attention to politics than to statesmanship.

Historically we have not been unique in this connection. Every new, developing country has rapidly amassed mountains of laws which read well but are unrealistic, fly in the face of the facts of life, and later have to be revised or abandoned in the light of experience, often painful and expensive. New countries have a passion for novelty, and a country like America, which grew out of conquest, immigration, revolution and civil war, is prone to speed social change by law, or try to do so, on the assumption that by such legerdemain it is possible to make people better by *force*. This seems possible because it is deemed to be right. This has been the cause of much misery and injustice throughout the ages.

It is almost axiomatic that it takes lots of time to change social mores, especially with regard to such hardy perennials as religion, race and nationality, to say nothing of social classes. There never being any unanimity about such things, sumptuary laws almost invariably become unpopular and the police power inevitably must be used to enforce compliance. The less popular they become, the more difficult and expensive is enforcement, and the less popular becomes the government which tries to enforce them because it is running counter to the wishes of a growing number of people.

Ferrero, the famed Italian historian, points out that the legitimacy of a government is gauged by the willingness of the people to accept and obey its acts and decrees, as shown by the ease or difficulty of enforcement. Widespread flouting of laws that are unpopular have frequently led to the downfall of governments; and as in a democracy this means the ultimate ousting of the political group in power—if it refuses to bow to the popular will. This is particularly true where the laws attempt to alter the public tastes and attitudes.

Millions of Americans believed that consumption of alcoholic beverages was wrong and physically injurious, and the temperance forces carried on a long and spirited campaign of an educational nature against indulgence. This was not entirely successful, and by World War I the liquor industry was on the defensive. It became regarded as "bad" to have and serve hard liquor in the home; the saloon was regarded as a den of iniquity and breeding ground for crime and destitution. Millions wore the white ribbon of temperance.

Then came the political triumph of the temperance forces with the passage of the Eighteenth Amendment. Education was not swift enough for them, so they turned to force. The saloon disappeared to make way for the speakeasy. Bootleggers came out of the mountains and invaded our cities and towns. Violations of the enabling laws became so frequent that law enforcement was crippled, and bribery and graft became endemic. Strengthened by easy money arising from whole sale violation of the law, the criminal element became so rich and powerful that it soon controlled what had hitherto been legitimate businesses; and now, thirty-odd years after Prohibition's end, it still does. Alcoholism is more widespread than it was in 1918, and its by-products today constitute a social problem and health hazard, despite Alcoholics Anonymous.

The Civil Rights Laws are another typically American attempt to use the force of law to compel the public to drastically change it attitude toward and treatment of a racial group, the so-called Negro, which the overwhelming majority population does not care to associate itself with, does not in the main wish to attend school with, does not chose to share its white collar and technical jobs with, and is opposed to sharing lodging with, and all the social contacts these involve. This has been the majority attitude since the earliest colonial days. It is morally wrong, nonsensical, unfair, un-Christian and cruelly unjust, but it *remains* the majority attitude.

This attitude has been progressively modified, however, especially with regard to individuals of color with the passage of time and continued intercourse and juxtaposition of the two groups. Anybody who has observed race relations during the past quarter century knows this to be true. Prior to the Civil War the position of the free Negro outside the slave area was most enviable, and Judge Taney was merely stating the truth that "the Negro has no rights that the white man was bound to respect." Indeed, the free Negro, North and South, was in about the same position, socially and economically. He was socially ostracized and severely restricted in employment. He was voteless in both areas until the 15th Amendment was enacted after the Civil War, and he was no more welcome in hotels, restaurants and first-class railway carriages in the ante-bellum North than in the South. He was denied an education in both areas, except in Massachusetts, Rhode Island, and Vermont, save for a few private schools, while college doors were generally closed. The North had less excuse in this connection than did the South, and yet there was little to choose between the two areas in day-to-day treatment.

Changes have been very slow since 1865, but there have been marked changes; and civil rights laws, state or federal, have had little to do with it. They have been enforced and accepted only when the dominant majority acquiesced, and have generally lain dormant in the law books. In short, custom has dictated the pace of compliance. The exception emphasizes the rule. Indeed, the complaint of the more impatient Negroes is that the pace of social and economic acceptance has been so slow that it is necessary to use extralegal force, such as picketings, demonstrations and boycotts to speed the pace of their progress.

Following the Civil War we had two civil rights laws and a Reconstruction Act to enforce the citizenship status of the Negro. The court calendars were full of cases of discrimination brought by Negroes until finally in 1883, the U.S. Supreme Court outlawed such legislation. The immediate reaction was the passage by former state legislatures of punitive laws which almost returned the Negro to slavery. This process was speeded in 1896 when the U.S. Supreme Court again bowed to the public will and handed down its infamous "separate but equal" decree. As Mr. Dooley observed, the Supreme Court always follows the election returns, and until 1915 when it outlawed the notorious Grandfather Clauses in Southern state constitutions designed to disfranchise Negroes, it had done nothing to repair the evil wrought by its 1896 decision. The nation was unready.

From 1922 onward various Congressmen introduced anti-lynching bills in almost every session. Not one was passed and there is none now, but lynching has become a rarity; whereas when I was a boy there were about two lynchings every week on the average, and terrorism was much more common. But times have changed along with public opinion, thanks to an aroused public conscience and the educational activities of the National Association for the Advancement of Colored People and numerous white agencies and individuals. Of course this change was not and could not be wrought overnight. It had to be educative and gradual.

As respect for and understanding of the Negro, and appreciation of his contributions and his patience increased, national opinion softened as the cultural gap between the two "races" narrowed. This was reflected in the American press, in the literature, in the common experiences of World Wars and the vicissitudes of the economic depression, in the influence of Negro music and the whole changing cultural community. Scores of white novelists, short story writers and playwrights (South and North, but mainly Southern) took the Negro and his tribulations as their theme and molded a more advanced public opinion through the years. Sociologists and economists joined forces with the fictionists to help create an atmosphere of social understanding and acceptance. The public image of the Negro slowly changed. This was not lost on the U.S. Supreme Court which from the late Thirties has successively issued opinions with regard to the franchise, property, education, transportation and tax-supported recreation which are memorable, unprecedented, and unequaled anywhere else in the world.

It might be said here parenthetically that nowhere else on earth has the progress of a dissimilar racial minority been so marked in education, housing, health, voting and economic well-being. Not one of the foreign countries whose spokesmen criticize and excoriate the United States can equal its record in dealing with a minority group. After 4,000 years, India still has its cruel caste system with 70 million Untouchables. Soviet Russia has enslaved and decimated its racial minorities, and to this day has segregated schools and segregated housing for them. Japan retains its Etas and Ainus. Indonesia has appropriated the property of its three million Chinese and put them into restricted areas. Australia has its blacks on reservations. The social ostracism of the Negroes throughout Latin America is well known, and the most exploited Negro in rural Mississippi is better of than they.

Perhaps the most drastic coercive legislation to insure the Negro the vote was written into the 14th Amendment, Second section, in unequivocal language. That section reads:

"Representatives shall be apportioned among the several States according to their respective numbers, counting the whole number of persons in each State, excluding Indians not taxed. But when the right to vote at any election for the choice of electors for President and Vice President of the United States, Representatives in Congress, the Executive and Judicial Officers of a State, or the members of the Legislature thereof, is denied to any of the male inhabitants of such State, being twenty-one years of age, and citizens of the United States, or in any way abridged, except for participation in rebellion, or other crime, the basis of representation therein shall be reduced in the proportion which the number of such male citizens shall bear to the whole number of male citizens twenty-one years of age in such state."

This means that wherever a Negro or anybody else is denied the right to vote, the representation on the basis of population will be to that extent reduced.

Thus, should a quarter million Negroes of a state be denied the vote in any election, the State's representation in Congress would to that extent be reduced.

This 14th amendment was proclaimed in 1868, nearly one hundred years ago. To date it has been a political dead letter because no enabling legislation has been passed, no matter which party controlled the Congress. An attempt was made by Henry Cabot Lodge, Massachusetts Senator, over seventy years ago, and it was defeated. No other attempt has been made until 1957, 1960, 1964, and if such legislation had been passed, the political power of the south would have been sharply reduced because the vast majority of Negro citizens in effect had been disfranchised.

This would have weakened the South politically and strengthened the North and West in Congress. The South could only have regained its lost seats by re-enfranchising the Negroes so that they could be counted in the apportionment. Because of the failure of Congress to implement the 14th Amendment, the political enlightenment of the section was retarded almost to a standstill, the Negro's progress was held back and the South (which counted his numbers but stole his vote) was enabled to wield a disproportionate influence in the national legislature, and on the political course of the nation.

The present Civil Rights Law which would attempt cumbrously to enable Negroes to vote where registrars now deny them is thus quite unnecessary because the same thing can be accomplished by implementing the 14th Amendment. But Congress will not pass either the one or the other. Why? Because majority public opinion will not back such a law. It is more interested in white racial unity than interracial justice, and has no desire to punish the disfranchising of Negroes by penalizing the South.

However, without any Civil Rights Law more than 1,500,000 of the potential 5,000,000 Negro voters in the South are registered and voting today. In the next ten years (unless some great reaction sets in—perhaps because of just such a Civil Rights Law) I predict that almost all Negro potential voters in the South will be voting, and that numerous Negroes will be holding public office and civil service jobs, just as they are holding them here and elsewhere. The process is slow, of course, but it will be solid because it is based on a true public will.

Already there are dozens of cities in the South where Negroes are finding accommodation in hotels, motels, and tourist camps. Most of this has come about without any picketing or demonstrations. There will be more changes with time and education. For this we do not need any federal legislation. Such might very well react to the Negro's disadvantage as in the past. When the big hotels everywhere accept Negro guests and serve them in their dining rooms, the little establishments will shortly follow suit in the best interests of free enterprise. The number that does not will be so small as not to matter much. When Miami, Houston, Atlanta, Dallas and Nashville are doing this, can others be far behind?

The Civil Rights Law attempts to force fair employment practices, barring discrimination against Negroes in all jobs and professions, and guaranteeing fair employment to all qualified. Under pressure President Roosevelt issued an executive order on the eve of World War II which was designed to bring this about. After about four years it had to be permitted to die because it was found to be unworkable. It was complied with to a certain degree in precisely the areas one would expect, and ignored or evaded elsewhere. At the end, the FEPC apparatus was openly defied by the railroads and associated labor unions. After that it was quietly dropped down the drain. This was reminiscent of the outraged agitation following World War I against women bobbing their hair. The bellows could be heard from Coast to Coast but it simply made women more defiant, and within a couple of years it was rare to find a woman whose hair was not trimmed or bobbed, whether attractive or not.

Color discrimination in employment in mills, mines, commerce and transportation was nationwide when Wilson entered World War I. There was no FEPC law nationally or in any state. By war's end Negroes were working in almost every branch of industry and commerce, and had the conflict lasted as long as World War II did, the economic life would have been completely integrated, racially as well as sexually, by virtue of necessity. Incidentally, without any compulsory law, the Ford Motor Company integrated its operations racially even before World War I, a "first" for private enterprise.

Widespread popular education, industry, transportation and communication in the past century have wrought a real revolution in American thinking on the race question in this country. I have already mentioned the growth of liberal literacy output on this question from *Uncle Tom's Cabin* to the present. The transformation in periodical and press handling of this question has been phenomenal. A century ago supposedly educated people were debating whether Negroes were men or animals, inferior or superior by virtue of skin pigment; and whether or not they could survive in this civilization. This is today no longer a moot question, and the former cruel educational discrimination against Negroes in per capita school expenditures has progressively disappeared. Laws which have been passed to expedite this progress have followed rather than led public opinion.

Do we therefore need a federal punitive law to enforce civil rights Negroes already have? Have not the American people advanced sufficiently to let them decide in their several areas the pace at which Negro social acceptance is to move? Every recent poll of the nation shows that the white people are generally agreed on equal education, equal housing, equal travel and recreational facilities, and equal job opportunities for Negroes. Every important church group has gone on record officially in favor of these goals. Pockets of resistance there are bound to be, because everybody does not change at the same pace, time, and degree. But what reason is there to suppose that this pace will be really expedited by the passage of the federal law with its inevitable army of enforcers?

How much nationwide good will between the races is going to be engendered and enhanced by a punitive campaign against those who remain unconvinced? What will be the ultimate influence of the rise in Negro expectations? As I have pointed out, there is not a Jim Crow law on the books of any nation south of the Rio Grande, but all who have traveled know that the U.S. Negro is better off in every way than any Negroes anywhere else in the world. There are more college graduates among them than in the rest of the colored world combined. With ten percent of the U.S. populace, they have thirteen percent of all federal Civil Service jobs. By a simple directive of the President, the entire armed forces of the United States have been racially integrated in every branch the world over within the past fifteen years in both the enlisted and commissioned ranks. Hundreds of Negroes are in the U.S. Foreign Service, U.S.I.A. and A.I.D. Seven Negro judges sit in the federal courts and sixty-two are in lower courts across the country. There is not an important city in the United States without Negro police and firemen, to say nothing of hundreds in appointive and elective posts. There are an estimated two million Negro-owned homes and even a greater number of automobiles. This disproportionate number of unemployed Negroes reflects more than anything else the educational and cultural lag that still exists as a heritage of the past, and the demise of labor rights by organized labor.

The principal case against a federal Civil Rights law is the dangerous purpose it may serve. It is still another encroachment by the central government on the federalized structure of our society. Armed with this law enacted to improve the lot of a tenth of the population, the way will be opened to enslave the rest of the populace. Is this far fetched? I think not. Under such a law the individual everywhere is told what he must do and what he cannot do, regardless of the laws and ordinances of his state or community. This is a blow at the very basis of American society which is founded on state sovereignty and individual liberty and preference. We are fifty separate countries, as it were, joined together for mutual advantage, security, advancement, and protection. It was never intended that we should be bossed by a monarch, elected or born. When this happens, the United States as a free land will cease to exist.

King: No Help to Peace
(1964)

This article was so disturbing that mainstream black and white newspapers refused to publish it. Finally, it was published in New Hampshire's Manchester Union Leader, historically a pillar of right-wing conservatism. Schuyler would write a number of articles for the paper in his later years, as well as for American Opinion, the publication of the John Birch Society. This article represents, in my view, the point at which Schuyler becomes a political outcast in African American political communities.

Although accustomed to seeing the Nobel Peace Prize awarded to a succession of pious frauds for the purposes of political propaganda, the leading Norwegian newspapers were shocked and puzzled when they got the announcement that Dr. Martin Luther King, Jr. the peripatetic parson, was the 1964 recipient.

I shared their shock, but I was not surprised after seeing it given to Dr. Linus Pauling, whose lugubrious wails about nuclear warfare has served the Soviet purpose of searing freedom-loving people into surrender to communism; to Karl von Assietsky, the anti-Nazi pacifist, as a slap at Adolph Hitler; to Gen. George C. Marshall, who engineered the victory of Mao Tse-tung and his Red gorillas; to Albert Luthuli, the South African, whose agitation increased apartheid; to Lester Pearson, the Canadian Adlai Stevenson; and to Dag Hammarskjold, the conqueror of Katanga. Along with many predecessors, none of the above contributed anything to world peace, nor even to national peace.

It was stipulated in the will of Alfred Bernard Nobel, the Swedish discoverer of dynamite, that the annual award be given to those "who have contributed most toward world peace."

The naming of Dr. Ralph Johnson Bunche in 1950 was in usual accord with Nobel's wishes. A trained diplomat, he arranged with great skill the armistice between the warring Jews and Arabs, thus averting what might have become World War Three.

But neither directly nor indirectly has Dr. King made a contribution to the world (or even domestic) peace. Methinks the Lenin Prize would have been more appropriate for him, since it is no mean feat for one so young to acquire sixty Communist-front citations, according to the U.S. government.

Only Dr. W. E. B. DuBois and Paul Robeson surpassed that record, if we exclude Eleanor Roosevelt.

This is a tribute to Dr. King's mentors: CPUSA member, Hunter Pitts Odell and former Young Communist League alumni and professional pacifist; Bayard Rustin, generalismo of the march on Washington. They coached their protégé assiduously for years. It is all in Uncle Sam's books. Rustin won additional distinction by being jailed for homosexuality in Los Angeles after delivering a rousing speech at a big church rally.

Dr. King's principal contribution to world peace has been to roam the country like some sable typhoid-Mary, infecting the mentally disturbed with the perversion of Christian doctrine, and grabbing lecture fees from the shallow-pated.

His incitement packed jails with Negroes and some whites, getting them beaten, bitten and firehosed, thereby bankrupting communities, raising bail and fines, to the vast enrichment of Southern Law and order.

With his omnipresent bench men, Dr. King persistently entered cities (Albany Ga., Birmingham Ala., and St. Augustine Fla.), after local Negro leadership had begged them to get lost. In none of them was anything gained.

Possibly his only meritorious service was in directing the Montgomery bus strike—and that was won by the much-derided NAACP legalism which ended Jim Crow bus service everywhere by federal court order.

After this "nonviolent" crash program ended with crashing store windows and rifling of goods, Reverend Doctor joined other self-styled Negro leaders in suspending all demonstrations. He was one of the engineers of the midsummer madness in Mississippi which ended not in peace but in arrests, arson, and murder. Instead of improving race relations, they were worsened by these pixilated endeavors.

Alfred Bernard Nobel will probably whirl in his tomb on December 10th when Dr. King receives the bauble and the bankroll.

The Rising Tide of Black Racism
(1967)

Simply put, the title of this essay was cause for considerable concern in traditional civil rights circles. Schuyler submitted the essay to the North American Newspaper Alliance, but it was never published. During the period when African Americans were on the cusp of achieving basic equality under the law, Schuyler, in a daring but ill-timed gesture, argued that black people could be racists. Livid over the ways in which the misdeeds of Congressman Adam Clayton Powell had been dismissed by his black supporters in New York's Harlem, Schuyler berated the black masses for their misguided racial allegiance. Schuyler had a more personal grievance with Powell: the congressman had defeated him in the congressional election of 1964.

Negroes having inherited the old clothes, houses and churches from white folks, are now taking over their racial fictions. Having lugubriously wailed for generations over the cruelty of the color bar and the panting of the prideful so-called Aryans over the tomes of Count Gobineau, Madison Grant, Thomas Dixon and Judge Brady, the colored spokesmen more and more sound like the White Citizens Council agitators of yesteryear. The black reaction to the Adam Clayton Powell scandal is symptomatic.

Just at a time when the white civilized minority was priding itself on finally having buried the racist twaddle, the Negro civil rights leaders, editors, politicians and preachers exhume the corpse and proudly carry it aloft amid hosannas of hatred. They rushed with shocking speed and vehemence to disprove the hoary Nordic fictions about their alleged inferiority by attributing the Congressman's crimes to the fact that he was a Negro and for that innocent of all accusations.

It was, they shouted, another Dreyfus case, fiendishly contrived to rid the Harlem hotshot of his important committee chairmanship. Not a single one of these dark defenders of the big Baptist parson mentioned anything about Powell's packing of the committee's payroll, falsifying expense accounts, cheating with airline credit cards, or the little matter of being a refugee from New York justice. They were unanimous in contending that the Representative's trouble arose solely from race.

When these defenders learned that the heat was singeing the haunches of the reverend political boss, they mobilized their forces with a speed and fervor which would have been commendable in a more worthy cause. The venerable Socialist labor leader, A. Philip Randolph, sounded the tocsin, packed his union headquarters with three hundred Powellites, and mooed about "racism masquerading behind a screen of congressional piety and self righteousness." He trotted out the often reiterated suggestion that other congressmen's conduct was as bad or worse than Powell's, but failed, of course, to name any.

So also said Borough President of Manhattan Perry Sutton; Chairman of the New York City Commission William H. Booth, echoing the obvious that "he was elected by the people and only the people can get him out"; Livingston Wingate, former executive director of the scandal-ridden Haryou-Act and longtime aide of Powell, crying "It's not America against Adam Clayton Powell, oh no, it's America against the black people. They're not after Adam, they're after his black power." A banker, a furniture dealer and a state senator swelled the roster of protesters, but the biggest applause was given to Jesse Gray, Harlem rent strike leader and disciple of deceased Communist leader Benjamin J. Davis, Jr. who snarled "They better not try to unseat Adam. I'm not advocating violence, but I'm telling all white people to lay off Powell."

Rev. Benjamin F. Payton, director of the national Council of Churches' department of social justice, speaking at another meeting for the 400 Negro ministers of the Baptist Ministers Conference boasting 300,000 members shouted unnecessarily "It is not for other congressmen to say who should represent the people of Harlem." None had. The Baptist preachers signed a 17-page petition, "The Case for Adam Clayton Powell," without specifying the charges against him. Rev. Payton was one of the NCC cabal that organized the Delta Ministry which led the jacquerie of peasants that took over a military installation in the Mississippi Delta until driven out at bayonet's point.

Even the interracial National Association for the Advancement of Colored People resolved at its annual meeting on January 3rd: "We recommend that and insist that no action be taken in the Powell case because under present conditions any action would be subject to a charge of being tailor made to fit his conduct while not touching other congressmen who may be similarly situated." This was a typical begging of the question, since no other Congressman was being charged with such misdemeanors and crimes.

As in Harlem, groups of similar Negro leaders were organized hurriedly all across the country, and 1,000 preachers and politicians packed the Metropolitan Baptist Church in Washington on the eve of the opening of the 90th Congress for the purpose of supporting Powell and building a fire under the feet of the legislators to bulldoze them into letting Powell go scot free.

The important thing to remember is that the Powell case is not by any means the first in which this same element has used race as an alibi and excuse to cover up moral dereliction. Crimes have been excused on the ground of "cultural deprivation" of Negroes over three centuries of "unrequited toil" and actual *de facto* school segregation.

What must honest people think of these preachers who convert their pulpits into agitator's soapboxes spewing rabid racism, inciting the retardates to slick practices, delinquency, civil disobedience and crime. When people in positions of leadership in society condone and defend what is generally regarded as criminal conduct, does it not support the canard that Negroes defend criminals?

Unfortunately, this racist self-serving borrowed from the worst whites has characterized the black civil rights politicians and agitators for the past decade. Race! Race! Race! was dinned daily into the masses by those to whom they looked for leadership toward better things. The meanest motives have been attributed to all white people indiscriminately at the most promising period in race relations in our national history. Every distemper has been exaggerated into an epidemic while white-dominated legislatures passed numerous civil rights laws in excess of anything previously known.

With opportunities for education and employment unprecedented for Negro youth, agitators with picket signs under one arm and Bibles under the other go about the country moaning about how badly off is the colored brother, and blaming all of it on white people. Moderation and compromise, the essence of statesmanship have been decried by these agitators ever since the Negro "revolution" started. Self-denigration, absurd demands for preference, and unbecoming racial truculence have been poor fare and a profound disservice to young boys and girls struggling to surmount real difficulties and needing encouragement and cooperation.

Indeed, the real sufferers from this borrowing by Negro spokesmen of rabid racism is the rising colored generation. When they need to think in terms of individual excellence they are contaminated by a cloud of racist propaganda. When they see much-touted leaders rushing to cover up delinquency, immorality and crime because the perpetrators are colored, what must they think? Of what can they be proud? To what are they likely to aspire?

This is a real, present, and future danger.

The Future of the American Negro
(1967)

*Delivered to the Christian Freedom Foundation in New York City
on April 6, this speech is one of the most substantive documents
that Schuyler composed. His audience was undoubtedly white,
Christian, and conservative. By this point Schuyler had marginal-
ized himself from traditional black leadership through his
vilification of Dr. King and other race leaders, but therein lies
the paradox. In this speech he acknowledges the value of the liberal project and also reminds his audience of America's racial
caste system, celebrating the steadfastness and ingenuity of African Americans only a century removed from bondage. In other
words, Schuyler reminds his audience that the "Negro" home rests
on American shores.*

As the wise Dean Kelly Miller of Howard University wrote nearly two
score years ago, "the American Negro must either get out, get white, or get along."

Around ten thousand free Negroes left the United States for foreign shores
between the founding of the American Colonization Society in 1817 and the
onset of the Civil War. Emigration has since then been only a trickle and the
number of black expatriates can only be a few score despite the recurrent uproars
of self-styled Black Nationalists and Back-to-Africa advocates. For all his moaning, groaning, and caterwauling, the colored brother knows he has it so good
here that he does not yearn to go elsewhere to live even when he has the means
to do so. Neither, for that matter, does the white American. In this the two
"races" are in truth equal.

The American Colonization Society purchased and supported Liberia so
that the free Negroes who resented their place in American Society could have
a homeland of their own. As has been said, few Negroes went there or anywhere else, near or far. Emigration to the West Indies and Central America for
disgruntled Negroes came to naught. Even Marcus Garvey could not get them
to go, for all his propaganda, nor did he go himself.

American Negroes in large numbers would not be accepted today anywhere
on earth, although their training and education would undoubtedly be helpful to
the backward and newly-emergent states. Barriers of language and culture stand
in the way. Soil depletion, desiccation and the general impoverishment and

ignorance of quarreling ethnic groups indigenous to the Dark Continent make it most unappealing to people whose standard of living is in general superior to that of Europeans, to say nothing of Africans. American Negroes having nothing whatever in common with even the most advanced Africans would create and encounter more turmoil than did the Zionist beachhead in Palestine.

There is not a worthwhile country in Latin America which would welcome American Negro expatriates and some have specific legislation excluding blacks. Indeed, black is a lower caste throughout Latin America to an extent unrealized by most Americans. But being quite well aware that their position, with all of its drawbacks, is superior to that of non-whites elsewhere in the world, they do not pant to go abroad. America is their home, even if they cannot occupy some of the rooms in that home nor often eat at the dining room table.

What about getting white? That is a panacea of extremist dreamers who feel that juxtaposition will lead to miscegenation. It will not and has not, and at this juncture there is slight chance of either of our color castes disappearing through scientific fusion. Nor even on a basis of social equality are we to see an end to racism. The majority here has never seen the non-whites as equals and apparently never will. Actually, the proportion of extremely light-skinned and colored people in the population has successively declined since the establishment of a viable black society following slavery and Reconstruction. There are few who "pass" today and there will be much fewer in the future. What we have now is a Brown America, and in the future it will be even browner.

Personally, I regard this as deplorable because I believe that miscegenation would make for a more physically attractive American with a far wider variety of types. However, there is little indication that situation is ever to be, and we have to face reality. Certainly our experience in America (and the experience elsewhere) has demonstrated that there is in human affairs no propensity for ethnic propinquity.

In his excellent *Slavery in the Cities* Richard C. Wade shows that during chattel slavery there was greater urban residential integration than there is today, or will ever be again. In the pre-emancipation Southern cities, the two color castes lived in the same blocks, quarters and compounds but nevertheless the vast social distance between them remained. Then, as now, social intimacy was uncomfortable, occasional, and clandestine. Urban Negro slaves were happiest when hired out by their owners and thus enabled to often live apart from all whites. It was this predilection of the blacks rather than any local city ordinances that led to the establishment of the first all-Negro southern so-called ghettoes. These were, in truth, what they have traditionally been: places of refuge and protection from ethnic antagonists. Today in our large urban conglomerations the large proportion of the Negroes, like the whites, prefer to live among what they regard as their own. Whether they ought or ought not be that way, that is the way people are, and the road to reason is not through wishful thinking. Even when the colored folk move to the suburbs, they feel better with some other Negro families around; but of course not enough to create the dilemma of the so-called tipping point: that is, around 40 percent, which is said to begin frightening white families into moving out.

The separate Negro churches were founded not by whites but through the initiative and efforts of blacks themselves. The whites were satisfied to worship with Negroes under the same roofs—if the blacks sat in the balconies and did not praise the Lord too vociferously. Many Roman Catholic churches thoughtfully provided Jim Crow pews for the occupancy of the colored devout. These entirely vanished only a few years back, along with lily-white parochial schools, but some may still remain.

The founding fathers whom we all extol fathered a large proportion of mulatto children but made every effort to suppress interracial intimacy—save, in the dark. The first such case in the Jamestown annals of 1630 involved a white man punished for lying with a black woman. In typical American manner, however, the law was honored in the breach. This helps explain why the generality of Negroes today have liberal dashes of European, Amerindian and African genes, and a typical Negro meeting resembles a United Nations assemblage. While many of the first African arrivals in the Virginia colony, being servants rather than slaves, married the white women deported from the streets of European cities, the alarming practice was discouraged with severity and soon outlawed. However, slavery is always more conducive to miscegenation than is freedom. Which explains why free blacks and whites will have little of it, even in this amoral age, except on a legal marriage basis.

Freedom makes a difference for both black and white women, and as previously stated, there were more "white" Negroes before emancipation than afterward. In ante-bellum days kidnapped or purchased whites were sometimes sold as slaves into the deep south with no more camouflage than curling their hair before they mounted the block.

Not that it was unusual for unmixed Nordics to be sold into servitude, either in America or elsewhere. If they could not be sold on the wharves in Boston, New York or Philadelphia, they were marched manacled through the countryside to be sold to farmers for the passage money due the captain. It is the custom to illustrate every book on the slave trade with a picture of the manner in which the slaves were packed into the holds. What is rarely shown is the manner in which European servants were similarly packed in like sardines, often with lower ceilings than the slave ships had.

In the bad, dark days before World War I, there was a popular weekly movie serial called "Brown and White" comedies which depicted Irish maids and Negro porters cavorting in burlesque romances while colored cooks were romanced by their Nordic employers. It was all rather hilarious. Today, neither racial comedians nor dialecticians dare tread the stages for fear of arousing the umbrage of hypersensitive ethnocentric groups. Minstrel shows are now taboo and even *Little Black Sambo* has succumbed to the book burners.

While paradoxically surfeited with talk of equality and civil rights, our color castes increasingly prefer to pursue their separate ways in religious organizations. So-called progressive preachers querulously bemoan the fact that the so-called races are most segregated on Sunday mornings. This is understandable, considering the facts previously mentioned. What realist can envision the nation's vast proliferation of societies, associations, organizations and clubs becoming multi-racial? Logic has no more to do with it than the incantations of a Haitian houngan. The facts of life will not go away despite the appeals of professional integrationists.

Except in the dark of some secluded rendezvous, members of the two color castes are always socially uneasy, and what integration there is, is token. It is in this connection illuminating that after two decades of political independence, the castes in India operate just as they did in the pre-Nehru era. In Latin America prominent whites can joke about the black twigs on their family tree, but here only an insane white American would do so, although far more of them have African ancestry.

Is this far-fetched? Back in 1927, in the heyday of Virginia's Racial Integrity law, some fifty white children were removed from Richmond's white public schools on the ground that they were actually Negroes! This anthropological abracadabra was based on a study conducted by two Johns Hopkins University professors which indicated that there having been no Indians unmixed with Negroes on the Atlantic coast for two centuries, all self-styled descendants of Pocahontas automatically became suspect as Negroes.

By the same reasoning, an Indian on a Virginia reservation was regarded as white until he left, whereupon he became a Negro. With more rationality an Oklahoma Indian became legally white as soon as oil was struck on his land, which then made wealthy Indian squaws eligible to marry white men, as many did.

When Virginia's Racial Integrity Law was first proposed, the venerable *Richmond News-Leader* created a stir by saying that among those, living and dead, who would have to be classed as Negroes if the bill became law, were:

> Two United States Senators, a United States Ambassador to France, five generals, two Presidents of the United States, two Secretaries of War, three of the most distinguished of Southern novelists, three Governors of Virginia, a speaker of the House of Representatives, two bishops, three Congressmen, one Rear Admiral, two judges of the Virginia Supreme Court, and many of the foremost officers of the Confederate Army.

In the white and colored groups today there are pyramids of societies, institutions and enterprises paralleling each other and with vested interests to perpetuate. There is no discernible clamor for them to coalesce. It is not white company that the colored want but white rights and privileges. From the days when the blacks were snatched from the claws of voodooism and tossed into the clutches of Christianity they have borne no affection for their captors. From the earliest days here, the white communities could not conceive of living cheek by jowl with free Negroes. Jefferson, Lincoln and Taft alike regarded the colored brethren as inassimilable, and even the victorious Abolitionists would not face the harsh implications of emancipation. That extreme Negrophile, Thaddeus Stevens, believed a revolution in the South would be necessary for Negro freedmen to get justice. A century later they still don't have it—except on paper.

Wishful thinkers dream that if the two color castes are thrown closely together, they will eventually merge their bloodstreams and become one race. From now on this will have to be by legal marriage or not at all. As racial chauvinism intensifies there will be less and less of it. A half century ago William Benjamin Smith, a professional Negrophobe, argued in *The Color Line:*

> If we sit with Negroes at our tables, if we entertain them as
> our guests and social equals, if we disregard the color line in
> all other relations, is it possible to maintain it fixedly in the
> sexual relations, in the marriage of our sons and daughters,
> in the propagation of our species? Unquestionably, No! It is
> as certain as the rising of tomorrow's sun, that, once the middle
> wall of social partition is broken down, the mingling of the
> tides of life would begin instantly and proceed steadily.

Mr. Smith was, I think, unduly apprehensive, albeit most white Americans three generations later share his view. Even with the extreme propinquity of our sexy, urbanized age, Negro-white marriages remain a rarity here, but no more so than elsewhere in the modern world.

Brazil is often cited as an ideal example of an interracial, miscegenetic utopia. This is, to put it mildly, a gross exaggeration coming almost exclusively from white Brazilian apologists. Obviously there has been a tremendous amount of miscegenation in Brazil, as there has been in our own South (as indicated by the number of birth records rifled and court houses burned down to prevent disclosure) but Brazilian miscegenation has come about not through legal marriage but through adultery, concubinage, fornication and prostitution. Marvin Harris and other American investigators on the ground have disillusioning information for the dreamers. The rich-poor social division in Brazil coincides with the black-white one; and it is more obvious than in Mississippi—except that the Mississippi blacks are better off!

From a glance inside Brazilian tourist propaganda, inside banks, hotels, restaurants, foreign service offices and mercantile establishments, the population would seem to be as white as that of Switzerland, but this is actually due to the economic color bar, which is more marked than in big U.S. cities. Unlike in the United States, Brazilian passports are stamped with the color caste of the holder: white (branco), brown (pardo) or black (preto). Racial intermarriage is, as I have said, rarer than here. Brazil's Congress, pressed by some extremists passed anti-discrimination law in 1951. Since enactment it has been honored in the breach.

The harsh fact is that at a time when there is more talking and writing around the world about democracy, justice and fairplay than ever before in recorded history, racism is on the increase on all continents. When Madison Grant back in the Twenties wrote about the *Rising Tide of Color,* the liberals scoffed at him. His writings were really quite prophetic.

Recent sanguinary race riots between Malays and Chinese in Singapore (with both groups socially rejecting the Eurasians) revealed a disturbing situation. The continuing complaints of dark (so-called "Oriental") Jewish immigrants to Israel against color discrimination by the dominant Eastern European brethren have caused concern. Not long after the more recent race riot in Tel Aviv, a white Israeli official warned with Dixie-alike alarm that the "Orientals" would be in the majority in 1975, if more white Jews did not emigrate to Zion—as if that would doom the country! Arab-Jewish marriages are decried in this young "democracy" and only recently the Jewish rabbinate graciously approved marriage between the whiter Jews and a suspiciously dark tribe from India, after a 2,000-year separation.

Pessimism is rife among East Africa's 300,000 Asians confronted by the rising black chauvinism in the newly-independent states of Kenya, Uganda, Zambia, and Tanzania where they have traditionally been the trading class, owning big stores and plantations. Lost among the 20 million blacks, they are encountering dire experiences, and the native boycotts against them have not only impoverished them but seriously hurt the shaky economies. Their situation is worsened by their clannishness which inhibits them from socially intermingling or intermarrying with Africans. One white observer, George Dalf writes: "The observation of an African Kenya leader that an integrated society would include intermarriage aroused widespread indignation among Asians; some said they would not give their daughters to members of another Asian sect, let alone an African."

Faced with increasing discrimination in civil service and private business, many of the Asians are now following the example of the whites, selling out and leaving the area, spurred by the recollection of the massacre or deportation of the entire Arab population in Zanzibar in a jacquerie unequaled by the horrors of the Russian and Chinese communist revolutions.

In December 1964, India and Ceylon quietly signed a treaty, unsung in the halls of the United Nations, by which 525,000 Indian immigrants to Ceylon were to be returned to their nearby ancestral land. These two peoples neither socialize nor intermarry. The Indians were a thorn in the side of the Ceylonese and had to go. Not dissimilarly, the Indonesians are in process of deporting the three million Chinese from their fertile and charming land, sending them to make a new life in the land of Mao Tse-tung.

When Dr. S. M. Ambedkar, an Untouchable, a Columbian University alumnus and Nehru's first Minister of Justice wed a wealthy Bombay Brahmin lady, it was the first such prominent marriage in India in 4,000 years, and created a national stir. It is only dimly recalled now that Mohandas Gandhi was assassinated by a Hindu extremist for championing the cause of the Untouchables.

Whites outnumber nonwhites fifty to one in Britain but race antagonism and conflicts are increasingly more evident. Canon John Collins, Dean of St. Paul's Cathedral, warned on November 13, 1964: "There is a grave danger of racialism so growing in this country that we shall soon be faced with such a problem as confronts others who have practiced this hideous blasphemy."

Widely publicized have been the racial difficulties of African students in the Soviet Union, its European satellites, Red China and even India following attempts at racial commingling. Currently a score or more of China's racial minorities, including the hapless Tibetans, are genocidal victims of the "superior" Han people. It is significant that in the Sino-Soviet clash, the Chinese minorities in Sinkiang are voting with their feet for the adjoining Soviet Asian territories.

However, the Soviet Union is no interracial Valhalla. After forty years of Communist liberation, the twenty million non-white people of Soviet Central Asia suffer an *apartheid* similar to that in South Africa although naturally not as honest. A dependable observer, Geoffrey reports:

> "In the towns, the Russians and other Westerners continue to inhabit the separate European towns located apart from the native quarters. The new "Soviet" town sections, erected by the regime to house the offices and employees of the vast Communist bureaucracy are ethnically mixed, but they house only a small segment of the native population, namely a part of its urban intelligentsia . . . The Moslem and Russian populations on the whole continue to reside apart from each other . . . This residential separation of the two groups is made more significant by the lack of social contact between them . . . (and) almost complete absence of intermarriage . . . Social intercourse between the two groups is very limited, Moslems and Russians meet at work but rarely outside it . . . The tribal and clan systems remain at their most exclusive precisely in those areas where Russian colonization has been the most extensive."

So much for Communist brotherhood: A Russian commissar in Tadjikistan would no more marry a nonwhite girl than would a Texas congressman.

The turmoil in British Guiana between East Indians and Negroes is typical of ethnic conflicts elsewhere, as for example in the Fijian Islands where the Fijis and the Indian immigrants are at each other's throats. The same fuse burns slowly in Trinidad. The Indian-mestizo-black-white conflict in Central and South America is fundamentally a racial one. One life-long Martinique lawyer, himself a mulatto, could not recall when any Negro had ever been invited to the home of a member of the small white aristocracy. It is the same throughout the Caribbean. Puerto Rican blacks get more economic opportunities and social acceptance in New York City than they ever did in Mayaguez, Ponce or San Juan.

One observer, Hugh H. Smythe, now U.S. Ambassador in Damascus, writing on the multiplicity of minority groups in Thailand, described them as being uniformly despised and discriminated against by the haughty Thai ruling class.

Viewing the world racial situation as it really is and not as the romantic wishful thinkers would prefer it to be, one wonders whence came the notion that some place exists where the population is multiracial and the problems are being solved by miscegenation and intermarriage. Certainly American coloreds and whites are not doing so to any marked extent. Negroes are never going to get white and whites will not become more tarbrushed. So those who attach importance to bloodstreams and backgrounds can relax.

As was mentioned, the dominant white caste has strongly opposed extra-legal sexual relationships and racial intermarriages since colonial times. Maryland passed its first such ban in 1661, Virginia in 1691. Massachusetts in 1706, Delaware in 1721, Pennsylvania in 1726, and North Carolina in 1741. By 1932 thirty states prohibited such marriages with prison sentences ranging from a few months to ten years, and with fines that went as high as $20,000. By 1963, the number of such states has been reduced to nineteen. Those which have repealed such laws are Iowa, Kansas, Maine, Massachusetts, Michigan, New Mexico, Ohio, Rhode Island, Washington, North and South Dakota, Oregon, Colorado, Montana, Idaho, and Nevada. Among these also is California, a state whose very first legislative session banned intermarriages. Maryland repealed its 300-year-old law in March 1967.

Arguments supporting such legislation were always on the basis of mutual repulsion of the races, which if true would make such laws unnecessary. The United States Supreme Court has so far found these laws too hot to handle but may so be compelled to do so. Interestingly, Nazi Germany's and South Africa's racially restrictive laws were copied from our code. However, despite these barriers, interracial marriages continue to occur. There are probably not more than 50,000 here but that is more than elsewhere on earth.

Considering the difficulties, these unions will scarcely double by 2,000 A.D. when there will be 40 million nonwhites with aggravated frustrations. Increasingly, I fear, the colored caste will be like the evil djinn in the Arabian Nights who released by Ali Baba from a flask after several millenniums had the first impulse to slay his liberator. Presumption of such tribal animosity is implicit in the propaganda of many self-proclaimed civil rights spokesmen whose professed love for the whites and alleged desire to "save" them deceives nobody.

So this leaves us with the necessity of Negroes getting along, since they will not get out and they cannot get white. They have to find a way of getting along, i.e., with the majority of whites. Thus what the latter thinks of Negroes is the determinant of their future in America. A long report by Fred Powledge in the *New York Times* of September 21, 1964, is illuminating. It was based on an elaborate poll in depth of the New York City whites' attitudes toward colored and the latter's struggle. New York is our most metropolitan center and the two color castes have lived there in juxtaposition since the first settlement in 1609. The last Negro slaves were freed there in 1827, public schools were desegregated there in 1898, and it is reputed that in no other American metropolis are race relations better, considering that the first civil rights law was passed in 1845.

The New York Times poll disclosed that 45 percent of the whites believed that Negroes disliked them; 40 percent confessed they felt uncomfortable with numerous Negro families living nearby (57 percent said they wouldn't). Some 66 percent said they would not want to be the only white person living in a Negro block. Of the 80 percent opposed to school pairing, 45 percent would send their children to private schools, only 17 percent would let them go to the paired schools, and 11 percent were not sure.

The poll showed that 54 percent of the whites wanted a slowdown in civil rights agitation and only 12 percent wanted more speed. Some 49 percent of whites felt demonstrations had hurt the Negro's cause compared to 42 percent who felt that they had. Some 62 percent of the whites said the demonstrations had not changed their minds, and 27 percent were more opposed to Negroes than ever because of the outbreaks. Here was a poll taken in the allegedly most liberal city in the U.S.

Religious polls showed 42 percent of the Protestants, 46 percent of the Jews and 63 percent of the Roman Catholics wanted *less* speed in the Negro movement. In this connection 61 percent of the Irish wanted a slowdown; 67 percent of the Germans, 58 percent of the Italians and 49 percent of the polls. Interestingly, 46 percent of the respondents felt too much was being done for Negroes, and only 19 percent wanted more done for them. On the future of race relations, 70 percent of the whites held that it would be more than ten years before whites and coloreds would be able to live together without friction or that this would ever happen. At the end of his report Powledge added that "in the earlier survey of attitudes among Negroes, 44 percent said ten years, more than ten years, or never."

We are giving more thinking and planning to the job of getting along racially in the United States than ever before, and racial adjustment is the key to communal peace. America has always had a caste system based on so-called race, and despite reformist endeavors this everlasting stain will continue to color our national life as long as the Republic stands. Believe it or not, the dominant white caste has a vested interest, economically, sociologically, politically, and psychologically in the perpetuation of this racist voodooism. Adjustments can be made from time to time, however, which will permit these two societies to live more or less amicably in juxtaposition. Looking about the world, however, I think that America has gone further along this line than any other nation, criticism to the contrary notwithstanding. This is because since its very foundation this nation has been trying. No other has accumulated such a vast body of remedial legislation. Nowhere else have so many of the great individuals and institutions striven to realize the ideal of a peaceful multi-racial state. Slavery was a long and traumatic experience and its aftermath still curses us with the problems we have today; but where else is more being done to change with the times? Nobody really wants racial conflict and because this is so, we have a good chance of surviving as a viable state. The fact that the Negro is better off in every way here than are minority groups anywhere else on the globe when he could well have been exterminated attests to the vast reservoir of goodwill, justice and fairplay existing even in our most backward areas.

By 2,000 A.D., a mere generation hence, our global population will exceed six billion souls, with the inevitable concomitant of almost endemic world poverty, malnutrition, disease and racism. India launched the color problem, South Africa adopted it, with a sort of painless *apartheid* which in the long period of adjustment may prove to be salutary.

At that not-so-far-off time there will be 350 million Americans, with forty million of them nonwhites. In 1990, for instance, Chicago will have two and a half million Negroes in its metropolitan area, or a fourth of the total. Already the same picture of urban packing develops all about us. Seven out of ten Americans are already city dwellers, and Negroes will soon be almost entirely so. However, they are unlikely to be permitted to long preempt the choice, tax-producing central cores of our cities.

It looks now as if the 21st century megalopolis will consist of concentric circles of sprawling suburbs surrounding the steel, concrete and glass heartland of government, commerce and finance; upper- and middle-class high rise residences, theaters, museums, parks and plazas; with Negroes becoming proportionately and progressively scarce. There will be a proliferation of nonwhite enclaves in the suburban sprawl, similar to those in South Africa built for Bantu, colored and East Indian but on more gigantic scale.

Earl E. and Alma F. Taeuber in surveying the *Changing Character of Negro Migration* during the past century, show that residential segregation in all major cities except New York has grown from one to nine points on an index taking 100 (or complete segregation) as a base. Even New York rates 81.

Bernard Weissbourd predicts in his *Segregation, Subsidies and Megalopolis* that by 1980 urban congestion will increase by 55 or 60 million more people. He argues that in order to pay the mounting costs of municipal maintenance, there must be living in the central core areas a class of people capable of doing so. This is understandable. What with the cost of federal, state and local welfare having expanded from $3.4 billion in 1958 to twice that much today, the National Planning Association is recommending expenditures of $25 billion more annually by business and government to create jobs and aid the economy.

Mr. Weissbourd proposes moving welfare recipients and low income groups from their present slums on potentially tax-rich land to what he calls "new towns" in the suburbs hard by industrial and manufacturing plants. He argues that the "ghettos are still so large that only a major plan to induce a substantial part of the Negro working population to live in the outlying 'new towns' can bring about a more uniform and just distribution of these people among the population as a whole."

However, in envisioning these "new towns" as multi-racial, he presupposes that impoverished and low-income whites will be less opposed to living alongside Negroes in these suburban "new towns" than in the cities. In the past the reverse has been true. The growing enmity against open occupancy is strongest in these developing sub-urban areas as we know from the physical conflicts ensuing from the efforts of qualified Negroes to move there.

Put bluntly, these "new towns" will simply be an American version of South African "locations." Certainly bedeviled politicians will support the majority white caste in perpetuating the segregationist pattern, with some "token" integration to take the curse off it. These thinkers who disagree with Mr. Weissbourd are considerably less convincing than he.

Projecting our thought to a generation hence, the America of 2,000 A.D. will probably not be the cornucopia it was in the halcyon days of the Founding Fathers. Forests, farms, mines, oil wells and natural gas will be seriously depleted and potable water will be scarcer. Even now water levels are falling in many sections presaging growing drought conditions and dwindling of the food supply.

Since 1910 the total acreage for human food production has risen by less than one-half whereas population has increased by two-thirds. It requires three acres of cropland to provide food and fiber for one person. New lands ceased about 1920, and by 1975 we shall be short some 70 million acres. Productivity of Midwest soil is decreasing at the rate of seven tenths of one percent each year. Our virgin forest timber is almost gone already, and the decline in forest production is marked, compelling us to find new sources abroad to keep pace with consumption. As the process of industrialization grows, the greater is the drain on our capital resources; and it will be tremendous when we have a population of 350 million.

In the coming dog-eat-dog world, few of us will prosper as we once did, and perhaps Negroes quite the least of all, while the starving billions of the outer world beat on our portals begging for succor. This fact alone necessitates a greater national unity than ever previously envisioned.

How well the colored caste meets the challenge of the coming years is indicated by how well it has adjusted itself in the past and how it is doing now. Median school years completed by nonwhites over 25 years old was 8.2 in 1963 compared to 10.9 for whites. That year there were 6,541,000 Negroes between the ages of five and thirty-four years enrolled in school, and this has been vastly increased during the educational activities of the past two years. Negro income after taxes exceeds $21 billion, and this is a growing market despite the wails about poverty. About 76 percent of all colored are employed compared to 78 percent of all whites. As evidence of Negro thrift we can point to the ownership of more than two million homes and two and one-half million cars.

In professional fields the number of Negroes has increased thirty-two times since World War II, while currently 13 percent of the Federal civil service is colored, which is a higher number than would be expected from a group constituting ten percent of the population. Negro life expectancy has risen since 1900 from 35 years to 66 years. The latest agricultural census showed the number of Negro farms as 265,621. Of these 89,749 were fully owned, 37,534 partly owned and 290 managed. The successive Civil Rights Acts and government prodding have legally removed many of the Negro's disadvantages, but of course it would be inexcusably naive to put too much dependence on mere legalism.

Private industry has risen to the need for equal opportunity and the growing diversity of Negro employment is heartening. Today one sees Negroes doing jobs undreamed of a few years back: everything from the moon project to municipal administration. Thus we find that in education, employment, residence, health and general culture the Negro seems everywhere to be on the rise. And the significant fact is that this has come about not simply through his own effort but through the aid and cooperation of concerned whites.

There is a lot of talk about Christian brotherhood operating in race relations. Much of it is cheap and shallow but a tremendous amount of it is meaningful and encouraging. Nobody would have believed in 1776 that we would have come so far so quickly. While the dream of having ultimately a single people here of one blood is a vain one, I think a wonderful job has been accomplished by America so far. And as far as we can see ahead, the future of the Negro is probably as good as that of anybody else; that we shall all go up or down together; and that the wealth, strength and resourcefulness of the American people will survive the vicissitudes of the years ahead.

The Reds and I
(1968)

This autobiographical essay was first published in American
Opinion, *a forerunner to the* New American Magazine. *Both
are publications of the John Birch Society. By 1968 Schuyler's
essays appeared exclusively in ultraconservative publications, as
he had become an unequivocating conservative. This essay
recounts his early interest in and rejection of socialism and communism. In Schuyler's view, "Homo Aframericanus" has benefited
the most from conservatism and capitalism.*

How is it, the sincerely curious have asked, that an American who
is colored can be simultaneously a "Conservative" and unalterably opposed to
the Communist rumble-bumble?

In such matters, of course being colored is only incidental—like being right-
handed, green-eyed, or sleeping on one's left side. The important thing is being an
American . . . born, bred, and nurtured on the native soil, and having affection for
and allegiance to its basic customs and beliefs; its manners, ambitions, and its
goals . . . with full knowledge of what is on tap and display on foreign strands.

To be an American is to know that, for better or for worse, you could not
be, and do not want to be, anything else—however persuasively disgruntled
émigrés may sing the praises of other continents from whence all who could
and can pound on our gates for admittance. Being an American is also, because
of our historical background, to be curious about other places, pioneering and
footloose; to roam this continent and increasingly visit other lands to an extent
no other peoples have, and yet to always return here with relief, reinforced in
the conviction that this is, indeed, the Land of the Free.

In this the lampblacked and technicolored citizenry does not differ from
those of creamy complexion, for Americanism is more than skin deep, and the
Afro-Americans residing abroad without a paid-up, United States passport are
as rare as equality in India or security in the Soviet Union. It is noteworthy in
this connection that only the tiniest maudlin minority of paranoid professional
agitators pant for the plains of Uzbekistan or the free soil of Tanzania where
complexion allegedly cuts no ice—if you belong to the one and only Party.

In sum, Homo Aframericanus is fundamentally "Conservative" because,
as Bert Williams used to sing, "I May Be Crazy, But I Ain't No Fool"—knowing

that he has more to conserve in America than elsewhere on the globe. To this the million or more colored who have been abroad to the far corners will readily agree, having noted that welfare recipients in Dayton are living more expansively than the sable aristocracy in Dahomey, and without fear of a Leopard Society or the local Liberation Front.

Thus, I can claim no uniqueness in being black and "Conservative." In truth, I would be unique if I were not.

What the average American colored person feels was no better expressed than at the conclusion of the New York City convention of the American Society of Free Persons of Colour in 1831, when the forty-odd delegates unanimously resolved that: "This is our home, and this is our country. Beneath its sod lie the bones of our fathers; for it some of them fought, bled and died. Here we were born, and here we will die."

That was in the heat of the colonization drive to persuade free Negroes to emigrate to presumed freer lands in Africa where slavery and genocide had been endemic for millenniums, tyranny was everywhere (as it is today), and Christian missionism had not yet begun to "ruin" the continent by preaching the Gospel, personal hygiene, and literacy. The nearly half-million free blacks were a socially ostracized and economically excluded caste. But they had hopes for the better and faith in America. Although the colonization movement had distinguished backing, received large sums from private philanthropy, and got federal grants, only ten thousand freedmen moved to the Liberian Promised Land between 1820 and the Civil War. The motto of Liberia, the nation they founded, is "The Love of Liberty Brought Us Here"; to which later, some local wag said should be added: "The Lack of Money Keeps Us Here."

The free colored were well aware of the hazards of emigration. Many of them or their fathers had come from Africa in durance vile (assisted by loving relatives eager to replenish exchequers) and thousands employed in the merchant marine and in the American Navy of the time had returned to spread the news of African reality. At that time chattel or feudal slavery extended over much of the earth outside Western Europe. The free colored emigrant to Africa might well be ultimately destined for another plantation, a cemetery, or an abdomen.

While the Americans, British, and French were trying to suppress the slave trade, the rest of the Europeans, the Russians, the Indians, the Chinese, and the Moslems everywhere were engaged in the lively business. A free colored (or a free white) landing among them would promptly be sold to the highest bidder. So it is no wonder that the overwhelming majority of the free colored elected to cast their lot with the country where they had a lot of white well-wishers, sympathizers, and allies among humanitarians of all faiths and conditions. The ignorance and obtuseness of the current miniscule crop of Black Nationalist agitators is no better illustrated than in their professed belief that there is something in common between the colored here and those elsewhere.

None of my family having been slaves since the dawn of the Republic, but being well aware of the iniquity of the "peculiar institution," as well as the cruelty of the economic color bar against them imposed by the inrushing hordes of European job rivals, my forebears had no illusions about schemes for mob salvation through mass unity. Progressively since 1724, the few labor unions established were lily-white, and every effort to change this foundered on the rocks of racism, as every novice in history knows. Negroes harbored the cynical view that any such mass movements would "include them out," and so it happened.

For all the uproars of the National Labor Union, the knights of Labor, the I.W.W., the Anarchists and the Socialists screaming for mob action and control, it all left the Negroes cold. In resulting strife the black worker could play no active part except as strikebreaker, to be fired as soon as the conflict was settled. Indeed, while its record is none too good, it was white business rather than white labor which afforded colored folk a chance.

Most of the urban-settled European newcomers, of course, flocked to the Democratic Party. Collectivism was a way of life for many of them. But American Negroes knew better. Frederick Douglass, the great colored Abolitionist, anti-colonizationist, diplomat, and political leader had told us years before my birth that "The Republican Party is the ship: all else the sea." What Negro could dispute him on the record? Of course the Republican Party then differed from that aggregation which now bears its name; knowing no Rockefeller or Javits. In the days of my youth (yes, it was before Noah), it would have taken the Pinkerton Detective Agency to find a Negro Democrat.

As a lad, I was curious to learn from my stepfather that the white neighbor across the street was a Socialist, and more shocked to hear him relate that Socialists believed in dividing up everything. It was shocking because we seemed to have more to divide than he did, what with a fourteen-room house, square piano, and other furnishings to match—despite the two strikes (social and economic) against us. As I think back from the summit of my seventies that childhood definition or Socialism, while simplistic, was not far wrong.

At the time such matters did not disturb me. My mother was introducing me to Longfellow, Whittier, Cooper, Irving, Mark Twain, Kipling, and later I was discovering *King Arthur's Knights,* the *Tales of Froissart, Alice in Wonderland,* the *Arabian Nights,* and newspaper accounts of the Philippine Insurrection, the Russo-Japanese War, and sundry butcheries across the globe. Children then were seen and not heard (if they knew what was good for them!), and it was nor until years later when the New Education came along that one heard warnings not to teach children to read too early! So reading kept me abreast of news and opinion.

I always saved the remaining copy from my newspaper route for home consumption and there read occasionally about doings of the Socialists, notably the aborted 1905 revolution in Russia and the periodic beefs by the European

Socialists against voting funds for national defense. It was not completely a surprise, therefore, when I read in late 1917 of the overthrow by Socialists of the Kerensky regime that had deposed the Czar. They were, as I was told in early childhood, going to divide up everything—and I awaited the results with suspicion tempered by fascination. The resulting chaos, slaughter, rapine, and starvation over the next three years, which only American aid stemmed, was precisely what I had expected to occur when order and discipline died in a society.

It was Socialist propaganda that led me astray. Horrified by the Red saturnalia in Russia and Eastern Europe, the "respectable" Socialists quickly denied that they were the same breed as Lenin, Trotsky, and their ilk. The Bolsheviks called themselves Communists and promoters of instant revolution, sneering at the old Socialists of the Second Internationale as gradualists. I swallowed this and in 1921 was prompted to begin a long, tortuous reading of standard Socialist "literature" which culminated several months later in joining the local Socialist Party, partly because I was bored and craved some activity. My life was dull enough but Party associations were even duller, and the experience of devouring so much of sociological buncombe that acted like a sleeping pill created a revulsion from which I never recovered. Every tenet of Party doctrine was a lie and basically the goals of Socialism and Communism were identical. The only differences between the two were strategic.

By June of 1921, I was firm enough in my convictions to cut all connections with the Socialist Party, to challenge openly its basic assumptions, and to debate Otto Huiswoud, a Comintern agent from Dutch Guiana who was connected with the African Blood Brotherhood, the first Negro Communist Front.

Huiswoud, who was an alien, almost white, and spoke broken English, had attended the Fourth Congress of the Comintern in 1922 as a delegate representing the American Negroes! It was my first debate and I think I gave a good account of myself. It was held in the auditorium of the West 135th Street Branch of the New York Public Library. It was needed because the Communists were making their first play for the Negroes. Many of them, then fascinated by the phony Negro Renaissance, were gobbling Marxism in delicatessen fashion, although never tackling such formidable cures for insomnia as *Das Kapital*.

The Reds and I sniped at each other occasionally as it became clearer that I was not one of them. My first shots were fired in the pages of *The Messenger* (A. Philip Randolph and Chandler Owen, co-Editors), which called itself a journal of scientific socialism but tolerated my excursions off the orthodox Marxist reservation. From late 1924 onward, I got the cannonade roaring with increasing frequency through the years on the editorial page of *The Pittsburgh Courier,* until its demise in November 1966.

From 1926 until 1964 I was the *Courier*'s chief editorial writer. Its Editor, Robert L. Vann, and its Vice President and Business Manager (later President), Ira F. Lewis, were anti-Communist, anti-bureaucratic, and opposed to F. D.R.'s deficit financing, so I was in a safe haven. What I wrote pleased them and they did not tell me what to write. Circulation soared to a peak of 300,000 weekly in the mid-Forties, and the paper had wide influence on Negro thinking. Nevertheless I note that most of those who have written books on Communist activities among Negroes rarely quote a Negro-owned and Negro-edited newspaper, although mentioning what was said by white fly-by-night magazines with five thousand or ten thousand readers and widely unread by the colored.

After visiting two hundred Negro communities in 1925–1926, and spending four months in West Africa in 1931, I began concentrating on exposure of Red schemes and plots. I followed with particular closeness the notorious Scottsboro Case and the methods by which the Reds through the International Labor Defense exploited it, after the Communists' colored front man, Benjamin J. Davis Jr., cleverly stole the case from the NAACP

That Scottsboro business was a major source of income to the Party for years, and I was the only one to consistently expose the racket. Even the Reds' prize captive lawyer, Samuel Liebowitz, later admitted that the Marxist machine had "gone South" with about a quarter of a million dollars while legal expenses were a minimal few thousands. Numerous "mothers" of the imprisoned Scottsboro Boys were paraded over the country in Negro churches and union halls to spark collections. Agitators who had once ridden the rods were traveling in Pullman cars and wolfing down canvasback duck. Courier readers were regularly alerted to what was going on.

As unemployment worsened in the early Thirties, the Reds rushed to exploit it, sending agents hither and yon to head demonstrations and confrontations, presaging the later fashion of Martin Luther King, Jr. and the Sixties' squadrons of C.O.R.E., S.N.C.C., and the W. E. B. DuBois Clubs. It was the time of the Communists' "Self Determination for the Black Belt" drive as decreed by the Sixth Congress of the Comintern in 1928, and Red agitation in the South had aroused fears of colored and white alike. One white Communist agitator who sought to set up a sharecroppers' union around Camp Hill, Alabama, vanished after getting threats from white landowners, leaving his black dupes in the lurch. Result: five lynched, twenty wounded, and the burning of a Negro church and several homes. Similar outrages occurred in the Alabama-Mississippi area. It was the duty of Negro editors and columnists to denounce them and explain the background. I did my duty.

The Communists whom I knew in Greenwich Village asked me if I would go to Atlanta to lead a demonstration of agitators for relief. Of course I laughed derisively, understanding well that I had been marked as a sacrificial goat. So they got a light-colored Cincinnati Negro named Angelo Herndon to lead the mob of a thousand colored and white families on the City Hall. Of course he was promptly arrested, tried, and sentenced under an 1886 law—and a "Free Angelo Herndon" campaign was started. When Angelo was released on bail during appeal, it turned out that he was too light-skinned to be effectively exploited by the Reds and the expected dough did not materialize.

Reminding Courier readers of how the Communists sentenced in Gastonia, North Carolina for subversion in the mill workers caper had jumped bail and escaped to the Soviet Valhalla, I commented jocularly that Herndon might do the same. This did it! The Harlem middle-class "intellectuals" sent a long letter to my Editor demanding that I be fired. It was signed by a score of them. The Editor promptly forwarded the letter to me and for years afterward I periodically had fun naming these lovers of freedom of speech. To their distress and chagrin I remained on the job.

I further incurred their enmity by ridiculing the parties held by Communists and fellow travelers designing to "capture" unsuspecting Negroes, where liquor and girls were offered. The liquor and the "girls," while strong and willing, were shabby and unappetizing. I exposed the technique, pointing out that there was far more comely stimulation available without selling out to Moscow.

I was invited no more. Especially after I exposed the film written by Langston Hughes, then handpicked President of the Communist-organized League of Struggle for Negro Rights, and to be produced in Moscow by Soviet filmmakers. It was supposed to expose the slave trade (capitalist not Communist). A score of Negro "actors" who had never acted were sent to Moscow for the production, but it never was produced because the Kremlin was then seeking diplomatic recognition from the capitalist powers and decided not to offend them at that time. The thing never was produced, the "actors" being sent on tours of Black Sea resorts and to address workers meetings, using interpreters. As was fitting, boss Langston Hughes was sent home via Vladivostok, Tokyo, etc., meeting all of the top Communists en route. I panned this from start to ignominious finish. And, I may say, with relish.

The next Red effort to get me fired because of my offensive anti-Communism was the adoption of the new Soviet constitution. There were yawps throughout the Communist world. In the *Courier* I pointed out that the fine promises in it were meaningless in the face of Communist tyranny, mass murder, and millions of moujiks in concentration camps; that the American Constitution was by far the finer document, if enforced. Proof that the *Courier* was widely read came in the form of a bulky letter to the Editor signed by every Negro stooge in Moscow demanding my discharge. It came to naught, and I often referred to it through the years with special delight, printing the names of all signatories.

It was the same reaction I got when I exposed the Communist-created National Negro Congress, the Civil Rights Congress, and the rest of the solar system of Communist satellites designed to entrap colored and white Americans. My tirades, as I remember, were rather effective, culminating in the exposure of the Red-organized peace Conference at New York's Waldorf-Astoria in 1949, to which delegates were sent from all over the world, all expenses paid. The benefactor, of course, was precisely whom you might expect.

I learned a lot about the ramifications of the Communist conspiracy and techniques from my fifteen years of lecturing to Negro colleges and forums from coast to coast; from my coverage of forty industrial centers during the C.I.O. unionization drive; from my tour of the then forty-eight state capitals, examining the status of civil liberties; from my study of Negro rural and urban families; my tours of South America and the Caribbean; my appearances at the Congress for Cultural Freedom conferences in Berlin and Brussels; my subsequent journeys to Scandinavia, the Low Countries, Britain, France, Portugal, French West Africa, Nigeria, Angola and Mozambique; and, later, my lecture tours for the American Opinion Speakers Bureau.

Beginning with my "Negroes Reject Communism" in *American Mercury* in 1939, I have been able to reach a larger audience than the colored minority, in a half-dozen publications. I was gratified when Congresswoman Frances P. Bolton entered my Berlin speech, "The Negro Problem Without Propaganda," in the Congressional Record and Philip M. Kaiser, the Assistant Secretary of Labor, had mimeographed bundles of it sent to every U.S. Embassy and Legation in the world. Later when I rewrote it for Freeman as "The Phantom American Negro," it was somewhat condensed by *Reader's Digest* and printed for all its editions, local and international. Then for eight years I wrote for the Spadea Syndicate which reached some six million readers. Most of my writings, then and now, have been anticommunist because I regard the Communist Conspiracy as the great world menace to freedom, as it has been for a century and a quarter.

I have been gratified and rewarded by association with some of the most dedicated anti-Communists across the world, from whom I have learned as much as from books and personal observation. It has long been clear to me that the Conspiracy operating at home is more dangerous to American freedom and the system of capitalist enterprise upon which it is based than that operating abroad, and of which it is only a segment.

We got rid of chattel slavery at tragic expense in blood and money, but we shall never rid ourselves of collectivist slavery once it triumphs here. The chattel slave was assured a lease on life because of his economic value, and the more resourceful and intelligent were able to buy their freedom whether in Babylon, Athens, Rome, Richmond, or New York. Under collectivist slavery the victim's life is worthless, there's no hiding place, and the only escape is an improbable one under or over the Iron Curtain—or death. Britain has learned the hard way that once a nation starts coasting down the Fabian freeway there is no return. We should be learning it as we lurch along on Keynesian deficit financing and a mounting debt that presages bankruptcy.

Of course one has to pay for everything in this life, but my anti-Communism, while expensive in subtle ways, has not enabled my enemies to get me down. Many of them have been within the colored group and even among my professional associates. Through the years I have been dubbed irresponsible, anti-Semitic, and (since I hit so strongly at the Communist direction and control of the Negro "Revolution") anti-Negro and "Uncle Tom," all grimly amusing.

One snide method of reprisal is not to mention you at all in the ranks of the commendable. For example, when Irwin Ross wrote a portrait of Roy Wilkins in *Reader's Digest* for January 1968—and praised his dangerous visit to the Mississippi River Flood Control Project in 1932, accompanied by "another" investigator—he refrained from mentioning that the other man was that contemptible anti-Communist, George S. Schuyler!

The Reds, under whatever alias they use in their intensive campaign of corruption and subversion, can dish it out but they can't take it. Dominating the communications world, the stage and the screen, to say nothing of the publishing world, they cried like stuck hogs when the late lamented AWARE exposed their control. Infiltrated into all branches of our government, they shrieked bloody murder when Senator Joe McCarthy exposed just a fringe of them, so guilty was the pack. They are still busily trying to rehabilitate Alger Hiss, as they scream piteously to "Stop bombing North Vietnam!" And we of the American Writers Association will not forget the chagrin and frustration of the Red sponsors of the Cain Plan to control all literary output in the United States when we spiked that plot. It was funnier than current efforts to "get" The John Birch Society.

I have enjoyed crossing swords with the Reds, and still do. Of course I cannot use their weapons of lying, cheating, stealing, and libeling, but I can use the weapons with which He has armed me from the beginning; and I like nothing better than a Pier Six brawl with no holds barred. Just good breeding, I guess.

Dr. King: Nonviolence Always Ends Violently (1968)

This unpublished article, submitted to the North American News-paper Alliance, reveals one of Schuyler's principle reasons for opposing the protest tactics of the civil rights movement. Mass demonstrations, in his view, lead to greater civic disturbances. He clings unyieldingly to the belief that individual initiative pro-duces more political change than collective protest.

The assassination of Dr. Martin Luther King, Jr. tragically emphasizes again the fact that non-violence always ends violently.

Countless mass demonstrations which started to advance a good cause have ended in clashes with police, looting, vandalism and killing rather than the goodwill and understanding originally intended.

Behaviorists have long known that the larger the assemblage, the lower the mass intelligence, and the greater likelihood that hysteria will result.

It was Dr. King's determination to influence the course of an ordinary labor dispute by his charismatic presence that led him to Memphis, doubtless at the behest of his associates there, and exacerbated an already dangerous situation. The recent rioting, vandalism and casualties were a direct result, and there would probably have been more of the same had he led another demonstration. Labor disputes should be handled by officials of the AFL-CIO and the employers concerned, and not by demagogic outsiders with appeals to public passion.

It is noteworthy that Dr. King's idol, Mahatma Gandhi, who preached non-violence, on several occasions had to call off his drives and go into seclusion until his millions of adherents had cooled off and cured the wounds received from battling police dedicated, there as here, to preserving law and order, and upholding the rights of others not involved in the struggle.

From Dr. King's original effort, the Montgomery Improvement Association's boycott, he contributed very little to the solution of the touchy problems of race relations in the United States. If these problems are to be solved, it must be in moderation and through innumerable compromises rather than by use of abrasive tactics that produce irritation and ill will rather than understanding and cooperation.

Wherever the Negro lives in the United States, he prospers only to the extent that he has the goodwill, tolerance, and acceptance of his white neighbors and fellow-workers. This is necessarily a slow process, when trying to maintain the most delicate balance. It cannot be speeded by razzle-dazzle tactics which arouse suspicion and lend support to the propaganda of Negrophobes. Then action brings reaction. As President Eisenhower said, this is a matter of education.

Because Dr. King believed he was right and had Holy writ behind him, he continued to persist regardless of clear warnings of danger, even to the point of irresponsibility. It was scarcely calculated to help the Negroes of Alabama or to increase the esteem in which Dr. King and his cohorts were held in that state, to fruitlessly declare a boycott on all of its products from which, if effective, the Negroes would suffer more than whites.

It merely increased apprehension, exasperation and frustration in Chicago and environs when Dr. King and his janizaries boldly marched in, painted "End Slums" all over a section of the city, took over one landlord's property for rent collection and renovation without the owner's permission, and led parades through all-white near-suburbs where the marchers only escaped severe casualties because of the vigilance of the much-maligned police.

Because of Dr. King's stubbornness or extreme dedication, the Birmingham shambles was unavoidable. Warned by responsible Negro leaders not to visit the city; that they had the situation in hand as much as it could be, he and his staff came just the same. This persistence aided by the atmosphere of mob-mindedness among colored and white led directly to the deplorable events that followed.

Similarly, the troubles in St. Augustine, Florida, were deliberately provoked, and to this day nobody knows what was gained by it. To be sure there was a vast uproar in the press, radio, and television, there were threats and jailings, but no one in St. Augustine can say today what help it was to race relations— except for more speaking engagements for Dr. King.

There was an increasingly widespread belief among sober-minded Americans that Dr. King was, to say the least, unfortunate or unwise in the choice of his associates and advisers. They were largely of the Left-wing variety: individuals like Bayard Rustin, an alumnus of the Young Communist League and organizer of the 1963 March on Washington; Hunter Pitts O'Dell, one-time communist Party Organizer in new Orleans who later became executive director of King's Southern Christian Leadership Conference, and Carl Braden, the Communist ex-convict of the Southern Conference Educational Fund, headed by Rev. Ralph Abernathy, a close friend of King.

Added to these were the Vietnik peace forces headed by Dr. Spook and an assortment of Hanoi-lovers who influenced Dr. King to lend his endorsement and influence to elements inimical to the best interests of the United States, and even to allowing Mrs. King to accompany a delegation of women to the Ho Chi Minh capital. Moderate organizations like the National Association for the Advancement of Colored People and the National Urban League warned against tying the civil rights movement to the so-called peace movement, but Dr. King persisted stubbornly, even giving leave to one of his associates, Rev. James Bevel, to help organize the peacenik demonstrations in New York's Central Park and in the United Nations Piazza where King spoke and American flags were burned.

In short, as Dr. King's influence waxed, his judgment seems to have waned. No more was said about praying en masse for white folks but there was much talk about civil disobedience and defiance of the powers-that-be.

Dr. King was talented and adroit. He was never at a loss for words and he was evidently dedicated to the cause of improving race relations. It was the methods he used which, considering the high emotionalism which surrounded his goals, were objectionable. There are too many retardate, half-witted, criminally-inclined people in our population whose expectations have to be kept in check; that provide the fuel for great social conflagrations. This becomes truer every day as our population soars and our society becomes more complex. There are irresponsible individuals ever willing and eager to take advantage of the opportunities offered by unsettled times. A few years back in a New York department store, Dr. King was seriously injured when a crazed woman plunged a butcher knife in his chest while he was autographing copies of his book.

What will the followers of Dr. King do now that he has gone? We have already seen what has happened in the wake of news of his assassination, with a spate of vandalistic orgies across the country. Will those sub-leaders of the departed disciple of Gandhi (who was also assassinated) drop the policies and tactics that gained him world fame and chart a new course? Will they call off the scheduled mass demonstration of 3,000-odd trained "invaders" of Washington, D.C., and wait until things cool down? The present temper of the nation shows need for caution.

The goal of the overwhelming majority of American Negroes is middle-class co-existence. Millions have attained this status, and more are doing so all the time. There is lessening economic discrimination and everywhere they wish to vote, they are doing so. It will not speed the process to continue tactics of harassment and annoyance, but may well cause a retrogression in race relations to the disadvantage of all. Dr. King never learned this. His followers had better.

Malcolm X
Better to Memorialize Benedict Arnold
(1973)

*By this point all of Schuyler's articles appear in ultra-conservative
publications such as* American Opinion. *His acidic attack on
Malcolm X recalls his uncompassionate assessment of Dr. King in
"King: No Help to Peace" (1964). To my knowledge, this is
Schuyler's last published essay. The wit and clarity of expression
found in earlier essays are still evident, but Schuyler emerges
quite vexed, as he wrestles with ideological demons. In an interview with Professor Michael W. Peplow in 1973, Schuyler claimed
that he was not lonely, but the ideas set forth in this essay reveal
an intellect operating in isolation. As I argue in the introduction,
I believe Schuyler yearned to be a race man, to have the kind of
social and cultural power that both Dr. King and Malcolm X had
achieved, despite their respective shortcomings.*

No sooner was Malcolm X, one of the high priests of Black Power,
assassinated on February 21, 1965, than an outcry was raised that he be memori-
alized. In Omaha, Nebraska, where he was born on May 19, 1925, an official
holiday was demanded, black children were kept out of schools, and memorial
ceremonies were held. Similar demands were made repeatedly in other places
about the country, and local authorities surrendered to radical demands. On
October 10, 1969, his followers in the tiny Organization of Afro-American Unity
opened the Malcolm X Liberation University in Durham, North Carolina. And,
as with Dr. Martin Luther King, Jr., there is a continued movement afoot to
make him a national hero.

When Malcolm was fatally perforated by gunfire from fellow Black Power
zealots as he delivered one of his rants at Harlem's Audubon Ballroom, James
Baldwin, the black writer, shouted to newsmen: "You did it!" And later: "What
happened to Malcolm X can happen to us all." At Malcolm's funeral services in
New York, the principal speakers were such Reds as James Farmer, Bayard
Rustin, Dick Gregory, and Ossie Davis. It is significant that no important Negro
leader eulogized the "martyr," but neither did any condemn him. The black
masses did not mourn his passing, but were largely indifferent. Nonetheless,

the pressure to deify him proceeds apace and, considering the current mass madness, it might prove successful.

Like his erstwhile mentor, Elijah Muhammad of the Black Muslims, Malcolm X was an underworld character—an ex-pimp, a former dope peddler, and an ex-convict with a record of serving ten years in a Massachusetts prison for robbery. Mr. Muhammad himself did his bit in federal prison for defying the draft law and flirting with the pro-Japanese Pacific Movement of the East. On emerging from the federal stir, Mr. Muhammad concentrated on the Nation of Islam, organizing a paratrooper group, the Fruit of Islam, to do the necessary Hitler Youth chores and to preach the gospel of hatred of whites, all of whom were termed "white devils."

It was in prison that Malcolm X heard about Elijah Muhammad and his Black Muslims and promptly joined the hustle. He became a zealous and dedicated disciple, denouncing white people at every turn. Unlike most of the self-appointed spokesmen of blacks, he openly decried non-violence, declaring that "If ballots won't work, then bullets will." He warned the white devils that "Your little babies will get polio." When, in 1962, a French plane crashed killing 121 whites from Georgia, Malcolm told a Los Angeles audience: "I should like to announce a very beautiful thing that has happened. I got a wire from God today. He really answered our prayers over in France. He dropped an airplane out of the sky with over 120 white people on it because the Muslims believe in an eye for an eye and a tooth for a tooth. We will continue to pray, and we hope that every day another plane falls out of the sky."

Nevertheless, Malcolm should have been grateful to the white folks—especially newspaper reporters, the broadcast con men, and college professors. Otherwise he would have been completely unknown. It was they who, in search of colorful pieces, produced the feature stories about him and his undoubted eloquence, gave him time before their microphones, and invited him to speak on college platforms. To the Negroes he was just another of the growing number of black agitators promising a Black millennium. To unsuspecting whites, he was another black curiosity.

As you might suspect, Malcolm X knew more about Islam than did Elijah Muhammad. On several occasions I appeared on radio broadcasts with him and was initially astonished by his wide ignorance. When he launched into an excoriation of white people in the name of Islam, I called his attention to the fact that the majority of Moslems were whites, mentioning the millions in the Middle East, Southern Europe, and elsewhere. He was surprised to learn this and had no ready reply when I pointed out that the Moslems were more responsible for the African slave trade than were the Western Europeans and that the first big African slave revolt (869 A.D.) was against the Moslem slaveholders of Iraq, who required fifteen years to suppress the insurrection in and around Basra. But he had the all-Black complex, like his father, a Baptist preacher who had been a follower of the late Marcus Garvey, deceased head of the Universal Negro Improvement Association and African Communities League, whom I heard spout the same nonsense a generation earlier.

The unholy communion between Malcolm X and Mr. Muhammad, boss of the Muslim temple in New York, would have continued until the present, thus keeping Malcolm out of the Black Pantheon, if it had not been for the assassination of President John F. Kennedy. It being impossible for Malcolm to keep his mouth shut, during the period of national mourning he was impelled to state publicly that the killing was a case of "the chickens coming home to roost." Being an old farm boy myself, chickens coming home to roost never did make me sad; they've always made me glad.

This was too much even for Mr. Muhammad. Although the boss Muslim had himself said worse things about the white race, he was well aware that the whole country was looking for a scapegoat. Very wroth, he suspended Malcolm from his Manhattan sinecure, and cut him loose to hunger. It was the end of a lucrative era for Malcolm X, and he had to find another occupation. Gone forever were the days when he might convert the reigning heavyweight champion of the world, Cassius Clay, and persuade him to change his name to Muhammad Ali. Gone were the lucrative engagements on college platforms.

With the neckbone snatched from his plate by Elijah's summary action, Malcolm was quick to retaliate. Dispatching an open letter to the press, he accused the boss Black Muslim of having fathered eight illegitimate children by six teenage Black Muslim secretaries in Chicago, and dwelt upon the fleecing of the membership.

Thereupon, editorializing in his weekly newspaper *Muhammad Speaks,* Elijah warned: "Only those who wish to be led to hell, or to their doom, will follow Malcolm. . . . The die is cast, and Malcolm shall not escape." Along with several other defectors who followed Malcolm X out of the Black Muslims were two of Mr. Muhammad's sons. And Malcolm said prophetically: "The thing with me will be resolved by death and violence." Shortly afterward, Mr. X's home in East Elmhurst, New York, was firebombed and the family had to move in with friends.

It was now fish or cut bait. Booted out of the Nation of Islam, Malcolm suddenly left on a trip to Mecca, the Middle East, and Africa. It was never divulged from whence the money came for this prolonged hegira. Malcolm X had recently been hobnobbing with the Socialist Workers Party and praising its weekly sheet *The Militant,* but it is unlikely that the enfeebled Trotskyites could have financed him. More likely the subsidy came from the assorted Communist cells in the United Nations, which customarily advance funds to incipient comrades to bankroll international ventures. Malcolm was in no mood to quibble.

So Malcolm X made the hegira, and was hailed wherever he went as a famous American black. Little matter that he was actually yellow in color! And he returned to New York ululating: "During the past eleven days, I have eaten from the same plate, drunk from the same glass, and slept on the same rug while praying to the same God with fellow Moslems whose eyes were the bluest of blue, whose hair was the blondest of blond, and whose skin was the whitest of white. We are truly all the same [brothers] because their belief in one God has removed the 'white' from their minds, and the 'white' from their behavior, the 'white' from their attitude. I see from this that perhaps if white Americans could accept the Oneness of God, then perhaps, too, they could accept the Oneness of Man."

That one little trip had, it seems, changed Malcolm's mind. He declared: "My trip to Mecca has opened my eyes. I no longer subscribe to racism. I have adjusted my thinking to the point where I believe the whites are human beings as long as this is borne out by their humane attitude toward Negroes. . . . I'm not a racist, I'm not condemning whites for being white, but for their deeds. I condemn what whites collectively have done to our people collectively."

It was good to learn that Malcolm, after an eleven-day trip, had abandoned racism and now believed whites were human beings. He did not learn in eleven days that slavery was widespread in Arabia; nor about the slave traffic from Africa to Mecca where "pilgrims" are still sold for payment of their passage to the Holy City. And he did not add to this statement that he had visited radical and black racist groups in Africa, some of them Peace Corps workers. But he did admit that he had "been hypnotized" and "did many things as a [Black] Muslim that I'm sorry for now."

Had he really undergone a change? Prior to his return I received an invitation to join his new Organization of Afro-American Unity. Of course I didn't join, and my skepticism was rewarded when shortly his five-cent sheet, *The Blacklash*, headlined the same old racist bilge—swampwater pieces like "RACIST AMERICA" and "JOHNSON KNIFED AFRO-AMERICA IN BACK" and similar tacky screeds.

The French are not as gullible about people like Malcolm X as are Americans. When he flew into Paris to carry on as usual after his Asian-African trip, the French authorities would not let him address his radical followers but confined him to a waiting room under guard, warning him to take the first place out. He could decry non-violence in America, but not in France. They knew his connections.

And the boy from Omaha did not last long after his return. Mr. Muhammad spoke truly when he warned that "Malcolm shall not escape." He had scarcely opened his mouth to an audience that had been kept waiting an hour before a hail of bullets cut him down.

Less than thirty-six hours after Malcolm was shot, his O.A.A.U. mobsters firebombed Muhammad's Mosque Number Seven in mid-Harlem, flames shot thirty feet into a black sky, and six firemen were injured when a wall collapsed. In Chicago, Mr. Muhammad's nineteen-room mansion had to be guarded by police, and in Los Angeles the Black Muslim Mosque was put to the torch, but the firemen saved it. Malcolm had recently told a Tuskeegee University audience of three thousand cheering ninnies that the Black Revolution would roar in 1965. "It will no doubt be the longest, hottest, and the bloodiest of the Black Revolutions," he prophesied. He had not anticipated that it would be *his* blood.

But Malcolm X is now being eulogized as a great Negro leader. If this were true it would be a serious indictment of the colored people of this country. Malcolm was a bold, outspoken, ignorant man of no occupation after he gave up pimping, gambling, and dope-selling to follow Mr. Muhammad. Like most of the loud-mouthed black leaders, he had but a tiny following, perhaps not more than a couple of hundred . . . and all equally ignorant, if not more so. Even Mr. Muhammad's Black Muslims probably do not number more than ten thousand, just as Marcus Garvey's "millions" did not exceed thirty thousand in his heyday in the Twenties when there were only half as many Negroes as today. The NAACP, the largest Negro reform movement of all, has only a half-million members out of more than twenty-plus million blacks. All the rest are insignificant groups of hustlers and braggarts organized to bulldoze white people into handing out charity or to snatch a little transient graft. As among all peoples everywhere, first-class leaders, men of ability, training, and character, are scarce. During the past generation the black "leaders" afflicting the nation have been mediocrities, criminals, plotters, and poseurs like Malcolm X. Go down the list and you have to search hard to find even a few that are worthy of an invitation to tea.

How is it then that so many black charlatans have been able to get a following gullible enough to believe them?

In the first place, there are those in the black community who want to get something for nothing; who are allergic to honest toil and thus susceptible to the bamboozlement of sharpers who prey upon their fears, weaknesses, frustrations, and misfortunes. Such people can be easily led to believe that what they think is wrong can be righted by repeated chanting for a magic "solution."

Because of disabilities or disadvantages, such persons or groups are prone to be apprehensive, and when some witch doctor shows up with a scheme to ease their fears and handicaps by blaming them on somebody else, they will follow him as if he were the Pied Piper. Negroes since Emancipation have succumbed to countless charlatans without close examination, and thus have been led astray by their self-styled leaders—dreamers, hustlers, and incompetents in the main, whose first move is always to found an organization and start raising cash. This has been the case with every black movement started in the past century. And those who have questioned these movements and their self-anointed leaders have been bulldozed into silence or acquiescence. They do not want to be called enemies of their people. So they join and pay and pay. They are led even to condemn the critics of their fleecing.

Which explains the swamp of freedom, equality, and civil-rights groups that has flourished since the U.S. Supreme Court decisions on schools, voting rights, and non-discrimination. Now the vapors rising from this swamp have produced a national madness. We might justly call it the Malcolm X syndrome. And the whites are falling victim to it too—with far less to complain about— and are being similarly hornswoggled.

With the packing of our prisons, even during the current age of permissiveness, the worst elements in our society have been thrown together to enjoy the benefits of prison reform, to scheme and plot against society when shortly paroled, and to seek each other out upon return to civilian pursuits. The Black Muslims were organized and nurtured in our prisons. Their agitations have led to prison riots across the country. With their anti-white doctrine they have strained race relations and spread racial animosities. Much of the increase in group prejudices we are now suffering can be laid directly to the prison-spawned activities of these embittered weaklings and mental defectiveness.

When they emerge well-versed in criminality, they terrorize and dominate the areas in which they live and circulate: snatching purses, robbing stores, burglarizing apartments, and selling dope. Some join extremist organizations like the Black Panthers and vent their madness on the people by agitation for various and sundry reforms to be achieved by coercion. Some join the Black Muslims, while still others crowd the campuses on free scholarships to loaf at public expense. Others, tiring of the American scene, have hijacked planes to Cuba and Algeria and similar Hellholes beyond the reach of civilization.

The Eldridge Cleavers, the Hubert "Rap" Browns and the Malcolm Xs will continue their madness and bedevil society just as long as they can find encouragement to do so. Until the people demand a halt to it, politicians will continue to use them to shout up mobs for personal advantage. Legal hustlers will be ever ready to defend them in court. Sensationalist newspapers will gladly give them headlines. Sob-sister reformers will urge sympathy and lenience for them. And prison reformers will do their best to see that these criminal apes, when finally put behind bars, are parked fatly in motels with all modern conveniences, unlimited visiting hours, as little work to do as possible, and plenty of time to hustle recruits.

It is not hard to imagine the ultimate fate of a society in which a pixilated criminal like Malcolm X is almost universally praised, and has hospitals, schools, and highways named in his memory! What is amazing is that no one dares say that we might as well call out the school children to celebrate the birthday of Benedict Arnold. Or to praise a memorial to Alger Hiss. We would do well to remember that all societies are destroyed from within—through weakness, immorality, crime, debauchery, and failing mentality. It was so in Rome, Constantinople, Alexandria, and Mecca. We shall not escape their fate by using liniment to treat cancer.

George S. Schuyler, Writer
An Interview with Ishmael Reed and Steve Cannon
(1973)

This interview originally appeared in Yardbird II, *a publication founded by Ishmael Reed. Like Schuyler, Reed spent his childhood years in upstate New York. As a satirist, Reed is probably the most obvious heir to Schuyler's ribald perspectives and controversial politics. As Schuyler did during his career, Reed has established a considerable reputation in both fiction and nonfiction, but he has also written five books of poems, four plays, three television programs, and two librettos.*

By 1973, Schuyler's brand of conservatism had forced him into obscurity, but Reed and Cannon realized the depth of his experience. In this interview Schuyler, at age seventy-seven, holds forth on the remarkable and tumultuous changes of the twentieth century.

George Schuyler, whose career has often inspired bitter controversy, was born in Providence, Rhode Island, in 1895. He is a distinguished journalist whose work has appeared in *The Messenger, The Pittsburgh Courier, The Crisis, The American Mercury, The World Tomorrow, New Masses, Modern Quarterly, Opportunity* and *The Nation.* He is the author of *Black No More* (1931), the first science fiction novel written by an Afro-American, and whose plot has been widely imitated. He is also the author of *Slaves Today: A Story of Liberia* (1931), and *Black and Conservative* (1966), his autobiography. Mr. Schuyler is presently the book reviewer for the *Manchester Union Leader.*

Mr. Schuyler discussed his stormy career and other matters with Steve Cannon and me in October of 1972 at his handsomely furnished apartment on Convent Avenue in Manhattan, full of sculpture, paintings, photos of his friends: authors, artists, and Presidents, and memorabilia concerning his hauntingly beautiful daughter, the late Philippa D. Schuyler. During the course of the interview Mr. Schuyler exhibited some of the spunk and bluntness that once required him to keep a gun next to his typewriter when threatened by some political opponents. When I asked Mr. Schuyler about the 1930s incident in which he was picketed for his comments on Angelo Herndon, a black Communist, he looked puzzled, trying to recall the case, saying, "I don't know. It's hard to remember. I've been picketed by so many people."

REED: Mr. Schuyler, in an essay you wrote called "Dr. Jekyll and Mr. Hyde and the Negro," you talked about a Negrophobe who exempted his maid from being a Negro. You talked about that as a metaphor for the Jekyll and Hyde nature of race relations in the United States. You said it explains to a large extent how our largest minority "has been able to survive regardless of Nazi-like laws and customs." You talked about the discrepancy between private and public attitudes regarding race relations. Would you like to elaborate on that?

SCHUYLER: When did I write this?

REED: In the early forties, I believe.

SCHUYLER: I don't recall just what it was.

REED: How would you feel about that generally? Some people are always talking about a "final solution" for black people in this country. You said that blacks have been able to survive because of a kind of schizophrenic attitude with which white America—the way white Americans regard them. This was an essay that was published in Mr. Sylvestre C. Watkins' *Anthology of American Negro Literature* [1944].

SCHUYLER: I'm trying to recall it. I don't recall it now. However, you can summarize the conclusion I drew and I'll elaborate on that.

REED: You said that there seemed to be a love-hate relationship between blacks and whites. You talked about the certain paradoxes illustrating this relationship in the South. You mentioned one incident in which black people were standing on a train. A white conductor wanted to give them more space and he broke the custom by allowing them to go into the section of the train usually reserved for whites.

SCHUYLER: There are a lot of peculiar things going on all sides. That is, the people are not all the same. You have immense differences between individuals, regardless of color. They both love and hate, sometimes at the same time. These things were apparent to me very early. There's really no validity to the generalization that white people or black people per se think a certain way. They don't at all. They think as individuals, unless they are childish, and then they rush to concede the generally accepted thing. But I find so many exceptions to the rule.

REED: You started off the essay—I'll have to send you a copy of it—by an amusing anecdote about this man suffering from what you called Negrophobia. He hated Paul Robeson and he hated black people. They asked him about his maid, and he said, "Oh, Ann, she's not black . . ."

SCHUYLER: "She's not a Negro." Yes, well, they don't regard people very close to them as Negroes, nor do Negroes regard white people who are very close to and intimate with them as white. That's the last thing they think about. I remember being asked down in Georgia, how did it feel being married to a white woman? I said, "I'm not married to a white woman; I'm married to Josephine. That's my wife. It doesn't occur to me; I know that she's white, but it doesn't occur to me except when somebody like you mentions it." I said, "I didn't marry a white woman. I married a certain individual." I think that happens in many parts of life and in human relations, that people don't think about certain individuals being Jewish, for example. Easily, I say, "So what? I don't care about him being a Jew. I'm interested in his character and his manner and whether we get along or not."

CANNON: That's what you were saying in the essay, that in interpersonal relationships judgments are made in relation to the person and not to ethnic background or anything like that. Can I put it that way?

SCHUYLER: Yes, I think you can put it that way. Of course, in recent years we have adopted certain words and have worn them out. "Ethnic background" really doesn't mean a damn thing.

REED: Can you give some more examples of words you think have been worn out, or have lost their meaning?

SCHUYLER: Well, "black" is one.

CANNON: Back at the turn of the century, that was a negative word for Negroes to use, wasn't it? Or I would say in the twenties.

SCHUYLER: Some Negroes used it, although my recollection is of the struggle to get the word Negro capitalized, and I said at the time that it didn't make a damn bit of difference if it was capitalized or not. I'd just as soon have it an adjective or a noun, because it didn't change his position, it didn't change his character. Then with the "black" business going on, it was even less sensible than Negro.

REED: You use the term Afro-American in this particular essay.

SCHUYLER: Yes, I used it. I think James Weldon Johnson was the first one I knew to use it and I thought it was an accurate term, although even that is not completely accurate. Some colored people are of three or four different derivations. That is, they have Indian . . .

REED: You claim in *Black No More* that the real distinction, the real so-called pure African disappeared very early in this country and that most people are descended from Caucasians and Indians.

SCHUYLER: Yes, and a lot of whites are descended from Africans and Indians. As a matter of fact, these two anthropologists from Johns Hopkins University made a long study in Virginia about miscegenation of the white and Indian and they found that there were no unmixed Indians in the Eastern United States. The only place you find unmixed Indians is in the West, and in some remote places in the South where they had a reservation.

REED: You satirize people like James Weldon Johnson and W. E. B. DuBois and give them satirical names in *Black No More*—also Garvey. There's always a touch of whimsy about it; it's not really vicious satire.

CANNON: It bordered on how absurd that situation really was.

REED: The thesis of *Black No More* was that if blacks became whites all of a sudden, the civil rights movement would go broke. You were suggesting that a lot of these civil rights groups really thrive on the misery.

SCHUYLER: They profit on the grief, although since they make a profession of it, they cannot acknowledge that there are others who do not, who do not give a damn. Some of the very masses that they're trying to win over don't care. They're not as frightened as many of the so-called leaders and spokesmen.

REED: Another thing about *Black No More*. I notice that on page thirty-two of the paperback edition (Collier African American Library), when you talk about how this individual Max Disher becomes a white man [Matthew Fisher], all of this elaborate machinery Dr. Crookman has around, reminds me very much of the Paint Factory section in *Invisible Man*.

CANNON: "Pure and White."

REED: Where the young man, the protagonist, underwent an operation. He was in this hospital and had all this science fiction type apparatus around him. You were the first one to do that in *Black No More*. I would call it a science fiction novel.

SCHUYLER: Yes, it was in the direction of most of the science fiction.

CANNON: But it went inward instead of outward; can I say that?

SCHUYLER: Well, I wouldn't say that.

CANNON: I mean metaphorically, in terms of him going down to Georgia to meet this family as opposed to going to the moon. That's what I meant.

SCHUYLER: That's where a Negro usually goes when he gets a little money.

CANNON: Down South, right?

SCHUYLER: . . . Struts around in his shoes?

REED: You had a scene where Fisher starts out being black and goes to this cabaret and sees this girl and falls in love with her. A Dr. Crookman has the formula for changing black to white. John Howard Griffin did a book like that, *Black Like Me*. They never gave your novel credit for preceding that. I'll bring that up again. What Max Fisher does after becoming white is that he works for the most rabid, racist organization. Will you make comment on parallels to Sartre's *The Inauthentic Jew*, where the people who really probably hate Jews are their own group. I have just read that the head of Hitler's Luftwaffe was Jewish and so dedicated that the German High Command looked the other way. Were you trying to make that comment in *Black No More?*

SCHUYLER: No telling.

REED: Why did you have him become an anti-Negro organizer in this book?

SCHUYLER: Because it was a pretty good plot.

CANNON: I thought so, too. I enjoyed the book.

SCHUYLER: You can get drawn easily into the race nonsense by that device.

REED: I want to return to that first question. I live on the West Coast and we have a different intellectual environment than in New York. In New York you hear a lot of the black intellectuals talking about the holocaust . . .

SCHUYLER: What holocaust?

REED: The one that's always around the corner, like *The Fire Next Time,* or there's going to be a final solution, like Nixon's going to take everybody to concentration camps. You mentioned in your essay that blacks really stimulate this country.

SCHUYLER: You mean do they make a cultural contribution?

REED: Yes.

SCHUYLER: Of course they do; they always have. They not only made it in this country; they made it in ancient Rome, and in Greece. This man at Howard University . . .

REED: *Blacks in Antiquity?* Snowden's book?

SCHUYLER: Yes, he goes into that. The first man to do that, of course, was J. A. Rogers. He preceded all these people and was a better researcher and scholar.

CANNON: Plus he published his own work.

SCHUYLER: Yes, and now Macmillan has put out two volumes of his. What is the name of it . . . *Great Men of African Descent* or something like that. It's well done and they follow the text almost completely. They leave out some things, those which were convenient to leave out. I was responsible for starting that.

REED: Is that right?

SCHUYLER: Yes, I was the one who got Rogers to start writing about the Great Men. He'd been talking about them over at the YWCA cafeteria and so we sat down and talked about these things. I was the managing editor of *The Messenger,* so I got him to start writing it. Then, when *The Messenger* fell and I went to Chicago to edit Ziff's publication—it was a supplement that went into all of the larger Negro weeklies—this supplement, in order to get better advertising notes, was edited in Chicago and published there. The printers just put the names and titles of the papers on as many thousands of copies as they used. So I got Rogers to write for that. I left New York for Chicago because there was a much wider circulation; it took in almost all the country. I think it had about 300,000 circulation combined.

REED: You mentioned dining with J. A. Rogers. Were you part of a circle in the twenties? A circle of intellectuals, poets, and writers?

SCHUYLER: Yes, although the word wasn't in use then.

REED: "The New Negro," Alain Locke said . . .

SCHUYLER: I had very little association with Alain Locke because Alain Locke was teaching at Howard University and he just came up here on occasion. But I moved around in that circle, because we met at some of the places. At one time, Theophilus Lewis was in that circle, and Wally Thurman and Langston Hughes—we used to have dinner in Langston's home.

REED: Did you know Zora Neale Hurston?

SCHUYLER: Sure, I knew her very well. In fact, I published one of the first of her short stories.

REED: You have very rigorous standards for writing. You wrote an essay called "The Negro-Art Hokum" which made everybody mad. Do you still maintain those views?

SCHUYLER: I don't know of any that have changed. I think that such art as Negroes produce will be American art, and all of the rest of this is hokum. Usually it's hokum because they don't know anything about Africa. They're not African. Knowing some African history doesn't make a person an African. Just as knowing Italian history doesn't make someone Italian. That was brought forcefully to mind when I was in Africa. Just being black didn't mean a damn thing.

REED: So even though an Afro-American may use African themes or African techniques like the young painters and sculptors are doing . . .

SCHUYLER: Painters and sculptors are a different thing. They could sculpt or paint Eskimo, and if they were good artists, they could sculpt or paint good representations of Eskimo.

REED: So you meant writers?

SCHUYLER: If you're talking about writers, now you're dealing with the culture of the people, and these people here don't know a damn thing about African culture. In fact, there are so many cultures in Africa that one would have to be historian, traveler, philosopher. I visited about twelve different tribes, or nations, as they call themselves—they're more honest than we are—in the backcountry of Liberia. They all had different hairdos, they had different language, they had an interpreter to talk through, and they stayed in their own areas. In other words, they were just small nations or tribes.

REED: There's a great deal of fanfare about a long awaited book by Alex Haley, the man who tape-recorded the autobiography of Malcolm X. He's doing a new book in which he traces his ancestry back to the Mandingo. But you did that already. You traced your ancestry back to the Mandingo tribe.

SCHUYLER: I traced them back on the maternal side to Madagascar. That's not so far back—a couple of hundred years. Then there were some Indians back there. Of course, there are some Indians in practically every Negro's background.

REED: I see a thread running through your comments on this which leads me to believe that by not acknowledging Caucasian or Indian ancestry, blacks are not being true to themselves and that maybe much of the politics and culture are based on false premises. Would you say that? Like, a lot of stuff that we hear today about the emphasis on "black pride" and this kind of thing.

SCHUYLER: I think the "black pride" ploy is horsefeathers. Now, people have pride, I mean individual pride. Usually it's based on something, not on nothing, like they make it now. A man has pride because of his family, because of his prowess or his accomplishments—that's what he's proud about. He can even be proud because he's got a small foot or something like that. He boasts that he thinks a lot of himself because of that. But what is there to think about being black or pink or red. So you're that. There's nothing to be proud about; you didn't cause it. If a man caused it, then he could be proud.

REED: It seems that a lot of our politics that we hear about—and I'll get to that in a minute, because you did a great study on certain liberal newspapers in *Black and Conservative* in which you talked about the lopsided ideological viewpoint in reference to blacks. It always seems to be the left-wing type of viewpoint that's promoted. There seems to be a lot, like today, on the campuses, you have teachers and professors who are pushing this idea of a collective, and "the people," and looking out for the group as opposed to the individual. They talk about the "luxury of individualism." Of course, my point of view is that individuals and secret societies have done as much to change history as mass movements. What do you see as the future of the black individual who does want to achieve things on his own terms and wants to express his gifts?

SCHUYLER: Well, I think he can do it. As a matter of fact, most of those who have accomplished something and have some kind of reputation have done it. You can't go into a man's factory or mill and say, "Here, I'm black"—he doesn't want that. He wants to know what you can do. For many years there was a Negro who worked over here at the *Newark News*. He was city editor, I believe. The *Newark News* is a very prestigious paper in this area. But, you see, he wasn't a race man and therefore only a few people knew about it.

REED: So he couldn't really go in there and say he's a race man; he has to be qualified as a journalist. And you made the comment: "Those who haven't accomplished something laud those who have."

SCHUYLER: Yes, and they also take credit for it.

REED: Take credit for it?

SCHUYLER: "Look what we've done."

REED: When they point to someone like Garvey, or DuBois, or yourself, or Wallace Thurman? That's an interesting point. Have you read Professor Nathan Huggins' book, *The Harlem Renaissance?* Did he talk to you? What is your assessment of that book? He said that the movement failed because it depended on white patronage. I never heard of anybody describing a movement of white writers as having failed when there could be individual successes in art—say individual poems. It seems that his idea is that they weren't radical enough for his taste.

SCHUYLER: This "Harlem Renaissance" is pretty much of a fraud. A lot of people connected with it were phonies, and there weren't many connected with it.

REED: That's Thurman's viewpoint—"the Niggerati."

SCHUYLER: There was a man [Thurman] with a sense of humor and not chained to any racist chariot. He had ability, shown by the fact that even in that early day he was able to get a job out in Hollywood as a writer.

REED: We've noticed, Mr. Cannon and I, that those writers who were independent, Rudolph Fisher, yourself, Wallace Thurman, even to an extent Zora Neale Hurston, who although she had patronage did do a lot of work on her own in the South—she recorded folklore and went to New Orleans.

SCHUYLER: And to Haiti.

REED: And to Haiti. And she wrote *The Voodoo Gods of Haiti* which you can't find, as you can't find *Infants of the Spring* or others. Why do you think the people who are more into the collectivist type of poetry and "for the people" have a bigger reputation than those who are independents?

SCHUYLER: Because they've been played up and built up.

REED: Who builds them up?

SCHUYLER: Well, people who are interested in building them up. It's a clique. Who would ever think of Malcolm X as a leader?

CANNON: Really.

SCHUYLER: Lead what?

CANNON: Every time we talk about that, we get shouted down.

REED: You can't say that. He's a holiday now.

SCHUYLER: This was a man who was so ignorant that, until I informed him, he didn't know that there were more white Moslems than there were black. I had to tell him on the radio. I used to be on this program—"The Editors Speak." He was on there frequently, and I had to tell him about this criticism, this denunciation of the white man—and you say you're a Moslem—that most of the Moslems were white. And moreover, I criticized him because of these people using X and Y after their names. You take the name Muhammad itself—that's taken from a white man. And these names that the Negroes have in Africa, that is, those that are Moslems, all come down from the white people who conquered them. I just told him, publicly, "You just don't know what you're talking about." And then when he went to Mecca, and saw it himself, it changed his whole outlook on things. Then, Mr. Muhammad fired him and that made him go off independently to be a leader.

REED: You talked about this clique. Would you describe this clique and how it works?

SCHUYLER: They use the same tactics, or similar tactics, to those they accuse white people of using. Now, you know, at my age and with my experience, I'm not eager to become a member of anything.

REED: What is your age?

SCHUYLER: I'll be seventy-eight in February. They have various organizations around here, this clique does, which they haven't invited me to join anyhow.

REED: Why is that?

SCHUYLER: Well, they know I won't. I don't regard them as top flight. I belong to the Authors Guild and things like that that are of some value to me. I belong to ASCAP by virtue of my daughter having belonged to it, and I inherit her interest in it.

CANNON: I was sorry to hear what happened to her. I met her when I was a little kid; I must have been about sixteen years old and she came down to Southern University to play—a very long time ago.

SCHUYLER: [Pointing to poster on the wall] That was her rehearsal at fourteen to play with the New York Philharmonic Orchestra at Lewisohn Stadium, which had never been done before by anyone except Marian Anderson. That was her standard, too.

REED: You were trying to instill a standard of excellence in your children?

SCHUYLER: Yes. Now, let's see. From whence did we wander?

CANNON: We were talking about the clique organizations, about the "Harlem Renaissance" being a fiasco.

REED: Langston Hughes was an excellent poet, don't you think? There were individuals within the Harlem Renaissance who were accomplished. Countee Cullen was a fine poet. And Wallace Thurman was excellent; he's considered part of the Harlem Renaissance, for some reason. There were fine musicians, too, isn't that correct, like James Weldon Johnson, who wrote Lyrics for Noble Sissle and Eubie Blake. You're criticizing the public relations aspect; the title.

SCHUYLER: You can put it on one way and say that there were many people in the nineties and the hundreds, and after that, who were exceptional. If you gather them all together, you could probably call it a renaissance. But some of these people they put in the Harlem Renaissance didn't even live in Harlem.

REED: Like who?

SCHUYLER: Well, James Weldon Johnson was associated with the NAACP; so was Walter White. They were here by virtue of the NAACP being here. There were others, like Clarence Cameron White, who was a great violinist and composer and had his work played by symphony orchestras.

REED: What about Claude McKay?

SCHUYLER: Well, Claude McKay was just a transient. In his late years, he lived in Harlem when he came back from Marseilles. His accomplishments were not particularly in Harlem. I think he wrote "If We Must Die" down in the Village somewhere. He was with the Max Eastman crowd. But of course, I know that there are a lot of people who want to claim every Negro in the world.

CANNON: Well, tell me this. During that period when you were up here, in the twenties and thirties, was there much interracial intellectual gathering? Fusion of ideas? I'm trying to see if it was integrated on an intellectual level.

REED: They hung out at the cabarets.

CANNON: Yeah, well, I got that out of *Black No More.*

SCHUYLER: Well, they had cabarets all over New York. There were even some Negro cabarets downtown, but there were also other associations. There were labor union associations, there were forums of all kinds. In fact, there were more forums in the twenties and the thirties than there are now, although there are three or four times as many Negroes as there were then. But I would say that the intellectual standards have fallen, if anything, because I think the people who were trying to be intellectual were aiming at higher standards than they are now.

REED: You're talking about Harlem?

SCHUYLER: Yes, in Harlem, and, as a matter of fact, you can go outside Harlem!

REED: You know, we have some pretty good contemporary writers here now. William Melvin Kelley has been compared to you. His book *Dem* has a science fiction plot. And also your idea in *Black No More* of what would happen if all the blacks disappeared, is taken up in *A Different Drummer.* There are a number of good writers. We may say that the standards are better than in the twenties, you know!

SCHUYLER: It just happens that I've gone through this whole period of literature from the mid-twenties on to the present.

REED: And you think that the standards are lower now than they were in the twenties?

SCHUYLER: I should say that they are, not only for Negroes, but for whites as well.

CANNON: For the whole publishing world, huh?

SCHUYLER: Great art and literature has traditionally come out of and been sup- ported by people of means and education, what is called the upper class. As a matter of fact, Upton Sinclair did a book once on that very theme and showed how all the Greek art and sculpture had been subsidized by people of means. Where a fraternity or a church has the means to subsidize an artist, they very seldom do it, because they don't understand it. Presumably, you've got to under- stand what you pay for, and know what it's all about. You can imagine, as in Rome, for example, Ovid and Horace were subsidized by the people who appreciated what they were doing.

REED: Would you consider Duke Ellington's music great art?

SCHUYLER: No, it's not great art.

CANNON: What's missing from it?

SCHUYLER: Variety, for one thing. Duke, whom I know and respect very much, has cleaned up on this trend. I think that some of the things Duke wrote thirty years ago are more pleasant to me than these growls that he puts out now.

REED: Do you think that what is called Afro-American music—what's generi- cally called jazz, ragtime, blues—that this . . .

SCHUYLER: That's a horse of another color. It's original.

REED: But original doesn't necessarily have to be great.

SCHUYLER: No. You make it great by the addition of artistry.

REED: *Time Magazine* did a review of my book and then compared it to your work and they called you "the black Mencken." Did you know Mencken?

SCHUYLER: Yes, I knew Mencken well. I was his houseguest several times. When- ever I passed through Baltimore I would call him up, and if he was not busy, I would go by there for an evening, and try out his cellar. He had a wonderful cellar. There were other people, too, during that period who were prominent in the literary world, even in the South, that I visited and shared their hospital- ity. And they solicited me. This was especially true after I wrote for *The Ameri- can Mercury* in 1927. At the same time, in 1927, my first piece came out, and it was the lead piece, too. I came to be known by a lot of people who were writ- ing. I think that other colored people with skill can get the same respect and cooperation. It's being done all the time. It's probably being done more now than it was then, because there are more Negroes now and there are more Negroes of education and training now than there were then. Because, after all, a so-called intellectual, even if he was connected with church or with one of the race-saving organizations, was not much in the labor movement because there weren't many Negroes in the labor movement on a higher scale. Once in a while you'd run across some colored man who was secretary-treasurer of a union, but, you see, Negroes couldn't join most of the unions at those times.

REED: There are still some unions they can't join, like the construction union in New York they're having difficulty with.

SCHUYLER: Oh, yes. Well, the labor movement started out in this country on Jim Crow. Not on Jim Crow, but on exclusion. The first labor union in the United States was in Boston and that was before the Revolution. They specifically put in their constitution that they weren't going to have any men of color, whether they were free or not. At the time of the Civil War, there were only about three unions in the United States that permitted Negroes membership. And so in that field you had very little representation. But the fields in which you did have representation didn't produce so much either. That is, in the field of education.

REED: There's a controversy now about "Black English."

SCHUYLER: Hogwash.

REED: You said there are no racial or colored dialects, only sectional dialects in *Black No More*. There are really no racial differences, only class differences, you said in *Slaves Today*, 1931. On the other hand, you do seem to hint that there is a unique style of African choreography or music.

SCHUYLER: I wouldn't say African choreography. I would say there's choreography in the dance, because I've seen that, and it was African, too; it wasn't any bogus thing. I might say, to digress, that in 1960 I was in Nigeria celebrating the first black Governor General of Nigeria, and we were there for a week when they gave the dance festival, which included tribes of people from all parts of Nigeria. When you say that, it makes it international because each one of those big tribes is a nation, you know. They got nothing in common. That's some idea they built up here in Harlem about that. As a matter of fact, half the Negroes in Nigeria enslave the other half. But now there you had marvelous dances and with no influence from anywhere else. It was indigenous. It came out of their lives. Now, as for the music, there's very little to African music. There are some tribes that make beautiful music. Other tribes are just percussion. In fact, I don't know why, as well trained as so many Negro musicians are, in the United States, that they haven't composed more on African themes.

REED: Still there are a lot of jazz musicians who at least use African titles.

SCHUYLER: Yes, but speaking of orchestral composition . . . they have to embody root music that comes out of the people that they are writing about. And they [have to] refine it and make something very artistic out of it. Now, they haven't done that. Somebody may have done it. I don't claim to know the history of music, but I know my daughter was the only one who did it. Because she wrote

"The Nile," which was premiered in Cairo by the Cairo Symphony Orchestra on—this was 1965, December 10.

CANNON: Was that ever recorded? Or do you know?

SCHUYLER: Well, it was played here. At her memorial service. They played it here at her memorial service, which was held in Town Hall. And that embodied the music, the basic music of Ethiopia, Uganda . . . well, all the four countries that bordered on the Nile, so that was the name of it, "The Nile." It was applauded very highly there by the critics in Cairo. But those are my views about art and literature and all. And . . .

CANNON: Did you and Mencken ever get in heated discussions about American language or was he working on that at the time?

SCHUYLER: I gave him many items for his *American Language*. We discussed. We didn't argue about it, of course. There wasn't any argument.

CANNON: No, you know what I mean. Just differences of opinion.

SCHUYLER: Just contributions to Americana.

REED: Are you an optimist about the—this is the kind of question they ask—an optimist about the future of race relations in this country?

SCHUYLER: Well, in a sense I am. But they're not going to continue so good if it's left up to the Negro intellectuals to stir things up and frighten people. It's a very bad thing, you know—to frighten people—especially if you don't have anything. Like I remember a vaudeville skit, you know, and the blackface comedian makes a pass at his back pocket, you know, as if he had something in there, and then later when he got the other man scared, when the other man began to retaliate, he would say, "I was just joking."

CANNON: That means that you knew Bert Williams and George Walker, doesn't it?

SCHUYLER: I didn't know them.

CANNON: I mean, as far as having seen their performances.

SCHUYLER: *The Messenger* office was just two doors north of where Bert Williams lived on Seventh Avenue.

CANNON: How was their material? I've never seen them. How are they as comedians? Were they very good as compared to what was happening in the world at the time?

REED: You're talking about Williams and Walker.

CANNON: Because I think what's-his-name was just coming on the scene when he was a little boy . . . what's his name? Leon Earl and people like Eddie Cantor—they were very young at that time. Earl was older. He was close to Williams, I think.

SCHUYLER: Well, Earl was better than most of them. You know, one time in one of the Ziegfeld Follies, Williams and Earl had a skit together and it was really immense.

REED: Bert Williams worked with Eddie Cantor.

SCHUYLER: I don't doubt it.

REED: Yeah, they had a routine. Williams was called Rufus the Red Cap. Of course Williams always upstaged him and you know that W. C. Fields said he was the funniest and saddest man he ever saw perform. But a lot of the younger black comedians, with the notable exception of Richard Pryor, who I think is a genius, consider the black comedians of the past to be Uncle Toms.

SCHUYLER: These people were comedians and they were good ones, too. And they took the life around them and made a joke out of it. As a matter of fact, lots can be said for Uncle Toms. I remember he said, "You can have my body but you can't have my soul."

REED: That's interesting that you would say that. Because it seems that Black-Negro-Afro-American behavior is always—always has to be restricted. You have to be angry. There's only one mask you can wear. I was reading in the *I Ching* the other night that there is a kind of parallel in Confucius to what we call Uncle Tomism—what they call taking abuse from the outside by preserving your inner light all along.

SCHUYLER: Well, now, how do you think these free Negroes—whose position was very difficult—in this country—how do you think they survived and, in some instances, prospered? And not only in the North.

CANNON: In the South?

SCHUYLER: In the South. Because, as I say, it was the individual. And if the individual has it within him then he can go to Harvard, Yale, Chicago, and all the other universities. And he'll just be a mediocrity. You run across them every day. Humpback with degrees.

REED: I notice in the universities, and Steve has too, a lot of the children are really undergoing an emotional, intellectual, psychological crisis because they've been badgered into thinking they have to be—you know.

CANNON: Well, use Mr. Schuyler's words, "race people." They think they have to be race people before they can be individuals.

REED: And some universities, instead of designing courses, they're like conflicts between those people who . . . really have like a Communist orientation when you come on out with it . . . and, say, those who want to make it within the system or treat Afro-American culture as a serious entity instead of using it as a political rally hall. How do you see us resolving that?

SCHUYLER: What other system is there for them to make it in?

CANNON: No, he means in terms of—let's look at it this way—in terms of Frederick Douglass and those people came up here. I'm going back now to the nineteenth century. Now, you had an awful lot of free Negroes living up around here. You mentioned one earlier in the conversation. You were talking about Thomas Fortune. Now, how did they react to the rabble-rousing Douglass and what those people were doing? I mean, did it affect their livelihood at all . . . or their "consciousness"?—that's the kind of word they use now.

SCHUYLER: Well, all of them were opposed to slavery of course. But they disagreed with the means which were being advocated. Douglass himself did not follow John Brown. John Brown, he gave him hell for not going along with him, but of course Fred Douglass was saying, in a way, in accordance with the old song Bert Williams popularized: "I may be crazy but I ain't no fool." And then you had a long debate among free Negroes in this country from the 1820s on about emigration to Africa.

CANNON: Yeah, right, that so-called Colonization Society. And if I remember correctly Douglass came out totally against it.

SCHUYLER: Yes, he was against it, but there were a lot of Negroes who were not against it. There were about ten thousand Negroes who went to Liberia and Captain Paul Cuffee had plans for an organization to carry a lot of them to Sierra Leone.

CANNON: The guy's name—you know who I'm thinking about—Delany. Martin Delany was another one of them who supported the movement.

REED: He always came back here though.

SCHUYLER: Well, he only went there once.

CANNON: Well, in other words that whole Garvey thing was nothing else than echoes and . . . the rounding out of that whole thing that started in the 1820s.

SCHUYLER: Yes. What had been said and done before. Only he could get a strong voice . . .

REED: Only he could talk louder. Lots of style. Lots of style.

SCHUYLER: Louder . . .

REED: How do you think Garvey will be evaluated when all the fuss dies down?

SCHUYLER: Well, I think he'll be evaluated like others who have had this dream of migrating to Africa. There are many of them who have had it, you know.

CANNON: Well, Chester Himes did a pretty good job of doing parody on that. I don't know if you read that *Cotton Comes to Harlem*, which was a parody on that whole Garvey thing. The movie version wasn't but the book itself was.

REED: But of course, there are people in the country—leaders—who use African or quasi-African-based philosophies and have success like Elijah Muhammad and Amiri Baraka.

SCHUYLER: Well, now, Elijah Muhammad—he's another hustler. However, he's not bereft of ideas and has much more fruitful ideas than most.

REED: Like the farms and the businesses?

CANNON: In other words and from what you know about this country, being your age, would you see him as an American phenomenon somewhat similar to the Mormons? Would you be able to draw a parallel to them?

SCHUYLER: No.

CANNON: Because the Mormons are supposed to be an American religion—right?

SCHUYLER: No. Not unless he did as the Mormons did.

CANNON: Going out and getting some state.

SCHUYLER: Yes. Some territory. But you see the thing is about Elijah Muhammad's followers, they don't want to go anywhere and they don't even want a segregated state. They just want to be aloof as a sect.

CANNON: That goes back to what we were talking about in that interview you had, Ish. I think in *Changes* you were talking about this other guy who was around in the twenties, you know what I'm thinking about. Where everyone had cards saying they were Asians . . .

REED: Abdul Sufi Hamid?

CANNON: Yeah. He was up in Harlem at that time, wasn't he?

SCHUYLER: He was strictly.

REED: No . . . excuse me, I meant Noble Drew.

CANNON: Yes.

REED: The Moor.

SCHUYLER: The Moor. Well, they were authentic Moslems, weren't they?

REED: Well, they called themselves Moors.

CANNON: They had little cards they ran around with.

SCHUYLER: Of course the Moors had only been Moslems since about the seventh or eighth century, before that they had another faith.

REED: I want to ask you this question. In *Black and Conservative*, you talked about the hassle you had with the Angelo Herndon people . . . where you had to get a pistol because they were in the South organizing and you pointed out that he was a Communist too! . . . and that they weren't particularly ready for criticism, I guess, so they picketed your house.

SCHUYLER: I don't recall the name . . . I've been picketed by so many people. I knew Angelo Herndon. I also know that he turned against the Communists.

REED: He did, huh?

CANNON: Recently?

SCHUYLER: No, no, he's dead now. You see, they exploited Angelo Herndon as they do everybody else, only he detected it.

REED: You feel he parallels today. I'm thinking of Angela Davis, for example. Do you think she's being exploited?

SCHUYLER: Well, undoubtedly . . . she's been exploited and she has swallowed this mob-hokum hook, line, and sinker, and it's unfortunate, I think, because she seems to be a bright person. But she's gone too far and the thing she's advocating now, most of the intellectual rich gave that up years ago.

CANNON: Back in the thirties.

SCHUYLER: Well, back in the thirties and forties. I know very few real intellectuals today—I'm not speaking about color now—who swallow Marxism and Stalinism and that sort of thing. That's been discredited, even the Bolsheviks can't make it.

REED: They're building Pepsi-Cola factories now in the Soviet Union, I understand. China wants Coca-Cola.

SCHUYLER: Well, hell, everybody wants Coca-Cola well cooled. But I suppose you saw that comedy that James Cagney starred in—*One, Two, Three*—that was based on the rivalry between Coca-Cola and Pepsi-Cola to get a contract from the Russians? Oh, it was a classic! And it was laid in Berlin and so they were all trying to get these Russians' contracts and the Russians were trying to get the Coca-Cola, and so on. Well, I mean, that bubble has burst and I hate to see people at this late date, you know . . .

CANNON: Come out with archaic ideas.

SCHUYLER: I don't bother now. I don't have anything to say about it at all.

CANNON: Well, let me get back to that question that Ish tried to ask you about the school situation—that's the one I'm fighting. The question was this: now, you see, what's happening out there in the case of the community college is that you've got some bright kids out there, you've got some who aren't too smart, you got—whatever you have—the school kids. Anyway the whole emphasis on the school is on this whole "blackness" thing.

SCHUYLER: The whole what?

CANNON: "Blackness." In your days it would have been "race." It's making it very difficult for some of these kids to go to school because they're there to learn how, you know, to learn technique on what they want to do. They're not too interested in learning to be black because they know that already, you see. So, considering that, what do you think is going to happen at those schools? What's going to happen with that generation when they find out that the country isn't really put together that way?

SCHUYLER: I feel sorry for them.

CANNON: In other words they've read Angela Davis, and they have to read George Jackson.

REED: Eldridge Cleaver.

CANNON: Eldridge Cleaver, and things like that

instead of . . .

SCHUYLER: That's an ordeal.

REED: Instead of *Black No More*; Al Young, my friend (he's editing the issue in which this interview is going to be), wrote a novel called *Snakes* and two books of poetry; he's a professor. He taught *Black No More* recently. He said it was real controversial and the kids liked it very much.

SCHUYLER: Well . . .

REED: But that's another point of view he exposed them to.

CANNON: Yeah, completely different point of view from most of the stuff they're getting right now, you know.

SCHUYLER: Oh, yes, they can't conceive of laughing at this situation. They actually take this seriously.

REED: You had a character in *Black No More* who said that the solution for blacks in this country is either to get out, get white, or get along.

SCHUYLER: Yes, that came from Kelly Miller. Kelly Miller was professor of mathematics and later dean at Howard University, and he wrote a lot of sound stuff. And during the war, he wrote an open letter to Woodrow Wilson on the disgrace of democracy. Now, it sounds like some of these people just wrote it yesterday. But that was fifty-odd years ago and another thing Kelly said. His definition of a Negro radical was an over-educated West Indian without a job. Now, another very capable man that came up here during that period was Dean Pickens, who was one of the officials of the NAACP. That man had a tremendous sense of humor and many a Saturday afternoon we sat up in *The Messenger* office and discussed things, what they call rap sessions here now. And then there was another man here, you hardly ever hear his name mentioned, Hubert Harrison. He was what you'd call an overeducated West Indian. But he used to speak on corners here and he had a very brilliant delivery and all. That's one thing they didn't do during the Renaissance . . . they didn't attempt to speak any black English.

CANNON: How did Julian fit into all that? Was he just a showman, Or what? You know who I'm talking about—Black Eagle.

SCHUYLER: I know . . . Black Eagle. And I been knowing him since those days. He came here by way of Canada. He was West Indian of course, claiming to be an aviator. He wore puttees that you could shave by and fine uniform but I don't think he got a student's license to fly until he'd been here about ten or fifteen years. But he got in dutch with Garvey because Garvey was talking about sailing back to Africa and he was talking about flying there. And so he and Garvey fell out. But I must say that Julian's been a good hustler.

CANNON: He's still around, isn't he? He doesn't make his home here, does he?

SCHUYLER: In the islands. See, he got in with these munitions sellers, and that's a very lucrative field. He even sold munitions to the Finns and to the Guatemalans. He was trying to sell munitions to the Congo but that didn't make it. They were getting munitions, but not from Julian.

CANNON: Well, was Jack Johnson a big thing in New York at that time? Or would he just come through?

SCHUYLER: Part of the time. He lived here for a long time. He used to live next door to me when I lived up here at 321 Edgecomb Avenue.

CANNON: Bert Williams was living right down the street from you.

SCHUYLER: I told you Bert Williams lived two doors from *The Messenger* office. *The Messenger* office was first at 2305 and then at 2311 Seventh Avenue, and a lot of notable people lived along there as they did along Edgecomb Avenue, what they called Sugar Hill.

REED: DuBois lived up there.

SCHUYLER: I think he did. I don't know whether he lived up there or not. I know Walter White did. Roy Wilkins did when he got here.

CANNON: The Johnson brothers probably did too.

REED: James Weldon and Rosamond Johnson. How did you get along with DuBois?

SCHUYLER: Oh, I got along all right, except in the thirties—around about '34 or '35, when he came out for segregation, you see, after being for integration all those years. And of course I took exception to that. He said that, in effect, Negroes should cut their communications and associations with whites as much as possible. Of course I said that was ridiculous because Negroes wouldn't have any jobs then. They couldn't live without working and who had all the jobs? And who had all the government? But staying aloof—you can't stay aloof from a thing you're living in the midst of. However, I had high respect for DuBois but not for some of his opinions, which I think were too farfetched and which, if adopted, would just have the Negro worrying himself to death. He's got enough worries as it is. No, there are a lot of people that I've crossed their path, among Negroes, I mean, for whom I have great respect and in many instances admiration as individuals. For example, I knew a man in Charleston, West Virginia—Mr. James. Now, this man had a wholesale fruit and vegetable business and he had agents—this was back in the twenties—who went around and bought up crops from the farmers and all and he had a big warehouse, and a spur on the railroad coming in there. And I don't think you could find his name on anything in any of these Negro histories but this was an important thing. It made some Negroes ambitious to do likewise. And if anybody said they couldn't do it they could point to him.

CANNON: They had a model there.

REED: Schuyler, what are you working on now?

SCHUYLER: Well, I work on films and books.

REED: What do you think of the current wave of black films that are out? Have you seen any of them? *Superfly*?

SCHUYLER: Most of them that I've seen are terrible. Of course the boys are hustling and making money and they taught the Jews how to do the same thing, you know. I've seen very few of any merit.

REED: Which ones would you say had merit?

SCHUYLER: That's a tough question.

REED: A lot of people are talking about *Sounder* right now.

SCHUYLER: *Sounder's* just an ordinary film but it's better than most of them and I thought it was pretty well done.

REED: What are you working on now?

SCHUYLER: Oh, I just review films, generally. For the *Review of the News*, Belmont, Massachusetts, a weekly news magazine. And then of course books—I've been fooling around with books since 1923. Sometimes I don't want to see any more books. Although I just finished a very good novel last night—but that novel *Augustus* [by John Williams] is very well done in a different way. That is to say, its story is told through a series of diaries and letters and other communications of that kind, one character with another. And it's very effective.

REED: Who are the younger writers you read? You don't have to mention us. Have you read any of James McPherson's work?

SCHUYLER: No.

REED: *Hue and Cry,* or Barry Beckham, Ernest Gaines, author of *Bloodline,* and *The Autobiography of Miss Jane Pittman* . . .

SCHUYLER: No.

REED: Cecil Brown? *Life and Loves of Mr. Jiveass Nigger.*

SCHUYLER: No. I didn't read them.

REED: Do you see any plays?

SCHUYLER: Sometimes. When I have the time. You know, I have very little time because in the first place, except for this boy [John, his assistant] here, there's nobody comes here. I do everything myself. Well, I guess my bar's not far. It's around the corner.

CANNON: Do you see any old-timers over there—guys you knew back in the thirties and forties?

SCHUYLER: No.

CANNON: But they all know you over there, though.

SCHUYLER: Oh yes. Frank's is closed, you know, and there are bars where I'm known and if I happen to be in the neighborhood I drop in and take a spot.

CANNON, REED: Thank you, Mr. Schuyler.

SELECTED BIBLIOGRAPHY

Originally compiled by Michael W. Peplow
Updated by Jeffrey B. Leak

PRIMARY SOURCES
Novels, Monographs, and Autobiography

Black and Conservative: The Autobiography of George S. Schuyler. New Rochelle, N.Y.: Arlington House, 1966. Rpt. 1971.

Black Empire. Boston: Northeastern Univ. Press, 1991.

Black No More: Being an Account of the Strange and Wonderful Workings of Science in the Land of the Free, a.d. 1933–1940. New York: Macaulay, 1931. Rpt. New York: Macmillan, 1971. African-American Library Series. Washington, D.C.: Consortium Press, n.d.

The Communist Conspiracy Against the Negroes. New York: Catholic Information Society, 1947. Sixteen-page pamphlet.

Fifty Years of Progress in Negro Journalism. Pittsburgh: Pittsburgh Courier Publishing, 1950. Seven-page pamphlet.

The Red Drive in the Colonies. New York: Catholic Information Society, 1947. Fifteen-page pamphlet.

Slaves Today: A Story of Liberia. New York: Brewer, Warren and Putnam, 1931. Rpt. New York: AMS Press, 1969.

Short Stories, Essays, Reviews, and Articles

"America Caught Up with Him." *Crisis* 49 (June 1942): 194–95.

"At the Coffeehouse." *Messenger* 7 (June 1925): 236–37.

"At the Darktown Charity Ball." *Messenger* 6 (Dec. 1924): 377–78.

"Black America Begins to Doubt." *American Mercury* 25 (Apr. 1932): 423–30.

"Black Art." *American Mercury* 27 (Nov. 1932): 335–42.

"Black No More." *Negro Digest* 8 (Apr. 1950): 64–69. An excerpt from the novel of the same name.

"Black Paradise Lost." *Opportunity* 13 (Apr. 1935): 113–16.

"Black Warriors." *American Mercury* 21 (Nov. 1930): 288–97.

"Blessed Are the Organized." *Messenger* 8 (Nov. 1926): 347.

"Blessed Are the Sons of Ham." *Nation* 124 (Mar. 23, 1927): 313–15.

"The Caucasian Problem." In *What the Negro Wants,* ed. Rayford Logan. Chapel Hill: Univ. of North Carolina Press, 1944.

"Craftsman in the Blue Grass." *Crisis* 47 (May 1940): 143, 157–58.

"Do Negroes Want to Be White?" *American Mercury* 82 (June 1956): 55–60.

"Do We Really Want Equality?" *Crisis* 44 (Apr. 1937): 102–3.

"Dr. Jekyll and Mr. Hyde and the Negro." In *Anthology of American Negro Literature,* ed. Sylvestre C. Watkins. New York: Random House.

"Emancipated Woman and the Negro." *Modern Quarterly* 5 (Fall 1929): 361–63. Rpt. in the Little Blue Book Series.

"Forty Years of 'The Crisis.'" *Crisis* 58 (Mar. 1951): 163–64.

"Freedom of the Press in Mississippi." *Crisis* 43 (Oct. 1936): 302–3, 306.

"Freedom Through Finance." *Sepia* 11 (May 1962): 55–58.

"From Job to Job." *World Tomorrow* (Apr. 1923).

"Garner at Home." *Crisis* 47 (June 1940): 170–71, 178.

"Haiti Looks Ahead." *Por Americas* 1 (Dec. 1949): 6–8.

"Hitlerism without Hitler: A Review." *Crisis* 48 (Dec. 1941): 384, 389.

"Hobohemia I: The World of the Migratory Worker." *Messenger* 5 (June 1923): 741–44.

"Hobohemia II: The Folk Farthest Down." *Messenger* 5 (Aug. 1923): 787–88, 796–99.

"Jim Crow in the North." *American Mercury* 68 (June 1949): 66–70.

"John A. Lankford." *Messenger* 6 (June 1924): 192–93.

"Keeping the Negro in His Place." *American Mercury* 17 (Aug. 1929): 469–76.

Krushchev's African Foothold." *American Mercury* 88 (Mar. 1959): 57–49.

"A Long War Will Aid the Negro." *Crisis* 50 (Nov. 1943): 328–29, 344.

"The Lord's Work." *Globe,* July 1937.

"Madam C. J. Walker." *Messenger* 6 (Aug. 1924): 251–58, 264, 266.

"Malcolm X: Better to Memorialize Benedict Arnold." *American Opinion* (Feb. 1973): 31–36.

"Memoirs of a Pearl Diver." *American Mercury* 22 (Apr. 1931): 487–96.

"Monrovia Mooches On." *Globe,* July 1937.

"More Race Riots Are Coming." *American Mercury* 59 (Dec. 1944): 686–91.

"Mortimer M. Harris." *Messenger* 6 (May 1924): 14–44.

"The Negro and Nordic Civilization." *Messenger* 7 (May 1925): 198–201, 207.

"The Negro-Art Hokum." *Nation* 122 (June 16, 1926): 662–63.

"Negroes and Artists: A Letter." *Nation* 123 (July 24, 1926): 36.

"Negroes Reject Communism." *American Mercury* 47 (June 1939): 176–81.

"The Negro in the New Order." *Modern Quarterly* 11 (Fall 1940): 85–87.

"A Negro Looks Ahead." *American Mercury* 19 (Feb. 1930): 212–20. Excerpted in *Review of Reviews* 81 (Mar. 1930): 91.

"The Negro Press." *New Leader* (June 26, 1943).

"The Negro Voter Comes of Age." *American Mercury* 84 (Mar. 1957): 99–104.

"New Job Frontiers for Negro Youth." *Crisis* 43 (Nov. 1936): 328–29.

"Not Gone with the Wind." *Crisis* 44 (July 1937): 205–6.

"Our Greatest Gift to America." In *Ebony and Topaz: A Collectanea*, ed. Charles S. Johnson. New York: Opportunity, 1927. Rpt. in V. F. Calverton, ed., *Anthology of American Negro Literature*. New York: Modern Library, 1929.

"Our White Folks." *American Mercury* 12 (Dec. 1927): 385–92. Excerpted in *Review of Reviews* 77 (Jan. 1928): 93–94.

"The Phantom American Negro." *Reader's Digest* 59 (July 1951): 61–63.

"Racial Intermarriage in the United States." *American Parade* 1 (Fall 1928). Rpt. in the Little Blue Book Series, number 1387.

"Reflections on Negro Leadership." *Crisis* 44 (Nov. 1937): 1, 327–28, 347.

"The Reminiscences of George S. Schuyler." Transcript, 1960. Oral History Collection, Columbia Univ., New York.

"Richetta G. Randolph." *Crisis* 49 (Dec. 1942): 382, 396.

"The Rise of the Black Internationale." *Crisis* 45 (Aug. 1938): 255–57, 274–75, 277.

"Scripture for Lynchers." *Crisis* 42 (Jan. 1935): 12.

"Seldom Seen." *Messenger* 8 (Nov. 1926): 342–44, 347.

"The Separate State Hokum." *Crisis* 42 (May 1935): 135, 148–49.

"Some Unsweet Truths about Race Prejudice." In *Behold America*, ed. Samuel D. Schmalhausen. New York: Farrar and Rinehart, 1931.

"Teaching Negro History Is Questionable." *Globe Democrat*, Aug. 13, 1968, p. 6A.

"To Boycott or Not to Boycott? A Deadly Boomerang." *Crisis* 41 (Sept. 1934): 259–60, 274.

"Travelling Jim Crow." *American Mercury* 20 (Aug. 1930): 423–32. Condensed in *Reader's Digest*, Aug. 1930.

"A Treatise on Mulattos. *Crisis* 44 (Oct. 1937): 308–9.

"A Tribute to Caesar." *Messenger* 6 (July 1924): 225–26, 231.

"Uncle Sam's Black Step-Child." *American Mercury* 29 (June 1933): 147–56.

"The Van Vechten Revolution." *Phylon* 11 (Fourth Quarter 1930): 362–68.

"What's Wrong with Negro Authors?" *Negro Digest* 7 (May 1950): 3–7.

"What's Wrong with the NAACP?" *Negro Digest* 4 (Sept. 1947).

"What the Negro Thinks of the South." *Negro Digest* 2 (May 1945).

"When Black Weds White." *Modern Monthly* 5 (Feb. 1934). Rpt. as lead article in June issue of German magazine *Die Auslese.*

"Why I Want to Stay in America." *Negro Digest* 9 (June 1951): 52–56.

"Woman Palaver." *Globe,* Mar. 1937.

"Woof." *Harlem* 1 (Nov. 1928): 17–20.

"The Yellow Peril: A One-Act Play." *Messenger* 7 (Jan. 1925): 28–31.

"The Young Negro Co-Operative League." *Crisis* 39 (Jan. 1932): 456, 472.

Secondary Sources

"Author George S. Schuyler Dies at 82 in New York." *Jet* 53 (Sept. 29, 1977): 56.

"Blame for the Riots as a Negro Writer Sees It." *U.S. News* 63 (Aug. 14, 1967): 10. Schuyler's views on Watts.

Bone, Robert, A. *The Negro Novel in America.* 1958. Rpt. New Haven, Conn.: Yale Univ. Press, 1965. Bone views *Black No More* as an "assimilationist" rather than "nationalistic" novel. A standard reference work.

Brawley, Benjamin. *The Negro Genius: A New Achievement of the American Negro in Literature and the Fine Appraisal of the Arts.* New York: Dodd, Mead, 1937. Brief paragraphs on Schuyler and helpful comments on the Harlem Renaissance.

Brown, Sterling A. *The Negro in American Fiction.* Washington, D.C.: Associates in Negro Folk Education, 1937. Rpt. New York: Arno Press, 1969. Probably the most significant study of black letters prior to the 1960s. Good on the Harlem Renaissance. Brief paragraph on Schuyler's *Black No More.*

Calvin, Floyd J. "Schuyler's Book Dedicated to 'Pure' Whites." *Pittsburgh Courier,* Jan. 27, 1931, p. 2-1. Favorable review of *Black No More.*

"Dark Slaves of Liberia." *Pittsburgh Courier,* Jan. 2, 1932, p. 1-10. Rpt. of the *New York Evening Post* review of *Slaves Today.* A favorable review.

Davis, Arthur P. "Black Satire." *Opportunity* 9 (Mar. 1931): 89–90. Even-handed analysis of *Black No More.*

———. *From The Dark Tower.* Washington, D.C.: Howard Univ. Press, 1974. Contains a chapter on Schuyler.

Du Bois, W. E. B. "The Browsing Reader." *Crisis* 38 (Jan. 1931): 16. Praises Schuyler's militancy and introduces the readers to "Black Warriors."

———. "The Browsing Reader." *Crisis* 39 (Mar. 1931): 100. An early and favorable review of *Black No More.*

———. "The Browsing Reader." *Crisis* 41 (Feb. 1932): 68–69. Negative review of *Slaves Today.*

Fabor, Martin J. "Building Black: Constructions of Multiple African American Subject Positions in Novels by James Weldon Johnson, Jean Toomer, Nella Larsen, and George S. Schuyler." Ph.D. diss. Univ. of Michigan, 1993. Abstract in *Dissertation Abstracts International* 54-07A (2000): 2577.

Ferguson, Jeffrey Brown. "The Newest Negro: George Schuyler's Intellectual Quest in the Nineteen Twenties and Beyond." Ph.D. diss. Harvard Univ., 1998. Abstract in *Dissertation Abstracts International* 59-10A (2000): 3818.

Fisher, Rudolph. Review of *Black No More. Books,* Feb. 1931, 5. Balanced review of the satire.

"George S. Schuyler, Iconoclast." *Crisis* 72 (Oct. 1965): 484–85. Editorial attacking Schuyler's outspoken comments on the Watts riot and Martin Luther King.

Gloster, Hugh. *Negro Fiction in the United States.* New York: Russell and Russell, 1948. Positive statements about *Black No More* and *Slaves Today.* Good survey of black authors through 1948.

Goodman, Jr., George. "George S. Schuyler, Black Author." *New York Times,* Sept. 8, 1977, p. 40. Long, critically balanced obituary.

Hughes, Carl Milton. *The Negro Novelist.* New York: Citadel Press, 1953. Brief comments on Schuyler's *Black No More,* but primary focus on the 1940–50 Negro novelists.

Janz, Janheinz. *Neo-African Literature: A History of Black Writing.* London: Faber and Faber, 1968; New York: Grove Press, 1969. (Published by Faber and Faber as *A History of Neo-African Literature.*) Surveys African and black American literature. Praises Schuyler.

Jones, Dewey R. Review of *Slaves Today. Opportunity* 10 (Jan. 1932): 27. Favorable comments on the sociological implications of the novel.

Larson, Charles R. Introduction to *Black No More.* New York: Macmillan, 1971. Develops the "urge to whiteness" theory about Schuyler's satire; agrees essentially with Robert Bone's interpretation.

Lee, Carleton L. Review of *Black and Conservative. Negro History Bulletin* (30 Jan. 1967): 22–23. Somewhat unfavorable review of Schuyler's autobiography.

"Liberia Today." *New York Times Book Review,* Dec. 27, 1931, p. 9. Reviews favorable and unfavorable aspects of *Slaves Today.*

Littlejohn, David. *Black on White: A Critical Survey of Writing by American Negroes*. New York: Grossman Publishers, 1966. Survey of prose and poetry, primarily twentieth century. Praises *Black No More*.

Locke, Alain. "We Turn to Prose: A Retrospective Review of the Literature of the Negro for 1931." *Opportunity* 10 (Feb. 1932): 43. Notes virtues and flaws of *Black No More*.

Mayer, Martin. "Recordings." *Esquire* 63 (Mar. 1965): 52.

"Meet the George Schuylers; America's Strangest Family." *Our World* 6 (Apr. 1951): 22–26. Not oriented toward literature, but nice background material on the family.

Mencken, H. L. "Check List of New Books." *American Mercury* 22 (Apr. 1931): Brief, somewhat unfavorable review of *Black No More*.

———. "Check List of New Books." *American Mercury* 25 (Feb. 1932). Critical review of *Slaves Today*.

———. "Editorial Notes." *American Mercury* 20 (Aug. 1930). Mencken introduces young Schuyler and includes a brief autobiographical sketch that Schuyler had submitted. Mencken's note also introduces "Travelling Jim Crow."

Ovington, Mary W. "Book Chat." *Pittsburgh Courier,* Feb. 6, 1932, p. II-2. Favorable review of *Slaves Today*, emphasizing its sociological significance.

Peplow, Michael W. "The Black 'Picaro' in Schuyler's *Black No More*." *Crisis* 83 (Jan. 1976): 7–10. Analysis of the picaro-trickster tradition in black literature and in *Black No More*.

———. "George Schuyler, Satirist: Rhetorical Devices in *Black No More*." *CLA Journal* 18 (Dec. 1974): 242–57. Analysis of the satiric devices Schuyler inherited and used in the novel.

Pfeiffer, John. "Black American Speculative Literature: A Checklist." *Extrapolation: A Journal of Science Fiction and Fantasy* 17 (Dec. 1975): 35–43. Argues that *Black No More* is topnotch speculative fiction, Swiftian in nature, "with the underlying message, 'Black is beautiful.'"

Rayson, Ann. "George Schuyler, Paradox Among 'Assimilationist' Writers." *Black American Literature Forum* 12 (1978): 102–6.

Reed, Ishmael. *Shrovetide in Old New Orleans*. New York: Doubleday, 1978. Contains the October 1972 interview "George S. Schuyler, Writer," which Steve Cannon and the author conducted. The interview was published in *Yardbird II* in 1973.

Reilly, John M. "The Black Anti-Utopia." *Black American Literature Forum* 12 (1978): 107–9.

Review of *Black No More*. *Bookman* 72 (Feb. 1931): 7.

Review of *Black No More*. *Boston Transcript*, Feb. 21, 1931, p. 2.

Review of *Black No More*. *Cleveland Open Shelf*, Nov. 1931, 144.

Review of *Black No More*. *New Republic* 65 (Feb. 11, 1931): 362.

Review of *Black No More*. *New York World*, Jan. 16, 1931, p. 14.

Review of *Black No More*. *Saturday Review of Literature* 7 (May 2, 1931): 799.

Review of *Black No More*. *Survey* 66 (June 1, 1931): 290.

"A Satire on Color." *New York Times Book Review*, Feb. 1, 1931, p. 9. Balanced review of *Black No More*.

Schraufnagel, Noel. *From Apology to Protest: The Black American Novel.* Deland, Fla.: Everette/Edwards, 1973. Brief mention of the historical significance of *Slaves Today* on pp. 16–17.

"Schuyler Calls for Historical Scientists." *Negro History Bulletin* 18 (Apr. 1955): 169–70. Describes Schuyler's address to students on the contributions of black historians.

Schuyler, Josephine. "Black No More." *Nation* 132 (Apr. 8, 1931): 132. Answers Dorothy Van Doren's comments about *Black No More*.

Smith, William Gardner. "The Negro Writer: Pitfalls and Compensations." In *The Black American Writer*, ed. C. W. E. Bigsby. Deland, Fla.: Everette/ Edwards, 1969. Brief reference to *Black No More* as a "semiclassic" on p. 72.

Tolson, Melvin B. "George S. Schuyler." *American Mercury* 28 (Mar. 1933): 373–74. The poet, then a young teacher, writes in praise of "Black Art," *Black No More*, and Schuyler's career in general to 1933.

Van Doren, Dorothy. "Black, Alas, No More! *Nation* 132 (Feb. 25, 1931): 21–29. Argues that *Black No More* is "poor white satire."

West, Hollie I. "A Black, Biting John Bircher." *Washington Post*, Sept. 6, 1973, pp. C-1, C-8. Biographical sketch of Schuyler.

Whitetow, Roger. *Black American Literature: A Critical History*. Totowa, N.J.: Littlefield, Adams, 1974. Brief yet objective report on Schuyler's career and major publications on pp. 96–100, 185.

"Who's Who." *Messenger* 5 (June 1923): 748. Editorial introduces readers to George Schuyler, one of the young, intelligent, and "radical" "New Negroes."

Williams, Harry McKinley, Jr. "When Black Is Right: The Life and Writings of George S. Schuyler." Ph.D. diss. Brown Univ., 1988. Abstract in *Dissertation Abstracts International* 49-08A (2000): 2354.

Williams, Oscar Renal III. "The Making of a Black Conservative: George S. Schuyler." Ph.D. diss. Ohio State Univ., 1997. Abstract in *Dissertation Abstracts International* 58-05A (2000): 1883.

Winslow, H. F. "George S. Schuyler: Fainting Traveler." *Midwest Journal* 5 (Summer 1953): 24–25.

BACKGROUND STUDIES

Anderson, Jervis. *A. Philip Randolph: A Biographical Portrait*. New York: Harcourt Brace Jovanovich, 1972. Significant study of one of the founders of the *Messenger* and of black history from the Harlem Renaissance to the 1970s.

Arnez, Nancy Levi, and Ceara B. Anthony. "Contemporary Negro Humor as Social Satire." *Phylon* 29 (1968): 339–46. Discussion of contemporary black satirists and their major themes.

Bergman, Peter M., and Mort N. Bergman, comps. *The Chronological History of the Negro in America*. New York: New American Library, 1969. A year-by-year compilation of significant events through 1968.

Bontemps, Arna, ed. *The Harlem Renaissance Remembered*. New York: Dodd, Mead, 1972. Essays on major figures of the Harlem Renaissance. One of the better anthologies.

Brown, Sterling A., Arthur P. Davis, and Ulysses Lee, eds. *The Negro Caravan: Writings by American Negroes*. New York: Dryden, 1941. Rpt. New York: Arno Press, 1970. A milestone in black literature anthologies. Includes selections from *Black No More* and "Black Warriors."

Brown, William Wells. *Three Classic African American Novels: Clotel, or the President's Daughter, Iola Leroy or Shadows Uplifted, The Marrow of Traditions*. New York: Vintage, 1990.

Carter, Dan T. *From George Wallace to Newt Gingrich: Race in the Conservative Counterrevolution, 1963–1994*. Baton Rouge: Louisiana State Univ. Press, 1996.

———. *The Politics of Rage: George Wallace, the Origins of the New Conservatism and the Transformation of American Politics*. Baton Rouge: Louisiana State Univ. Press, 1996.

Cooke, Alistair, ed. *The Vintage Mencken*. New York: Vintage Books, 1956. Invaluable introductory essay and good collection of Mencken.

Cooper, Anna Julia. *A Voice from the South: Schomburg Collection of Nineteenth-Century Black Women Writers*. 1892. Rpt. New York: Oxford Univ. Press, 1990.

Dorson, Richard M., ed. *American Negro Folktales*. 1956. Rpt. Greenwich, Conn.: Fawcett Publications, 1967. Valuable collection of black folktales.

Dundes, Alan, ed. *Mother Wit from the Laughing Barrel*. Englewood Cliffs, N.J.: Prentice-Hall, 1973. Important collection of essays of black folklore.

Ellison, Ralph. *Shadow and Act*. New York: Vintage, 1953.

Fishel, Leslie H., Jr., and Benjamin Quarles, eds. *The Black American: A Documentary History.* Rev. ed. New York: Scott, Foresman, 1970. Standard collection of historical documents.

Forgue, Guy J., ed. *Letters of H. L. Mencken.* New York: Alfred A. Knopf, 1961. Includes letters from Mencken to Schuyler.

Franklin, John Hope. *From Slavery to Freedom: A History of Negro Americans.* New York: Alfred Knopf, 1967.

Gayle, Addison, Jr., ed. *The Black Aesthetic.* Garden City, N.Y.: Doubleday, 1971. Significant collection of essays by modern black scholars on a "black aesthetic" for the modern black artist or critic.

————. *The Black Expression: Essays By and About Black Americans in the Creative Arts.* New York: David McKay, 1969. Another collection of significant essays on black literature, art, and music.

"Harlem Renaissance Revisited." *Black World* 20 (Nov. 1970). Entire issue devoted to reappraisal of Harlem Renaissance and its major personalities.

Harrison, John M., and Harry H. Stein, eds. *Muckraking: Past, Present, and Future.* University Park: Pennsylvania State Univ. Press, 1973. Collection of essays on the art of muckraking. Excellent background materials.

Highet, Gilbert. *The Anatomy of Satire.* Princeton, N.J.: Princeton Univ. Press, 1962. One of the standard studies of the art and techniques of satire.

Holman, C. Hugh, comp. *A Handbook to Literature.* 3d ed. New York: Odyssey Press, 1972. Revised and expanded version of the Thrall and Hibbard *Handbook.* Invaluable for students of literature.

Hopkins, Ernest J., comp. *The Ambrose Bierce Satanic Reader.* Garden City, N.Y.: Doubleday, 1968.

————. *The Complete Short Stories of Ambrose Bierce.* Garden City, N.Y.: Doubleday, 1970.

————. *The Enlarged Devil's Dictionary.* Garden City, N.Y.: Doubleday, 1967. The three volumes edited by Hopkins are the standard collection of Bierce's work. Each volume is accompanied by an informative introduction.

Huggins, Nathan I. *Harlem Renaissance.* New York: Oxford Univ. Press, 1971. A modern and valuable critical overview of the era.

Hughes, Langston, ed. *The Book of Negro Humor.* New York: Dodd, Mead, 1966. Standard collection of folk and modern humor and satire.

Hughes, Langston, and Arna Bontemps, eds. *The Book of Negro Folklore.* New York: Dodd, Mead, 1959. Invaluable collection of tales about High John de Conquer, Brer Rabbit, and other trickster-picaros.

Hurston, Zora Neale. *Mules and Men.* 1935. Rpt. New York: Harper, 1990.

Johnson, Charles. *Oxherding Tale.* 1982. Rpt. New York: Plume, 1995.

Johnson, James Weldon. *Autobiography of an Ex-Colored Man.* Ed. William Andrews. 1915. Rpt. New York: Penguin, 1990.

Larsen, Nella. *Passing.* Ed. Thadious M. Davis. 1929. Rpt. New York: Penguin, 1997.

Lewis, David Levering. *The Race to Fashoda: European Colonialism and African Resistance in the Scramble for Africa.* New York: Weidenfeld & Nicolson, 1987.

Locke, Alain, ed. *The New Negro.* New York: Boni and Liveright, 1925. Rpt. New York: Atheneum, 1970. One of the most important Harlem Renaissance anthologies; includes the "The New Negro," by the editor. Indispensable resource.

Meier, August, Elliot Rudwick, and Francis L. Broderick, eds. *Black Protest Thought in the Twentieth Century.* (Formerly *Negro Protest Thought in the Twentieth Century.*) 2d ed. Indianapolis: Bobbs-Merrill, 1971. Standard resource work and perhaps the most comprehensive compilation of original texts and manifestos beginning with Booker T. Washington.

Mintz, Lawrence. "Langston Hughes' Jesse B. Semple: The Urban Negro as Wise Fool." *Satire News Letter* 7 (1969): 11–21. The urban trickster defined.

Morrison, Toni. *Paradise.* New York: Knopf, 1998.

———. *Playing in the Dark: Whiteness and the Literary Imagination.* Cambridge: Harvard Univ. Press, 1992.

Murray, Albert. *The Omni Americans, Black Experience and American Culture.* New York: Da Capo, 1970.

Nower, Joyce. "'Foolin' Master." *Satire News Letter* 7 (1969): 5–9. Important discussion of the trickster tradition in black folklore and literature.

Osofsky, Gilbert, ed. *Puttin' On Ole Massa.* New York: Harper and Row, 1969. The editor's introduction, especially "A Note on the Usefulness of Folklore," discusses the trickster role as revealed in the slave narratives collected in this text.

Peplow, Michael W., and Arthur P. Davis, eds. *The New Negro Renaissance: An Anthology.* New York: Holt, Rinehart, 1975. Thematic arrangement. Includes excerpts from *Slaves Today* and two essays: "The Negro-Art Hokum" and "Our Greatest Gift to America."

Robinson, Randall. *Defending the Spirit: A Black Life in America.* New York: Plume, 1999.

Rosenblatt, Roger. *Black Fiction.* Cambridge: Harvard Univ. Press, 1974. Provides important background information on black trends and themes. The section on "Exceptional Laughter" analyzes black humor and satire.

Schechter, William. *The History of Negro Humor in America.* New York: Fleet Press, 1970. Brief passages on emergence of the rural and urban trickster.

Shaw, J. D. "William Cowper Brann." In *Brann the Iconoclast: A Collection of the Writings of W. C. Brann.* 2 vols. Waco, Tex.: Herz Brothers, 1898.

Sutherland, W. O. S. *The Art of the Satirist.* Austin: Univ. of Texas Press, 1965. Good discussion of the craft, technique, and history of satire.

Toomer, Jean. *Cane (A Norton Critical Edition).* 1923. Rpt. New York: W. W. Norton, 1989.

Turner, Darwin T., comp. *Afro-American Writers.* New York: Appleton-Century-Crofts, 1970. Standard bibliography of black authors and background studies.

Wagner, Jean. *Black Poets of the United States: From Paul Laurence Dunbar to Langston Hughes.* Urbana: Univ. of Illinois Press, 1973. Translated by Kenneth Douglas from the original French edition of 1962. Carefully researched and documented study of black poetry.

Walden, Daniel, ed. *W. E. B. DuBois: The Crisis Writings.* New York: Fawcett, 1972. Important collection of Du Bois's editorials and columns, 1910–34.

Wicks, Ulrich. "The Nature of Picaresque Narrative: A Modal Approach." *PMLA* 89 (Mar. 1974): 240–49. Catalogues major themes and methods of picaresque fiction.

INDEX

Rac[e]ing to the Right was designed and typeset on a Macintosh computer system using PageMaker software. The text and chapter openings are set in Berkeley. This book was designed by Vernon Boes, typeset by Kimberly Scarbrough, and manufactured by Thomson-Shore, Inc. The paper used in this book is designed for an effective life of at least three hundred years.